DISCOVER NORTHERN EUROPE

Reader's Digest

PUBLISHED BY THE READER'S DIGEST ASSOCIATION LIMITED

LONDON   NEW YORK   SYDNEY   MONTREAL

DISCOVER NORTHERN EUROPE

Translated and edited by Toucan Books Limited, London
for Reader's Digest, London

Translated and adapted from the French
by Alex Martin

For Reader's Digest
Series Editor: Christine Noble
Editorial Assistant: Caroline Boucher
Production Controller: Martin Hendrick

Reader's Digest General Books
Editorial Director: Cortina Butler
Art Director: Nick Clark

First English language edition Copyright © 2001
The Reader's Digest Association Limited
11 Westferry Circus, Canary Wharf, London E14 4HE
www.readersdigest.co.uk

We are committed to both the quality of our products and
the service we provide to our customers. We value your
comments, so please feel free to contact us on 08705 113366,
or by email at cust_service@readersdigest.co.uk
If you have any comments about the content of our books,
you can contact us at gbeditorial@readersdigest.co.uk

Copyright © 2001
Reader's Digest Association Far East Limited
Philippines copyright © 2001
Reader's Digest Association Far East Limited
All rights reserved

ISBN 0 276 42513 8

Discover the World: NORTHERN EUROPE
was created and produced by
AMDS (ATELIER Martine et Daniel SASSIER), Paris for
Selection Reader's Digest S.A., Paris, and first published
in 2000 as *Regards sur le Monde:* SCANDINAVIE ET PAYS BALTES

©2000 Selection Reader's Digest, S.A.
212 boulevard Saint-Germain, 75007, Paris

CONTENTS

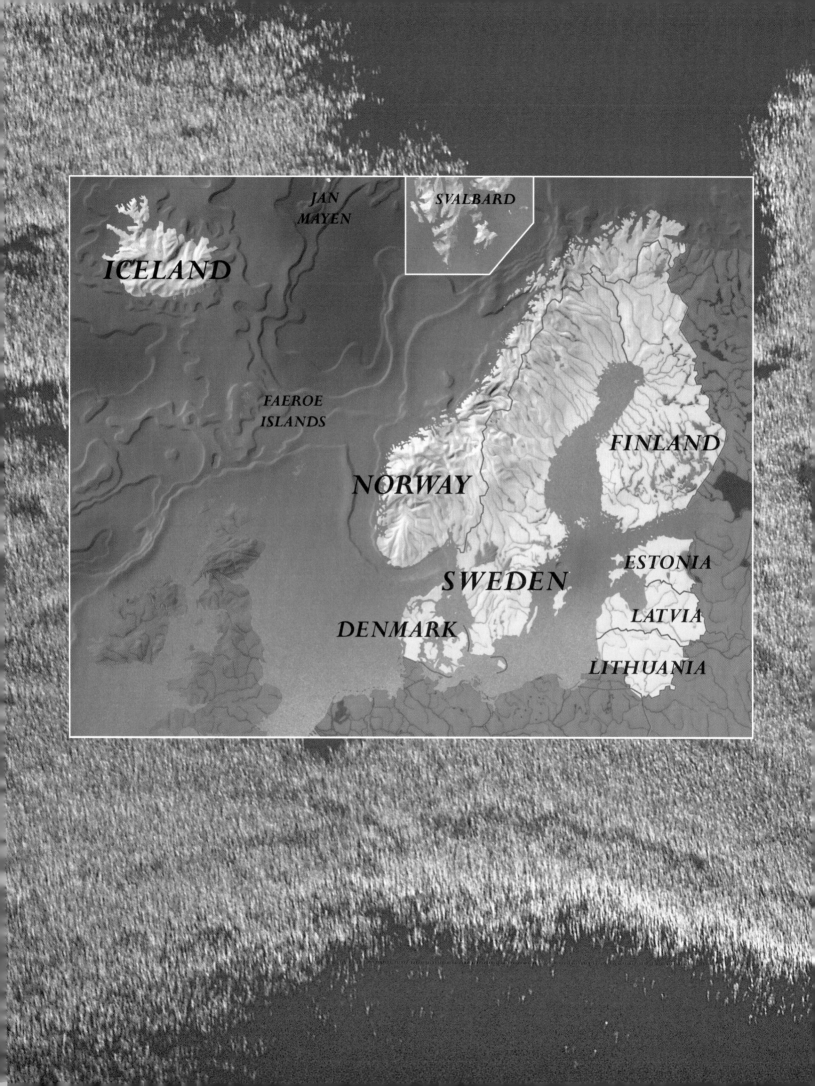

INTRODUCING
NORTHERN EUROPE

Stretching from Denmark's border with Germany to deep inside the Arctic Circle, the countries of Northern Europe contain a fascinating range of scenery, from the primeval landscape of Iceland's volcanoes and lakes of boiling mud to Norway's dramatic, mountain-shadowed fiords and the serene forests and lakes of Finland. The diversity is matched by the social and political cultures of the region's inhabitants. The Scandinavian countries – Denmark, Finland, Norway and Sweden – are committed to public welfare policies and human rights, while the Baltic States of Estonia, Latvia and Lithuania are rediscovering their indentities following the collapse of the Soviet Union.

Northern lands

Barely 10 000 years ago, the vast region stretching from Iceland to Estonia, from the North Atlantic to the Baltic Sea, lay under a thick layer of ice. Gradually, as the climate changed and the earth grew warmer, the ice sheet melted. The glaciers – billions of tons of frozen water – thawed and slid down from the higher ground, grinding and gouging the landscape as they went. The Gulf Stream bathed the shores of Iceland and Norway, bringing warm coastal waters and mild weather to these frosty latitudes. The Scandinavian lands soon teemed with wildlife, as birds and beasts migrated north into the newly hospitable terrain. Humans followed, hunting reindeer and other game, and the first settlements began to appear.

Conditions were harsh for the early settlers, who had to take their opportunities where they found them. Avoiding the dense inland forests and frozen tundras, they preferred the more welcoming coasts, rivers and lakes with their plentiful supplies of fish and shellfish. Prehistoric communities lived close to water, and they became skilled in boatbuilding and navigation. This was the start of a long Scandinavian tradition that continues to this day. The Vikings' seafaring skills took them trading and warring across Europe, around the Iberian peninsula and deep into the Mediterranean in the 9th and 10th centuries AD. They opened up inland trade routes to the south, exploring the rivers of Eastern Europe until they came to Constantinople, linking the Baltic and the Black Sea, and founding the city of Kiev on the way. Striking out across the Atlantic, they colonised the Faeroe Islands, Iceland and Greenland. They even reached the shores of North America.

Traditionally seen as destroyers and pillagers, the Vikings were also superb sailors, craftsmen and traders. They were builders as well as destroyers. Much of their heritage has survived: the great Norse sagas remain as a record of their turbulent lives; their magnificent ships, weapons and jewellery, preserved in the museums of Oslo and Copenhagen, bear witness to their outstanding skills of hand and eye. It is tempting to see the old Viking spirit of discovery in later explorers, such as Fridtjof Nansen, Roald Amundsen and Thor Heyerdahl; and their instinct for business and global trade in some of today's leading brand names – Volvo, Nokia, Bang & Olufsen, IKEA, Lego, Ericsson.

There is another side to this success story. The Scandinavians have long been devoted to ideals of equality, social justice, education for all, the spread of knowledge and the arts, and women's rights. In the 20th century, the political scene was dominated by Social Democratic parties with their commitment to social change. They created a model of the welfare state, which has been widely envied and copied, despite criticism from devotees of the free market. On the international stage, too, the Scandinavians have been outstanding champions of human rights, often leading the search for peaceful solutions to conflicts around the world.

The Baltic States, only recently freed from subservience to the Soviet Union, have a long way to go to catch up, especially in the economic sphere. Like their neighbours in Eastern Europe, they have gone through a period of rapid and profound change – politically, culturally, and in the way their inhabitants live their lives. Yet questions still remain. Perhaps the biggest of these is membership of the European Union and its single currency. Both Norway – outside the European Union – and Sweden have indicated a wish to retain their currencies. The choices are complex, difficult and beset with uncertainties. But one thing is sure: the rich diversity of these countries, their vitality and individuality, will remain.

A view from space   A satellite picture of the area between the Arctic Ocean and the Baltic Sea shows the fretwork of land and water that characterises the region, with its deeply indented coasts, islands, peninsulas and archipelagoes. Some of Finland's 188 000 lakes, covering a total area the size of Belgium, are also clearly visible.

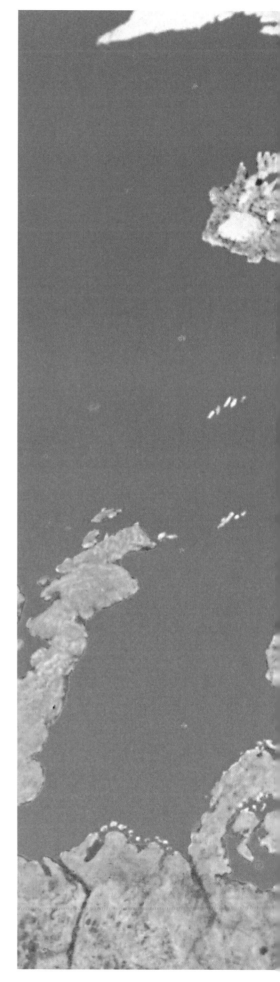

Naming the land It took little inspiration on the part of the Scandinavian mariners who first sailed into these forbidding waters to name the place Ice-Land. The ice floes in the picture (right) are fragments of the huge Vatnajökull, or Vatna Glacier (seen in the background), which is 3300 sq miles (8540 km²) in area and 3000 ft (900 m) deep at its thickest point. As the glacier slowly slides towards the south-east coast, pieces break off and melt in the sea. Despite its name, Iceland has a mild climate: it is a land of streams and rivers, rich grasslands, hot springs, and volcanic landscapes of lava, ash and rock. Glaciers cover just one-tenth of the island, remnants of the Ice Age that survive only in the highest mountains and areas like Vatnajökull that are cut off from the effects of the Gulf Stream.

Realms of fantasy *Strange, ghostly presences inhabit the valley of the Tenojoki, slicing through the far north of Scandinavia, along the border between Norway and Finland. In these high altitudes, visitors may come face to face with magnified images of themselves projected onto a screen of mist and mirroring every movement they make. The phenomenon is a trick of light, but it has given rise to a widespread belief in guardian spirits that watch over people in the barren wildernesses. The same effect can make Lapp herders think that their reindeer are twice as numerous as they really are. All kinds of fantasies become possible, including tales of a giant who during the long winter months travels up and down the snowclad landscape rescuing local people who have got into difficulties.*

King of fiords *Excavated by great glaciers from the ice sheet that thawed 10 000 years ago, the fiords of Norway are coastal valleys that have flooded with seawater. Sognefiord, known as 'the king of fiords', is 128 miles (204 km) long and plunges to a depth of 4290 ft (1308 m) below sea level, while the mountains that enclose it rise 3280 ft (1000 m) above the dark waters. Spectacular waterfalls cast glittering ribbons of spray down the mountains' rock faces.*

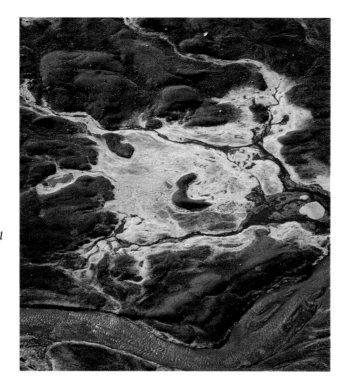

Volcanic colour *A bright swirl of crystallised sulphur creates a flame-like pattern among solidified black lava flows from one of Iceland's 200 volcanoes. These bursts of colour are short-lived, however. Grimmia, a silvery green moss, colonises the ash and lava as soon as they cool – and can be seen here.*

Meltwater flood *In October 1996 clouds of volcanic smoke began to drift across the Vatna Glacier in south-east Iceland (below) – the first evidence of an eruption beneath the ice. A few days later the huge meltwater lake created burst out and poured into the sea, sweeping away a stretch of coast road as it went.*

River of ice *The glaciated volcanic massif of Öraefajökull (right) rises 6952 ft (2119 m) above sea level. As the glacier melts it becomes a river of ice, ash and lava, spilling in a great fan shape down to the sea. Two key processes in the shaping of the Earth's surface are at work here: erosion and deposition. Despite the primeval splendour of the scene, these mountains are geologically young: just 23 million years old.*

Giant's bones   The coast of Norway is craggy and harsh. This steep and forbidding shore (left) is near Narvik in the north of the country. The hazards of navigation in these stormy waters are increased by frequent fogs, formed where the warm water of the Gulf Stream meets icy Arctic air. According to Norse mythology, the land was made from the bones of a giant, Ymer, born of snow and mist.

Watery maze   Forested islands lie scattered across the entrance to the Finnish port of Turku (top right of the picture), making navigation a hazardous business. The larger Åland Islands to the west continue the barrier across the southern end of the Gulf of Bothnia, which lies between Sweden and Finland. These islands are the highest parts of a shelf that is gradually rising out of the sea. The average depth of the Gulf of Bothnia is only 200 ft (60 m), and the large number of rivers pouring into it keep the salt content low, so that it can remain ice bound for five months of the year.

Meandering to the sea   The coast of Iceland presents many different faces. Some parts are so flat that water can barely flow. The Markarfljot (below) is a small river, only 7.5 miles (12 km) long, that begins as a raging torrent 4750 ft (1450 m) above sea level in the ice-capped heights of the Myrdalsjökull. After a steep descent, it lands on a soft flat bed of volcanic ash that absorbs and disperses its energy, reducing the river to lazy, drifting meanders before it finally – and very reluctantly – reaches the sea.

Peat bogs and tundra Sixty per cent of the plateaus of Finnish Lappland are covered in stagnant waters where sphagnum mosses grow and, year on year, break down into peat. Among the low, scrubby vegetation of the tundra a few trees bring a note of colour and variety to the landscape. Trees are a sign of the transition zone between tundra and the taiga forests farther south.

Glacial erosion Deeply scored by rivers of melting snow and ice, the landscape around Lake Inari in Finnish Lappland (below) shows the traces of the glacier that covered this region until 10 000 years ago. As glaciers melt and slide they grind the rock below them, leaving broad strips of boulders to mark their path.

Hot and cold In a landscape sculpted by erosion and fissured by volcanic activity, Iceland's rivers are often dramatic. The falls at Hraunfossar are in the centre of the country, a gigantic rocky staircase where icy melt-waters from glaciers are tumbled with hot streams rising from the depths of volcanoes.

A brief history

As the last Ice Age began to draw to a close, a narrow strip of coast around what is now Norway, Finland and northwest Russia was revealed. As the thaw continued, and the land was freed from the crushing weight of the ice, dramatic coastlines were sculpted, along with deep glaciated valleys, great cirques and thousands of gouged depressions – soon to be filled with water to form lakes. Rock carvings, found in Norway's Altafiord, show that human habitation must have begun at about the same time.

The first hunters

Nine thousand years ago, the Baltic Sea was an inland lake. The sea-level rose, creating the Danish archipelago and turning Scandinavia into a peninsula. As the climate grew milder, dense forests spread across the Nordic lands. Small bands of hunters settled in Denmark, southern Sweden and along the Norwegian seaboard. Few traces have remained of these early inhabitants, but some built dolmens (Stonehenge-style structures) and impressive tombs, with covered stone alleys leading to burial chambers. These can be seen at the neolithic site of Kong Asgers Høj on the island of Møn.

Low-lying land not covered by sea

The great thaw From about 8000 BC the ice sheet began to melt, starting with the coastal areas.

Prehistoric archer
Rock carvings at Alta in Norway reveal the presence of early man: here a hunter stalks reindeer with his bow and arrow.

Fluctuating fortunes

Beginning about 1800 BC, the Bronze Age in Scandinavia was a time of plenty: the climate was mild, agriculture developed and the population grew. Metalwork and trade flourished. The Nordic peoples travelled south along the German rivers, the Oder and the Elbe, to reach markets where they exchanged slaves, amber and furs for copper and tin, the raw materials for bronze. By 500 BC they were working with iron.

At the end of the Iron Age, in the 4th century BC, the Celts invaded south-west Germany, pushing out the German tribes. At about the same time, the climate changed for the worse. Torrential rains drowned the fields and farming and trade suffered. By the time of Christ the situation had improved, particularly in Denmark, where the rich, flat landscape encouraged agriculture, and a settled trade with the Celts was established.

Farmers and warriors

The Romans, who regularly exchanged goods with the Scandinavians, left few records of their impressions. The historian

The languages of Scandinavia

The first settlers spoke a Germanic language that has survived only in the form of a few hundred words found in inscriptions on stone, wood and metal. Known as Proto-Scandinavian, it remained the common language of the region until the Viking age, around 800-1000 AD, when it developed two different strands. East Scandinavian was spoken by the Danes and Swedes and around the Baltic Sea. West Scandinavian was spoken in Norway and Iceland and on the Atlantic seaboard. The two strands crossed again when Norway was ruled by Denmark in the 15th to 18th centuries, and the ruling élite adopted a variant of Danish. Swedish is today the most widely spoken of the six Scandinavian languages.

Fertility symbol This Bronze Age figure is the ancestor of Freyr, the Norse god of peace, fertility, sun and rain.

Rock art Ancient rock carvings at Tanum in Sweden show boats and four-wheeled carts.

Iron Age village On the Swedish island of Öland archaeologists have reconstructed Eketorp, together with its strong defensive wall.

Tacitus, writing in the 1st century AD, speaks of the *Svioner*, or Svears, and mentions only their fine weapons and boats. Later sources emphasise the physical size and warlike temperament of the Nordic warriors. Archaeology helps us to fill out the picture: fortified sites in Jutland and the island of Öland are rich in remains. The people lived by farming, fishing, trade and war. They became skilled navigators, exploiting the rivers and the sea.

In the 6th century, the Nordic peoples were caught up in a great movement of populations around Europe. The Scandinavians had a definite culture of their own, with a common language, Old Norse. This derived from the same Indo-European roots as the languages of the Letts and Lithuanians. Only the Finns and Estonians spoke a separate and very different tongue: Finno-Ugric. This is similar to Hungarian, and betrays their origins in a people who migrated to the Baltic lands by a different route – westwards from the Ural Mountains.

Raiders from the North

In 793, a band of Norse raiders landed on Holy Island, off the coast of Northumberland. They pillaged the monastery of Lindisfarne, a centre of manuscript illumination and Christian culture founded in 635 by St Aidan. In 794, they sacked the monastery at Jarrow. By 802, these sporadic raids were being coordinated into full-scale military expeditions. Godfred, King of Denmark, sent a fleet of 200 ships to ravage the Frisians, who were allies of his enemies, the Franks. With Viking raids now a constant threat, the Christian world lived in terror. Defenceless communities were attacked and robbed by these raiders from the North, whom they called Northmen, Norsemen or Normans. For more than 200 years their power held, and they accumulated treasures and established vast kingdoms.

Defensive layout The Iron Age citadel of Ismanstorp was designed so that people could shelter from danger.

Precious possession Large beads of highly prized Scandinavian amber are the main ornament of this necklace found in Gaul.

Pirates of the fiords

In Old Norse, the word *Vikinkgar* means 'people of the creeks' – pirates who lay in ambush in hidden bays and fiords, and would rush out from nowhere to surprise their victims. At the end of the 8th century, when the Vikings made their first raids across the North Sea, there were around 2 million inhabitants in Scandinavia. They enjoyed a mild climate and good harvests, but the land could not sustain a growing population. Only eldest sons inherited their fathers' land and possessions, which meant that younger sons had to seek their fortune elsewhere. The prospect of overseas adventure and unlimited loot must have been too tempting to resist.

The restless Rus

Long before their westward voyages, the Vikings had opened up other routes to the south. From the 5th century the Rus, a Swedish tribe who lived on the western shores of the Baltic, had carried out raids on other tribes in Finland and around the Baltic. In time they reached a great waterway, the Dniepr, where they enountered the Finns and Slavs, tribes who lived in a strip of land between Lake Ladoga (north of Novgorod) and the Black Sea. The Rus set up trading stations at Novgorod and Kiev, then set off along the Dniepr, bound for the Black Sea. From here it was a short voyage to Constantinople, a huge trading metropolis. The Rus tried to capture the city, but failed. In 945, a treaty was drawn up that forbade them to enter Constantinople in groups of more than 50, or to spend the winter there. But the Byzantine emperor was so

Dragon ship
Oslo's Viking Boat Museum, the Vikinskiphuset, on the Bygdød peninsula, houses many superb examples of naval architecture. This is the Oseberg boat.

impressed with these men of the North that he recruited his bodyguard, the Varangian Guards, from among them. Other Rus took a different route, along the Volga to the Caspian Sea, where they established a trading camp. Some travelled as far as Baghdad.

Secrets of the dragon ship

The Viking warship had a solid keel, a flexible clinker-built hull, a central removable mast and a square sail. The symmetrical design – the stem and the stern are identical in their shape – meant that the boat could go in either direction. With a draught of about 3 ft (1 m), the vessel was equally suitable for seagoing or river use. When the wind dropped, the crew of up to 100 men could row instead. The ship's design combined lightness and strength. The prow was often carved in the shape of a dragon's head – hence the name 'dragon ship'. The Vikings' main instrument of navigation was a form of sundial, but they also made use of the ocean currents, prevailing winds and the flight of birds.

The Vikings in Britain

At the end of the 8th century, the Danes and Norwegians made regular voyages to the west. They raided and pillaged many parts of the British Isles, including Shetland, Orkney, Northumbria, East Anglia, the Isle of Man and Ireland, ending the flowering of Celtic civilisation. They founded Dublin as a trading post in 831, and by 866 they ruled northern Scotland, the Hebrides, and north-east England, where they levied a tax known as the *Danegeld*

Fine horsemen
The Scandinavians were at home on horseback, but even in the heart of continental Europe they preferred to travel by boat, using great rivers such as the Danube and the Don.

A place in the sun

With their insatiable desire for conquest, the Vikings sailed through the English Channel and along the coasts of France, Portugal and Spain, laying siege to the cities of Lisbon, Cadiz and Seville. They passed through the Straits of Gibraltar and attacked North Africa, the south of France and Pisa on the west coast of Italy. By AD 1000, however, these raids had stopped. In their place the Normans, who were themselves of Viking descent, established kingdoms in southern Italy and Sicily.

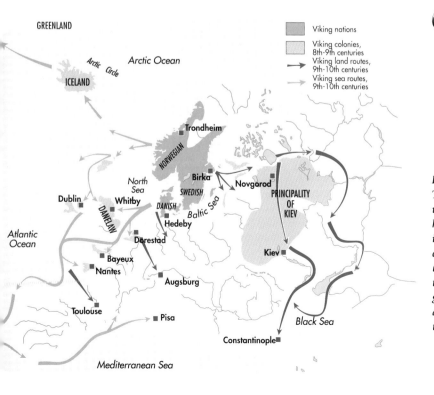

GREENLAND

Arctic Ocean

Arctic Circle

ICELAND

Trondheim

NORWEGIAN

Birka

SWEDISH

Novgorod

North Sea

Dublin

Whitby

DANELAW

DANISH

Baltic Sea

PRINCIPALITY OF KIEV

Atlantic Ocean

Hedeby

Dorestad

Bayeux

Nantes

Augsburg

Kiev

Toulouse

Pisa

Black Sea

Constantinople

Mediterranean Sea

Viking nations
Viking colonies, 8th-9th centuries
Viking land routes, 9th-10th centuries
Viking sea routes, 9th-10th centuries

Norman conquest *A Viking fleet carried William of Normandy with his army to England in 1066.*

(Dane's money). They did not conquer Wessex, however, and it was from here that Alfred the Great organised a successful resistance, defeating them at the Battle of Ashdown in 871. As a result he was able to force the Danes in England to accept Christianity and keep to the east of the Roman road Watling Street in the area called the Danelaw. Many traces of their culture have remained in Britain – from place names ending in 'by' (Whitby, Derby, Rugby) to dialect and standard English words.

After Alfred the Great's death in 900, peace was maintained for another 75 years. Then a weak king, Ethelred, came to the throne, and Viking incursions began again. In 1016 England submitted to the Danish king, Canute. Although his rule only lasted until 1042, when the Danish empire split up, the Vikings had not quite finished with

England. In 1066 King Harold had to fight off an attempted Viking invasion of Yorkshire at the Battle of Stamford Bridge. While he was there, William of Normandy landed in the south. Harold rushed down to Hastings to face William in battle, taking only part of his army with him. His forces were too weak. With Harold's defeat at the Battle of Hastings, English culture was changed for ever.

A foothold in France

The Frankish kingdom, so brilliantly ruled by Charlemagne, broke up on his death in 814. In its weak state it was an easy prey for the Vikings. They set up camps on islands and estuaries, and sailed up the Seine and Loire in their dragon ships, bringing terror wherever they went. In 842 they attacked Nantes and massacred its inhabitants; in 861 they sacked Paris. In 911 the French king, Charles the Simple, offered their leader Rollo a fiefdom: 5000 Vikings were to be allowed to settle the fertile country of Normandy – 'land of the Norse men'. It was from here that Rollo's descendant William, Duke of Normandy, set out to conquer England in 1066.

Voyaging westwards

In 865 a band of Vikings colonised Iceland. They were rebel chiefs and their followers, mostly Norwegian, who had broken away from their king, Harald Fairhair. They found an almost virgin

Mythical horse *The upper part of this runic stone shows Odin, king of the Norse gods, galloping on his eight-legged horse, Sleipnir.*

Discovered in America *This necklace is rare evidence of Leif Ericsson's landing in Newfoundland.*

land, inhabited only by a few hardy Irish monks. They built settlements on the coast and organised a government based on the *Althing*, an assembly of free men. This was effectively the first parliament in Europe.

Just over a century later, in 982, Eric the Red was forced into exile for manslaughter. He sailed west and discovered a land that he called Greenland. Sailing down the east coast, searching for a place to land, he eventually managed to beach his ships at Brattahild near its southern tip, where he founded the first Viking colony.

It is now proven beyond doubt that Eric's son, Leif, discovered America in the year 1000 – nearly 500 years before Christopher Columbus. He was on a mission from his king to bring the Christian religion to Iceland, but was blown past his destination and landed in what he called Vinland, after the wild vines growing there. Traces of the brief Viking stay – including the remains of some ancient dwellings – have been found on Newfoundland's north coast.

Knights, priests and kings

In a little over two centuries the Vikings had seized vast territories. At the same time their own society was changing: kingdoms formed, requiring laws and settled patterns of administration. One by one, the kings became Christians, and instead of pillaging they started contributing to the civilisation of medieval Europe.

Harald Bluetooth, King of Denmark, was converted to Christianity in around 965. The people of Iceland followed in 1000, then the Norwegians under their popular king, Olav II Haroldsson. When he died at the Battle of Stiklestad in 1030, he became

Norse sagas

The Viking poets, the *scalds*, told tales of gods and heroes in a way that mixed reality with the supernatural. Long poems known as sagas describe endless family feuds, full of heroic and bloody deeds. Like Homer's epics of Ancient Greece, the sagas recounted historical events, but added mythical elements to help people understand and find guidance for living.

Danish king *This 14th-century manuscript illumination portrays Knut the Great (1016-35), whose empire included England.*

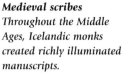

Medieval scribes
Throughout the Middle Ages, Icelandic monks created richly illuminated manuscripts.

Viking church
This wooden church at Vik in Norway dates from the 12th century.

the first Scandinavian saint. Finally, Sweden joined the Christian fold at the end of the 11th century. Under the Church's influence, old customs, beliefs and institutions passed away. Blood feuds were suppressed and the monarchy took over the administration of justice. Feudal armies replaced Viking bands. Knights were landowners who provided men for military service.

By the end of the 11th century, Norway, Sweden and Denmark had found ways of coexisting in peace. Finland remained a chaos of competing tribes. Under the pretext of converting the Finns to Christianity, King Eric of Sweden invaded in 1157. Swedish rule lasted until the beginning of the 19th century, although the Finnish language and culture managed to survive.

Power at the heart of Europe

In 1230, the Lithuanian tribes united under Mindaugas to form a Grand Duchy that became one of the most powerful states in Eastern Europe. In the reign of Gediminas (1316-41) they fought off the Teutonic Knights, a brotherhood of mercenaries founded in the Holy Land in 1190. Gediminas's grandson Jogaila married Queen Jadwiga of Poland in 1386, uniting the two nations as a formidable power. With his cousin Vytautas, Jogaila finally destroyed the Teutonic Knights at the Battle of Tannenberg in 1410. Over the next 160 years the dynasty he founded, the Jagiellons, ruled a vast area including Byelorussia, Western Ukraine and, for a time, Hungary and Bohemia.

From Romanesque to Gothic

From the 12th century, wooden churches were built in Norway. In the rest of Scandinavia, the Romanesque style of architecture spread from Western Europe. The favourite building material was stone – as in the enormous granite church at Viborg in Denmark – but brick was occasionally used, in a distant echo of the Lombard style of northern Italy. The first basilicas in stone were built at Lund in Denmark (1145) and Uppsala in Sweden (1164). Gothic architecture began to appear in the mid-13th century: the Danish cathedral of Odense is a superb example, as is the cathedral of Uppsala, completed in 1435.

Gothic masterpiece This polychrome statue of the Virgin Mary was created in Sweden in the 13th century.

The Valdemar supremacy

Despite efforts to maintain peace and stability in the region, struggles for power frequently broke out. Denmark suffered particularly badly. In 1131, a member of the royal family, Knud Lavard, Duke of South Jutland, was murdered, triggering a civil war that lasted 25 years. In 1157 Knud's son Valdemar was proclaimed king and a time of peace and prosperity followed. The Danish population grew, the city of Copenhagen was founded, and military threats from abroad were repulsed.

The Valdemar dynasty reigned for more than 200 years. Denmark became the most powerful of the Scandinavian countries. Valdemar II, known as *Sejr* (the Victor), ruled a sizable part of northern Germany as well as his own country, and conquered Estonia in 1219. A written constitution, limiting the king's powers and establishing an annual *hof,* or parliament, was agreed in 1282.

Valdemar IV, the last of the line, was a shrewd administrator who helped the country recover from the Black Death

(1349-50) and reformed the economy, the army and the constitution. After his death in 1375, his daughter Margaret became Queen of Denmark.

Margaret's achievement

An important influence on trade and foreign policy at this time was the Hanseatic League, an association of German cities on the Baltic and North Sea, set up in the 12th century to control the trade of northern Europe. As its influence grew, it established banks in a number of key locations, and its economic leverage was such that it could dictate policy to entire nations, including Denmark. In 1361, the Danish king, Valdemar IV, attempted to reduce the power of the League by seizing Gotland. Sweden and the Hanseatic League reacted angrily, attacking Denmark by sea and land. In 1370, Valdemar made peace, handing over trading rights in Denmark and control of three key ports in southern Sweden.

Danish hopes of standing up to the power of the Hanseatic League at last became a reality, thanks to Valdemar's daughter, Margaret. In 1363, at the age of ten, she was married to Haakon, heir to the Norwegian throne. In 1380 Haakon died and their son Olav became king of

Tallinn and Riga, Hansa ports

In the 13th century, the Baltic was an economic battleground between the Germans and Scandinavians. In northern Livonia, the Danes installed a bishop whose diocese extended as far as Riga, a city founded by Germans. The Danes then fortified Tallinn to consolidate their hold on the surrounding area of Estonia. In the 14th century the military strength of the Teutonic Knights shifted power back to the Germans, while the Hanseatic League ran the ports. The Hansa merchants built splendid houses and depots for their goods. The stepped gables of these buildings can be seen as far south as Amsterdam.

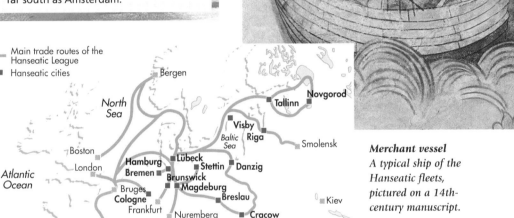

— Main trade routes of the Hanseatic League
■ Hanseatic cities

Merchant vessel
A typical ship of the Hanseatic fleets, pictured on a 14th-century manuscript.

Denmark and Norway. When Olav died in 1387, Margaret ruled in his place. The following year, she was offered the Swedish crown by rebellious nobles who wanted to depose their German king, Albert III of Mecklenburg. Margaret defeated Albert in battle in 1389, although the war for the Swedish throne dragged on for another eight years. In 1397 the union of the three crowns was proclaimed at Kalmar. Margaret reigned until 1412, and nominated her nephew, Eric of Pomerania, as her heir. The Kalmar Union between Denmark and Norway was to last for another 400 years – although Sweden soon broke away.

Bloodbath in Stockholm

In 1448, the Swedes elected a king of their own, Karl Knutsson. He was succeeded by three members of the Sture family. Swedish

Banking centre In 1361 the Danish king, Valdemar IV, seized Visby in his war against the Hanseatic League. This 19th-century painting by Carl Gustav Hellqvist imagines the wealth of the city.

independence did not please the Danes, who tried repeatedly to seize control of the country. Finally, in 1520, Christian II of Denmark entered Stockholm with his army and was crowned king after promising an amnesty to all those who had opposed him. Almost immediately, he broke this promise and beheaded 82 leading Swedish noblemen and priests. Far from destroying the opposition, this spurred them on. A young Swedish noble, Gustav Vasa, organised a rebellion. He defeated the Danish army in 1521, rallied support for his cause from abroad, and in 1523 forced Christian back to Denmark. Gustav was elected king that same year, with the title Gustav I Vasa.

The Reformation

King Gustav was attracted by the new religious ideas of Martin Luther, the brilliant German theologian and preacher who believed passionately in teaching ordinary people to understand the Bible, and questioned the Catholic Church's doctrines on salvation and the infallibility of the Pope. These ideas were spread through

Modern monarch
The true founder of modern Sweden was Gustav I Vasa, who was crowned in 1523. This painting by Julius Kronberg (1850-1921) shows Gustav being presented with the first Swedish translation of the Bible.

Scandinavia by German preachers and Hansa merchants, with the help of the new technology of the day – printing.

Sweden was the first Nordic country to convert. Lutheranism was adopted as the official state religion in 1527. King Gustav saw in the reformed church a means of consolidating his power. He also saw a financial opportunity: by confiscating the property of the Catholic Church he was able to add to the royal exchequer.

In Denmark, events followed a similar pattern. King Christian III (1534-59) needed money for his army. The clergy refused to help, so the king reacted swiftly, arresting most of the country's bishops and seizing all the Church's property in a single night. The Lutheran religion was officially adopted and was soon imposed on Norway and Iceland (which had been ruled by Denmark since the previous century). The task of translating the Bible into Danish was begun.

Baltic wars

At the start of the 16th century, after a series of military setbacks, Denmark came to terms with her German neighbours, making a peace that lasted more than 200 years. Relations with Sweden, however, remained hostile. The two countries were fierce rivals over trade around the Baltic Sea. Sweden at that time was in expansionist mood. Gustav's son, Eric XIV (1560-8), took Tallinn and its surrounding territories in 1561, and fought the inconclusive 'Seven Years' War of the North' against Denmark and Norway in 1563-70.

Empire builder *Eric XIV, son of Gustav I Vasa, strengthened the power of the Swedish monarchy and fought wars against the Danes and Poles. He later went mad and died in prison in 1577.*

Hard times in Iceland

Iceland became part of the united kingdom of Denmark and Norway at the Union of Kalmar in 1397. Its natural poverty was exacerbated by corrupt royal governors and raiding parties of English and German mariners. With no markets nearby, fishing produced no income. A harsh political regime was imposed in the 17th century. In 1707, an epidemic of smallpox killed 18 000 people, more than one-third of the population. Although Frederik V (1746-66) tried to develop the country's agriculture, a series of natural disasters took a further toll of this beleaguered nation: more than 10 000 Icelanders were killed in volcanic eruptions between 1783 and 1786.

Vanquished *The Battle of Nordlingen (1634) was one of Sweden's rare defeats in the Thirty Years' War.*

Vitus Bering

The Danish navigator Vitus Bering (1681-1741) was employed by Peter the Great of Russia to find out if the continents of Asia and America were connected. He left St Petersburg in 1725 but found his way blocked by ice near the Kamchatka peninsula. In the spring of 1728 he set off again and sailed in a thick fog through the strait between Russia and Alaska that has since been given his name. In later years, Bering took part in the Great Northern Expedition to map the coast of Siberia, but died of scurvy after a shipwreck at Bering Island in 1741.

Insatiable for knowledge *A woman of great curiosity, Queen Christina is portrayed here having a geometry lesson with Descartes.*

Queen Christina

When Gustavus II Adolphus of Sweden died, his daughter Christina (1626-89) was only six years old. For the next 12 years the chancellor, Axel Oxenstierna, governed on her behalf. A popular and successful queen, Christina built several castles and gathered a brilliant court around her, attracting some of the greatest minds in Europe, including the French philosopher René Descartes. To the displeasure of her people and the astonishment of Europe, she abdicated in 1654, became a Catholic and moved to Rome. There she founded the first public opera house and supported numerous artists and composers, among them the sculptor Bernini and the composers Corelli and Scarlatti. She was also a great protector of the poor and the Jews in Rome.

Strategic genius
Symbolically protected by the king of animals, Charles XII of Sweden leads his armies into battle. His adventurous life was described in a biography full of passion and tragedy written by the French philosopher and writer, Voltaire.

A generation later, Sweden's Charles IX (1595-1611) led campaigns against Poland and Russia, then renewed the war against Denmark, but again without a decisive victory for either side. The Thirty Years' War, which ravaged Europe from 1618 to 1648, inflamed the old enmity between Denmark and Sweden. The Swedish king, Gustavus II Adolphus (1611-32), won some famous victories in Germany, and by the Treaty of Westphalia in 1648 his country was granted western Pomerania and a number of North Sea ports, including Bremen.

These triumphs irked the Danes, who attacked Sweden with disastrous results. Swedish armies invaded Jutland and marched on Copenhagen. Between 1643 and 1660 Denmark was forced to give up its richest provinces: Halland, Skåne, Blekinge, Bohuslän, and the island of Gotland. Sweden was now at the peak of its power, with ports in Poland and the Baltic lands. Riga became Sweden's second largest city after Stockholm, where the population had already reached 50 000.

Sweden's neighbours now became alarmed, and a military alliance between Russia, Saxony and Denmark was formed. They declared war in 1700. The 18-year-old Swedish king, Charles XII (1698-1718), was a dangerous opponent, crushing his enemies in a series of battles, including the Russians at Narva in 1700. He was not invincible, however, and an invasion of Russia in 1707 was unsuccessful. His army surrendered to the Russians at Poltava in 1709. Narrowly escaping capture, Charles fled with a few men to Turkey, where he stayed for five years, ruling his homeland as best he could from exile. His return to Sweden was dramatic: leaving Turkish territory on suspicion that he was about to be betrayed, he rode across Europe in disguise, reaching Stralsund on the Baltic in just 14 days. But Charles's time of glory was over. He was forced to hand over territories and make the best of his reduced military power. He laid siege to the Norwegian town of Fredrikshald in 1718, exposing himself to enemy fire, and was fatally shot.

After his death, the Great Northern War (1700-21) came to an end. Sweden, a spent force, ceded its Baltic provinces and a part of Finland to Russia. Even those parts of Finland that stayed under Swedish control were constantly harassed by the Russians. The former great power of the Baltic was too weak to react.

Baroque splendour
Decoration inside the Orthodox Church of the Holy Spirit in Vilnius.

Lithuania, land of the Baroque

At the start of the Reformation, Riga and Tallinn, the principal cities of Latvia and Estonia, adopted Protestantism. Lithuania, united politically to Catholic Poland, resisted, falling instead under the influence of the Counter Reformation preached by Polish Catholic priests and Jesuits. Splendid new churches were built around the country in the Baroque style, the official architecture of the Counter Reformation. Forty churches were built in Vilnius alone, among them St Casimir (1615) dedicated to Lithuania's patron saint.

From absolutism to enlightenment

The more or less continuous state of war in the 17th century meant that Scandinavian monarchs tried to keep political power in their own hands. In Sweden, Charles IX (1660-97) confiscated half the property of the nobles and used the money to fill the coffers of state. In Denmark, Frederik III (1648-70) was given absolute powers following the success of his campaigns against the Swedes.

This period of absolutist monarchy was followed in the 18th century by a time of political reform. King Frederik I of Sweden (1720-51) agreed to a constitutional form of monarchy, and in Denmark ministers of Christian VII (1766-1808), who suffered from dementia, introduced a number of liberal laws. His successor, Frederik VI (1808-39), introduced further reforms.

Meanwhile the Baltic States had, in 1721, become part of the Russian Empire, following Sweden's defeat in the Great Northern War. No enlightened reforms were seen here. Even the abolition of serfdom by the Russian tsar, Alexander I, in 1819 had little practical effect.

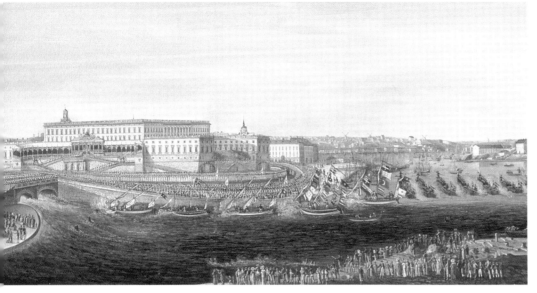

Napoleonic turmoil

The 19th century began stormily in Europe, with a series of wars unleashed by the French Revolution and the Napoleonic empire that followed. Gustavus IV Adolphus was fiercely anti-Bonapartist: he declared war on Russia, which at the time was an ally of France. The war did not go well, and by the Treaty of Hamina (1809) Sweden gave up the Åland Islands and the whole of Finland to Russia. Gustavus IV Adolphus had refused to negotiate, and was deposed by a group of officers. His successor, the senile Charles XIII (1809-18), had no heirs. In those dangerous times, with the threat of war ever present, the country needed a strong leader. The Swedes began to look around for a suitable heir to the throne. A young officer, Carl Otto Mörner, suggested a French marshal, Jean-Baptiste Bernadotte. After some controversy

Adopted country The arrival of Jean-Baptiste Bernadotte in Stockholm. Born in Pau, in southwest France, this marshal of Napoleon's army was elected to the Swedish throne.

Bernadotte was offered the job and became crown prince in 1810.

Denmark and Norway attempted to stay out of the Napoleonic conflict, but a treaty of armed neutrality with Prussia, Sweden and Russia was interpreted as hostile by the English, who sent Nelson to destroy the Danish fleet in 1801. The British navy returned to bombard Copenhagen in 1807. These actions drove the Danes to the French side, which by 1813 was on the way to final defeat. By the Treaty of Kiel in 1814, Denmark lost Norway (which Sweden then gained), but kept control of Greenland, Iceland and the Faeroe Islands.

A new world

After the devastation of the Napoleonic wars, the Scandinavian countries had to rebuild their economies. Norway's exports

Battle of Copenhagen In the Napoleonic wars, Denmark's 'armed neutrality' was seen as a provocation by the English, who destroyed the Danish fleet in 1801.

of timber and fish had been hard hit by the continental blockade. Denmark's economy was stagnant. Only Sweden had begun the process of industrialisation, although in 1850, 90 per cent of its people still lived on the land, and there was a mounting problem of overpopulation, coupled with a series of bad harvests. For many of Scandinavia's rural poor, migration to North America offered the only hope. From the mid-century on, as white settlers pushed westwards across the continent, building railroads and towns, the opportunities seemed limitless. More than a million Swedes emigrated to America between 1850 and 1900.

At the same time, a new society was being born at home. Industrialisation gathered pace, as did democratic reforms. With the new constitution of 1865 the Swedish parliament gained a second chamber, and its new members soon began to address a host of social issues: freedom of worship,

Royal, by invitation

In 1810, Swedish King Charles XIII was senile and childless. A regent was needed, as well as an heir to the throne. Baron Carl Otto Mörner, a young Swedish officer, was sent to discuss the matter with Napoleon, then the most powerful man in Europe. Mörner had served for a year in the French army, and had been impressed by one of Napoleon's marshals, Jean-Baptiste

Bernadotte. With help from allies in Sweden, Mörner persuaded the Swedish parliament to adopt Bernadotte as regent. He accepted the appointment and arrived in Stockholm in October 1810. He proved a wise choice, making shrewd military alliances with Russia and England against Napoleon. As a reward for his help, he was offered the throne of Norway in 1814, joining the two kingdoms in a union that would last until Norwegian independence in 1905. Bernadotte was crowned King of Sweden in 1818, taking the name Charles XIV. He was popular with his subjects, though he never managed to learn their language. He died in 1844 and his descendants have remained on the Swedish throne ever since.

Rural poverty Life in 19th-century Scandinavia was harsh and emigration to America attracted many people from Sweden, where 75 per cent of the population in 1900 still lived on the land.

women's rights, health care and education for the poor, alcoholism. The Danish king, Frederik VII (1848-63), gave up his absolute power to become a constitutional monarch. Men aged 30 and above were given the vote, and through new provincial assemblies local democracy was born. As elsewhere in Europe, this was a time of nationalist ferment. A series of wars were fought over the duchies of Schleswig and Holstein, which had mixed populations of Danes and Germans. Denmark lost the area to Prussia in 1866.

At the same time, an old dream of uniting Denmark, Norway and Sweden was revived. When Prussia invaded Denmark in 1848, volunteers from the other two countries flocked to her defence. The conflicts and rivalries of previous centuries gave way to cooperation.

Independence and identity

When Norway and Sweden were united in 1814, Norway kept its own constitution and parliament. Iceland, which had remained under Danish dominion, also began to clamour for independence. In 1874, legislative powers were granted to the *Althing*, the Icelandic assembly, although still under the sovereignty of the Danish crown. A further step towards independence was taken when Icelandic ministers became answerable to the *Althing* rather than to the Danish monarch.

Finland, for many years a Swedish possession, had become a grand duchy of Russia in 1809, with the capital transferred from Turku to Helsinki. The Finns enjoyed a large measure of independence, but resented the use of Swedish as their official language. A movement led by the philosopher Johan Vilhelm Snellman pressed for a change to Finnish. In 1863 Snellman's efforts were rewarded when Finnish was made an official language.

In the Baltic States the ideal of nationhood was much in the air, discussed by thinkers and writers as it had been since the 18th century. The university of Tartu in Estonia was a particularly vigorous and independent centre of political thought, but the Russian authorities did not look favourably on ideas such as autonomy and

self-determination. When an uprising against tsarist rule broke out in Lithuania in 1832, they responded by closing down the university. In the first Russian revolution of 1905, Lithuanian peasants took advantage of the situation to burn down landowners' castles.

United nations From 1814 to 1905, Sweden and Norway were joint kingdoms, as symbolised by the 19th-century Swedish royal coat of arms.

Patriotic composer Jean Sibelius (1865-1957) wrote music inspired by Finnish landscape and legend.

Schooldays The film Pelle the Conqueror re-creates the strict atmosphere of a schoolroom in bygone days. Education has long been highly valued in Scandinavia. Denmark in 1814 became one of the first countries in Europe to make schooling compulsory.

Economic awakening

By the early years of the 20th century, industrialisation in Scandinavia had become a serious business. In Denmark there was a boom in shipbuilding, while breweries and cement works multiplied. The population grew from 1.7 million to 2.9 million in the space of 50 years. In Sweden there was similarly rapid progress. Iron mines in Kiruna and Gällivare, in Lappland, were turned into massive industrial workings. The building of a railway to the Norwegian port of Narvik in 1902 allowed the iron to be exported across the North Sea. Meanwhile the engineering industry expanded, too, and Swedish ball-bearings quickly became known worldwide.

Commander-in-chief Marshal Mannerheim defended the independence of Finland in two world wars.

The Great War

During the First World War, Denmark, Sweden and Norway were neutral, despite their sympathy for the French and British cause. Although all three countries' overseas trade was boosted by the war, the Germans' use of submarines from 1917 caused significant losses to Scandinavian shipping. Throughout the war Denmark, still smarting from the loss of Schleswig to Prussia in 1866, was nervous of its German neighbour. When Germany was defeated, the Versailles Peace Treaty ordered a referendum in Schleswig to determine which state its inhabitants wished to belong to. In

Export boom Oslo in the early 20th century, a busy industrial port.

1920, 70 per cent of the people of North Schleswig voted for Denmark; 80 per cent of the southerners for Germany. The frontier was established between the two countries just north of the city of Flensburg. It has not been seriously contested since.

New states

The 1914-18 war had other consequences for Denmark. By the Act of Union of 1918, Iceland became a separate state, although the two countries continued to share the same monarch, and foreign policy was still decided by the Danish government. This arrangement lasted until 1940, when Hitler's armies invaded Denmark. Iceland, garrisoned first with British then with American troops, was legally free to follow its own path. In 1944, after seven centuries of foreign domination, Iceland became a republic, truly independent at last.

Finland, meanwhile, took advantage of the Bolshevik Revolution of 1917 to free itself from Russian rule. A year of civil war followed, as the 'reds' fought a stronger 'white' army led by Marshal Mannerheim and supported by the Germans. The communists were defeated at Tampere and in 1919 a Finnish Republic was proclaimed. The Baltic States also achieved independence. According to the principles of national self-determination, the Treaty of Versailles recognised three new states: Estonia, Latvia and Lithuania.

Years of social democracy

Between the world wars, political reform went on apace. The Swedish Social Democratic Party participated in government as early as 1917, rapidly becoming the dominant force in Swedish politics. It ruled the country either alone or in coalition from 1932 until the 1980s. Denmark's Social Democrats were equally successful, as were the Labour Party in Norway following the elections in 1927. Although there were differences in policy between these parties, social democracy in all three countries depended on a strong single labour union with enough negotiating power to stand up to the politicians and big business. In the course of the 20th century, great social changes took place. The class system was broken down through education and a commitment to equal opportunities for all.

The Nazi menace

In the Second World War, Sweden was the only Scandinavian country that stayed neutral. The Germans forced some concessions from the Swedish government, but the country remained independent and played an important role in taking in thousands of refugees from Denmark, Norway and the Baltic States, and from Jewish communities across Eastern Europe. Denmark, with its border with Germany, was particularly

Copenhagen protest The Social Democratic tradition was no guarantee against popular demonstrations such as this one in 1951.

exposed to the Nazi threat. A non-aggression pact between the two countries was signed in 1939, but this did not prevent the Germans invading on April 9, 1940. A coalition government of the four main political parties was formed, and struggled to retain its independence until 1943, when German military defeats abroad and shortages at home led to strikes, sabotage

Norway breaks free

Norway's growing prosperity in the 19th century, based on modernised timber and fishing industries, led to demands for independence from Sweden. On June 7, 1905, the Norwegian Diet abolished the union with Sweden, and this was backed by a referendum in August. Stockholm accepted this decision, and the constitutional monarchy of Norway was born.

The women's century

In 1906 Finland was the first country in Europe to give women the vote. Norway followed in 1913, Denmark in 1915, and Sweden six years later, although married women were allowed to vote in Swedish municipal elections as early as 1862. The first woman minister to serve in a democratic government was Nina Bang, who was appointed Danish minister of education in 1924. The first woman head of state to be elected by universal suffrage was Vigdis Finnbogadøttir, who was president of Iceland from 1980 to 1996.

First female president *The Finns followed Iceland's example in February 2000, when Tarja Halonen was elected president.*

and anti-Nazi protests. The Danish government refused to carry out German orders to use violence against Jews, saboteurs and protesters, and a state of emergency was declared. The Germans took control. The Danish ambassador in London placed his country on the side of the Allies, and the campaign of resistance within the country intensified.

Norway was rapidly overrun by superior German forces, and the king fled to London. Resistance to the occupying army was fierce throughout the country, and had some spectacular successes, including the destruction of a factory at Rjukan in Telemark used by the Germans to manufacture heavy water for a projected atom bomb. On May 7, 1945, British troops liberated Oslo. German troops in Denmark had surrendered two days before.

Finland's winter war

The Finns faced a threat from a different direction. The Soviet Union, freed temporarily from war with Germany by the Molotov-Ribbentrop non-aggression pact, demanded a part of southern Karelia in order to protect the approaches to the city of Leningrad. The Finns refused, and on November 30, 1939, Soviet troops invaded Finland. Despite heroic resistance under Marshal Mannerheim, the Finns were defeated. They were forced to give up a large part of Karelia, leading to a mass exodus of its people. When Hitler turned on Russia in June 1941, the Finns took advantage of the situation to resume their struggle against the Russians in the so-called 'War of Continuation' (1941-4). This was only partly successful, and at the end of the war Finland was left with a reduced territory, as well as 300 000 Karelian refugees, reparations of $300 million to pay to the Soviet Union, and large areas devastated by the Germans in the north. Despite these handicaps, the country recovered in the postwar years with surprising speed.

Looking to Europe

In Norway and Denmark, the bitter experiences of the Second World War led to a wholesale revision of foreign policy. The concept of neutrality now seemed hollow, and the two countries joined NATO in 1949. Sweden remained outside the treaty, but worked hard for global disarmament

Nazi hatred *When German troops overran Oslo in 1940, their occupation led to many heroic acts of resistance, including industrial sabotage.*

Collapse of communism *Lithuania declares independence in 1990. Huge crowds turned out to celebrate the end of Russian domination.*

and the protection of human rights. Finland kept up good relations on both sides of the Iron Curtain, signing an 'Agreement of Friendship, Cooperation and Mutual Assistance' with the Soviet Union in 1948 – a reflection of its geographical position and the 20 per cent of its exports that went to the USSR – while also joining EFTA, the European Free Trade Area, in 1961.

Denmark joined the European Economic Community (EEC) in 1973, but refused to sign the Maastricht Treaty in 1992 or adopt the European single currency. Finland and Sweden also joined the EEC, while Norway voted twice to stay out, once in 1972 and again in 1994.

Latvia, Lithuania and Estonia were freed from Soviet domination by the collapse of communism in 1989-90. They soon began to seek entry to the European Union. Although their economies remained some way short of the criteria for admission, their future as independent European states, living and trading in peace with their neighbours, was no longer in doubt.

THE PLACE
AND ITS
PEOPLE

Together, Iceland, Scandinavia and the Baltic States have a total population of 23 million, living in an area that covers nearly 560 000 sq miles (1 400 000 km²), six and a half times the size of the UK. These figures are significant: there are immense open spaces and magnificent landscapes protected against the depredations of man. The human communities are remarkable, too, with a rich cultural heritage going back to prehistoric times, and a special gift for inventiveness and creativity that includes technology, art and business.

CHAPTER 1

THE MAJESTY OF NATURE

Lakes and forests, long sandy beaches, mountains, fiords, volcanoes, glaciers, waterfalls…the countries of Northern Europe offer an amazing variety of landscapes. Like a kaleidoscope of the elements, the surprises are never-ending. Iceland is a cauldron of volcanoes, hot springs and geysers, yet it also boasts the largest glacier in Europe. The dark mountain landscape of Norway, gouged by the thawing glaciers of a retreating ice age, sparkles with immense waterfalls. The woods and the water are a paradise for animals: migrating birds, salmon, trout, deer, bears, lynx and lemmings. Most striking of all, as you approach the North Pole, is the quality of the light: sunlight that burns and sparkles with almost unreal intensity; moonlight that bathes the snow-covered landscapes in an icy, silvery sheen. And then, in winter, that dreamlike display of colours in the sky, the aurora borealis, or northern lights.

The North Cape, on the Norwegian island of Magerøya, is the northernmost point of Europe.

Where land and sea meet

From the spectacular fiords of Norway to the gentle green islands of the Danish archipelago; from the sandy beaches of the North Sea to the storm-battered rocks of the Baltic, everywhere land and sea interact in an endless and fascinating drama.

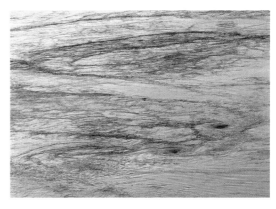

Turbulent waters *The original maelström is a fast-flowing current in the Norwegian Sea.*

Preconceptions can deceive: from Spitsbergen to Denmark is the same distance as from Denmark to Sicily and the differences in nature, climate and geography are equally striking.

Down the latitudes

Surrounding Spitsbergen and the whole north polar region is the Arctic Ocean. This is the world's smallest ocean – 4.7 million sq miles (12.25 million km^2) – yet its icy waters play an important role in driving the flow between all the oceans on Earth. Most of the Arctic is permanently covered in ice, which severely restricts animal life. Despite this, a food chain exists, from the microscopic floating plants known as phytoplankton through to the large marine mammals: whales, seals and walruses. These, along with polar bears and Arctic foxes, thrive in the frozen wastes inaccessible to man.

Farther south, the long western seaboard of Scandinavia crumbles into countless archipelagoes in the Norwegian Sea. Ten thousand years ago, as the glaciers melted at the end of the last Ice Age, the sea level rose, filling the mountain valleys, creating fiords and islands. The fiords are sea inlets. Many are very deep and surprisingly long –

Preserve of nature *The high chalk cliffs (left), woods and sandy beaches of the Danish island of Møn are celebrated beauty spots.*

The *Sund*

The Strait of Øresund, the *Sund*, which connects the Baltic to the North Sea, is 68 miles (110 km) long from north to south, but only 3 miles (5 km) wide at its narrowest point between the Danish city of Helsingør and Swedish neighbour Helsingborg. In 1432, Erik of Pomerania, King of Denmark, Norway and Sweden, imposed a toll on every ship that passed through the strait. Over four centuries, until its abolition in 1857, this toll provided two-thirds of the Danish kingdom's income. The imposing castle of Kronborg at Helsingør was built in the 16th century to protect this valuable source of revenue. Today Øresund is no longer a frontier. Ferry traffic between the two shores is intense. In 1991, plans were agreed for a combined bridge and tunnel which was opened in 2000. This brings the cities in the area, notably Malmö and Copenhagen, into a single, powerful network.

From conflict to coexistence

For a thousand years, empires have risen and fallen across the Baltic and North Sea. Political, economic and military rivalries between Scandinavian countries have led to a succession of wars and treaties, unions and separations. In the 11th century the Viking monarch Svend Forkbeard and his son Knut the Great ruled a kingdom that included Denmark, Norway and England. In the Middle Ages, Denmark was the foremost power in north-eastern Europe, and until 1814 ruled Iceland, Greenland and the Faeroes, Jutland and Norway. Sweden for many years controlled Finland, Poland and the Baltic States, and took over the Norwegian crown from 1814 to1905. Since Viking times Sweden and Denmark have fought each other 28 times for supremacy in the Baltic. They finally ceased to do battle in 1718 at the end of the Great Northern War.

some stretching as far as 60 miles (100 km) inland. The scenery of the fiords, with their steep green sides and still blue waters reflecting snowy mountain peaks, is breathtaking.

Farther south again lies the North Sea, a harsh and unpredictable environment, once with such plentiful fish that it fed the people living on its shores for centuries. A shallow, recently-formed sea – 150-300 ft (50-100 m) in depth, and, like the fiords, only flooded some 10 000 years ago – it has enormous reserves of oil, which have significantly boosted the economy of Norway.

Denmark's Jutland peninsula faces the North Sea, and at Skagen, its northern tip, two contrary currents meet, North Sea versus Baltic. The coast here is superb, with windswept moors and sand dunes as far as the eye can see.

Ice sculpture Small icebergs are dissolved by the action of the sea. This one has been eaten away to form an arch.

Rich harvest Around the mountainous Lofoten Islands in the Norwegian Sea are some of the best cod-fishing grounds in the world.

White and black One of the many faces of the coast of Iceland. This is one of the arms of the Vatnajökull, the largest glacier in Europe, as it reaches down into the sea at the south-east corner of the island. Elsewhere there are long black beaches of fine volcanic sand.

Moving east down the coast of Jutland, you come to a skein of over 400 verdant islands, sheltered by the peninsula from the buffetings of the North Sea and its prevailing winds. On the largest of these islands, Zealand, sits the capital of Denmark, Copenhagen.

Rounding the corner of Skåne, the Baltic Sea opens out between Germany, Sweden and Finland, touching Poland, Latvia, Estonia, Lithuania and Russia on the way. The Baltic is the world's youngest sea, only about 5000 years old, as well as its largest body of brackish water. Its low salinity and wide seasonal variations in temperature restrict the number of animal species that can live in its waters (cod, hake, herring and halibut are the most common), but stocks remain high and Baltic herring is a valuable export item. The coast is generally low-lying and fringed with dunes, woodland or fields.

Forged in a watery element

All of life in Scandinavia is connected with water: fiords, sounds, lakes, waterfalls and rivers. With their ancient maritime heritage and the sea always close at hand, the Scandinavians are born sailors. To them, the sea is never a barrier, but always a pathway, a means of communication with neighbours, and a source of wealth. All the great cities are ports, with merchant fleets that still rate as some of the largest in the world, and fishing industries to match.

The maritime spirit runs deep in the Nordic imagination: Iron Age burials took place in boat-shaped chambers; Viking longhouses had roofs in the form of upturned ships; sea-blue, the colour of youth, adventure and life, is a favourite colour. Yet, lovers of the sea as they are, the Scandinavians have no illusions. Behind the majestic scenery of the fiords, the colourful fishing villages, the beaches where children happily play, they know there lurks a cruel enemy – terrifying storms with 60 ft (20 m) waves, shifting sands that create unexpected shallows and shoals, dunes that can swallow up a house. Such threats are never taken lightly: the Scandinavians have a healthy respect for the sea that has shaped their moral character, making them careful, well-organised and straight-talking, brave but not foolhardy, and always ready to face the worst.

Volcanoes under the ice

Iceland, like the Azores, is a peak of the Mid Atlantic Ridge, a long geological fissure that runs under the Atlantic Ocean. Sunk deep below the sea for most of its length, the ridge is a gigantic crack between two plates in the Earth's crust.

The Icelanders are used to storms, extreme cold, earthquakes and volcanic eruptions, but one thing they fear above all else is floods. These arrive with terrible suddenness, as huge pockets of meltwater form inside glaciers and burst out with no warning.

Disasters waiting to happen

In 1973, a wave of heat from Hekla, the nearest active volcano to Reykjavik, caused the lowest layer of the glacier on its slopes to melt. A lake built up inside the glacier and, when it reached a critical size, rushed down the mountainside with the force of the Amazon in flood: a flow of 200 000 tons per second.

In 1996, the eruption of Bardarbunga turned part of the Vatnajökull, a glacier that covers the volcanoes of the south-east corner of the island, into an enormous invisible reservoir. When this great mass of water found a way out, it emptied itself with devastating force, carrying off several cubic miles of ash and volcanic rock, and sweeping a length of coastal road into the sea.

Natural disasters such as these are completely beyond human control and are a permanent threat. Icelanders live with this knowledge, accepting an element of danger in their daily lives. In other ways, though, the explosive marriage of water and fire that gives Iceland its unique character creates a beneficial environment – thermal springs provide free heating for houses, city pavements, greenhouses and swimming pools. Hot mud baths, volcanoes, thermal springs and giant geysers bring tourists from all over the world, who congregate around the Blue Lagoon, a vast open-air swimming pool filled with thermal waters in the middle of a lava field. They also stand and admire the famous *Geysir*, a jet of superheated

Tourist attraction *In Iceland many geysers, fountains of boiling water and steam, erupt from the earth.*

water and steam that bursts from the depths of Mount Hekla at regular intervals, shooting 60 ft (20 m) into the air. (This is the original geyser, which has given its name to all geysers worldwide.)

The volcanic landscape offers one of the greatest shows on Earth: lakes and rivers of fiery red lava seep out of the ground, often crowned with ghostly fountains of flame. The sight is spectacular, and usually quite harmless. The process has gone on for millions of years and continues today, on land and beneath the sea, without threat to life. Occasionally, though, an eruption of exceptional violence takes place.

Nature's palette

Ask people how they picture Iceland and most will probably describe something similar to the Jökulsarlön lagoon. This lies on the island's south-east coast – a beach of black volcanic cinders, a steel-grey sea with drifting white icebergs, and a snowy backdrop of mountains and glaciers under a leaden sky. But this is far from the whole story: Iceland is surprisingly green, from the grassy, sheep-nibbled steppes to the slopes of volcanoes where grimmia (a hardy local moss) creeps over the debris of ash, cooled lava, and scattered boulders, mantling every surface in green. Then there are the brilliant, almost dreamlike, mineral colours – sulphur yellow, carmine, burnt gold, Prussian blue – which are deposited in the form of crystals by the steam of geysers and thermal waters as they spout from the hot earth. Even the greys and whites of Iceland are more varied than you might imagine: they range from the pure ice-blue of fresh snow sparkling in polar sunlight to the dirty, molten-lead tones of glaciers.

Volcanic cone *The surface of this volcano near the Myrdalsjökull, a glacier in the south of Iceland, is covered in ash that has been colonised by plants. The lower slopes are deeply scarred by erosion.*

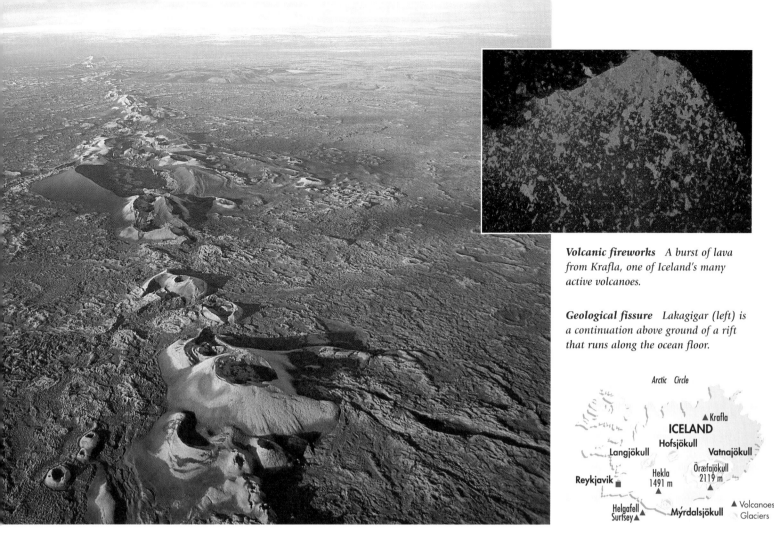

Volcanic fireworks A burst of lava from Krafla, one of Iceland's many active volcanoes.

Geological fissure Lakagigar (left) is a continuation above ground of a rift that runs along the ocean floor.

Arctic Circle

ICELAND

▲ Krafla
Hofsjökull
Langjökull   Vatnajökull
Reykjavik ■   Hekla   Öræfajökull
              1491 m   2119 m
Helgafell
Surtsey ▲   Mýrdalsjökull   ▲ Volcanoes
                              ▽ Glaciers

This occurs when a plug of cooled lava blocks the hot lava pushing up from below and pressure builds up until the plug is blown away. The lava, accompanied by blasts of smoke and poisonous gases, explodes from the ground in all directions. Such an eruption occurred in 1104 when Mount Hekla destroyed communities for 43 miles (70 km) around. This earned the volcano the reputation of being one of the gates of hell. Today tourists enjoy the sense of fear and awe that the volcanoes inspire. Perhaps the most spectacular of all is Öraefa-jökull (or Hvannadalshnukur), which rises 6950 ft (2119 m) from the southern shore of the island. Viewed from a boat, its huge conical peak encased in ice is a sight never to be forgotten.

Earth's building site

Scientists believe that Iceland emerged from the sea around 23 million years ago. As its fiery, unstable character shows, it is still in the process of being formed. New islands and volcanoes regularly appear from the deep. In 1963, an eruption on the seabed off south-west Iceland created the island of Surtsey. It took four years to form, and rose 1000 ft (300 m) from the ocean floor. Nearby, in 1973, a volcano on the island of Heimaey erupted, burying one-third of the local fishing port, Vestmannaeyjar, in ash and cinders.

The greatest show on Earth Iceland's marriage of ice and volcanic fire creates some stunning effects, unique in the world.

Iceland grows more rapidly than it is worn away. The forces of erosion are immensely powerful, with frequent storms, high seas, melting snows, floods, and the scouring of glaciers as they grind their way down the mountain slopes. But the forces of growth are even stronger, as magma oozes up from the depths of the earth, forcing its way through a fissure in the tectonic plates that has been widening at a rate of about 4/5 in (2 cm) a year for the past 60 million years. One-third of all the lava that has poured out of the earth in the past 500 years is estimated to have come from Iceland and its 200 volcanoes.

The fury of Laki

Laki is the Icelandic god of the underworld. It is also the name of the country's deadliest volcano. When Laki erupted in 1783, it tore a 30 mile (50 km) gash in the earth along the great fault that runs beneath the Atlantic Ocean and surfaces in Iceland's turbulent landscape. From this gash poured more than 2.88 cu miles (12 km³) of molten lava, which spread over 218 sq miles (565 km²) of land. Clouds of gas – carbon dioxide and sulphur dioxide – killed three-quarters of the farm animals in the region. A second eruption two years later killed more animals and caused devastating famine in which 9500 of the 10 000 inhabitants died. Compared with Laki, Hekla's eruptions, in 1766, 1947 and 1970, have been relatively harmless, although the underworld god has another weapon here: meltwater lakes that form inside glaciers and break out, causing massive flooding. This last occurred in 1973.

35

The Scandinavian Alps

A paradise for walkers and cross-country skiers, Scandinavia is often thought of as hilly rather than mountainous. Not so: ski-jumping was invented here, in an exciting mountain landscape that compares favourably with the Alps.

O ne of the most spectacular railway journeys in the world runs across the south of Norway from Oslo to Bergen. Although it never climbs higher than 6500 ft (2000 m) above sea level, the track winds along an astonishing succession of ramps, through tunnels, over viaducts and around hairpin bends, suspending the train in mid-air one minute, threading it along the bottom of a shadowy gorge the next. As it crosses Buskerud, Norway's central rocky plateau, the track burrows between glaciers and tightrope-walks along the tops of razor-like ridges, with dizzying views down to fiords on either side. After travelling on the railway line, you understand why the mountains are known as the Scandinavian Alps.

According to geologists, what we see today is only half the story – a layer of ancient bedrock that was once crowned with far higher peaks. The bedrock, known as the Baltic Shield, was formed of granite and other extremely hard materials

Mountains and fiords *A typical Norwegian landscape, patches of snow surviving into summer.*

Rise and fall *Scandinavia's mountains were shaped by the same geological forces as the Scottish highlands. The highest peaks are around 8000 ft (2500 m), but they look much higher. Lemmings (left) are part of a rich wildlife population.*

between one and two billion years ago. For 180 million years this area was under the sea, which added layers of slate, limestone, shale and conglomerate to a thickness of 330-500 ft (100-150 m). Part of the same Caledonian System as the British Isles, the mountains were created by folding processes around 400 million years ago, and subsequently eroded to about half their original height through a succession of ice ages and thaws.

If the two mountains could be placed side by side, Glittertind, the highest peak in Scandinavia (8103 ft/2470 m), would be dwarfed by Mont Blanc, the highest in the Alps (15 770 ft/4807 m). But in its context Glittertind is just as impressive a sight, and the same is true of all the Scandinavian mountains: they look and feel as high as the Alps, but in reality they are not in the same league.

Illusion and reality

Snow and ice play a part in the illusion. White peaks give a sense of mystery, distance and unreachable height. The presence of water adds to the deception: reflections in fiords and lakes double the apparent size of the mountains that rise sheer from their depths, and waterfalls tumbling from high clefts in the rock mark the distance of their plunge in slow-motion detail. Everywhere there is a feeling of energy, vastness and awe. Viewed from a boat or aeroplane, the brooding masses of these high snowy plateaus, rising like fortresses from the sea, are reminiscent of the Andes or Himalayas. Their forbidding grandeur is due not so much to their height, as to the way they are deeply slashed by fiords along 1250 miles (2000 km) of shore.

Like other coastal ranges, the mountains of Scandinavia turn a steep and rugged face to the ocean and a gentler one inland – in this case south and eastwards, down to the Baltic Sea and the Gulf of Bothnia. Sweden is generally flatter than Norway, but the north is mountainous, with the highest

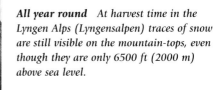

All year round   At harvest time in the Lyngen Alps (Lyngensalpen) traces of snow are still visible on the mountain-tops, even though they are only 6500 ft (2000 m) above sea level.

summits – Kebnekaise (6926 ft/2111 m) and Sarektjåkko (6857 ft/2090 m), both in Lappland – not far short of Norway's highest peaks. The line of Scandinavia's mountains stretches some 1180 miles (1900 km) from Cape Lindesnes in the south to Cape Nordkinn in the north, forming much of the border between Norway and Sweden on the way.

Three different types of mountain scenery can be found along this great spine of rock. In the south is the Hardanger Plateau, the largest in Europe, nearly 4600 sq miles (12 000 km²) in extent. It lies on average 2950 ft (900 m) above the sea, with deep valleys and numerous industrial towns. Farther north, in central Norway, is Jotunheim, land of the giants, wild and harsh, sharply incised by fiords and crowned by the twin peaks of Glittertind and Galdhoppigen.

Farthest north of all is the Dovrefjell, frozen, inhospitable and sparsely populated, sloping away gently to the east in the Finnmark Plateau, its rocky extremities entering the sea in the Lofoten Islands and the Svalbard archipelago.

Forbidding beauty Spitsbergen, high in the Arctic Circle, was also shaped by glacial erosion. These mountains are just over 5580 ft (1700 m) high.

Lands of waterfalls

Gaps in the steep sides of fiords allow mountain streams and torrents to take the shortest route down to the sea in the form of spectacular waterfalls. Norway alone has nine of the world's 50 highest waterfalls. Many are hard to visit, located as they are far up some of the longest fiords in the country, and accessible only by ship. Two of the most beautiful can be reached on popular

cruises: Voringsfossen at the end of Hardangerfiord, and the Bride's Veil waterfall in Geirargerfiord. Haugfossen, on the Tyrifiord north-west of Oslo, is the setting for open-air concerts in the summer months. Iceland has some fine waterfalls, too, notably Hraunfossar, Dettifoss, and Gullfoss – a wide, multilayered waterfall of sweeping grandeur in the centre of the country.

Cascading torrent   A waterfall spills from the side of Gudvangen, a classic trough-shaped glacial valley in Norway.

Resistance heroes

During the Second World War, Norway was occupied by the Germans, who had a plant for the manufacture of deuterium oxide, (heavy water, essential for their bid to build an atom bomb) at Rjukan, halfway between Stavanger and Oslo, in the Telemark region. The Norwegian resistance, one of the most active and courageous groups in Europe, formed a plan to destroy the factory, which was located in a narrow gully below Mount Gausta in a spot almost impossible to attack by air. On a snowy night in February 1943 the Norwegian partisans, led by Captain Knut Haukelid, approached across country and blew up the factory in a daring night-time raid. Although the

factory was devastated, the stocks of heavy water remained untouched in underground caverns deep below the installation. In November the same year American bombers tried and failed to destroy them. In February 1944 Haukelid and his men had one last chance: to attack the rail convoy carrying the heavy water to Germany. As the line itself was heavily guarded, they laid timed explosive charges on a ferry where the wagons would be loaded the next day. The plan worked perfectly, sinking the ferry and its cargo in 1300 ft (400 m) of water, thus fatally delaying the German attempt to build a nuclear weapon. The episode inspired the 1960s film, *Heroes of Telemark*.

A maze of lakes

Finland's lake district, the largest in Europe, is a haunting world of dark forests reflected in still waters. Norway also has lakes – no fewer than 160 000 – while Sweden has 90 000, many of them so intricately shaped that they are hard to show in detail even on the largest-scale maps.

The advance and retreat of glaciers that has gouged the Scandinavian landscape has left it filled with countless lakes. The great Finnish lake system is the largest and most spectacular of these, but both Norway and Sweden also boast lakeland scenery of exceptional variety and splendour.

The lake of 1000 islands

North-east of Helsinki lies the huge expanse of Lake Saimaa, 1700 sq miles (4400 km²) in area, an endless labyrinth of bays, promontories, inlets and channels. Bathed in the dreamlike light of summer nights, with a thousand hues of blue and green, it is a place of

Waterland
In the Norwegian highlands the Otra valley, or Setesdal, (below) contains a variety of landscapes, from tumbling waterfalls to more peaceful lakeland scenery.

enchantment and unearthly beauty. From June to September an old steamboat plies between the towns on its shores and islands: places like Savonlinna, with its medieval fortress and summer opera festival, bring visitors from all over the world. There are famous spas around the lake, too, such as Lappeenranta in southern Karelia, which was popular with the fashionable classes of St Petersburg in pre-revolutionary Russia.

In the autumn of 1939 the eastern part of the Finnish lake country was a theatre of war. The invading Red Army made painfully slow progress along its winding roads; the defending Finns, meanwhile, knew shortcuts and hiding-places in the forests. They opened the sluice gates of the Saimaa canal and trapped the Russian forces in a mire of mud and water. Only when the winter freeze came, and the watery landscape turned to ice, were the Russian tanks able to advance more rapidly.

Even today, iced-over lakes are used as roads in winter to cut journey times. Locals keep boats for summer use, whether for shopping in the nearest town, or exploring and picnicking among the hundreds of wooded islands.

It is hard to say where one lake ends and another begins: what looks like the opposite shore may be an island, what seems a channel may have no exit. Saimaa's neighbour, Päijänne, is shaped like a giant octopus, its tentacles reaching round headlands or deep into calm, reed-fringed bays. Rivers and streams often pass from one lake to another, forming a network of more than 225 miles (360 km) for canoeists to enjoy.

Making lakes   The long, slow process of glacial erosion is invisible until the ice melts. Then water fills the hollows gouged out by the glacier, forming lakes.

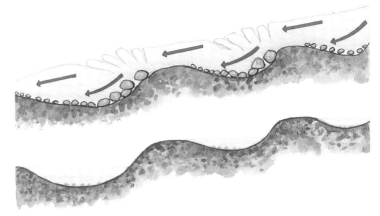

Largest lakes   Vättern, the second biggest lake in Sweden, is over 770 sq miles (2000 km²) in area.

Fabled outlook *Lake Pielinen in Karelia, seen from the hilltop of Koli, one of the most famous viewpoints in Finland. The islands and forests are typical of Finnish lakeland.*

Hiking in national parks

North-east Sweden is a mountain area with numerous long, thin lakes connected by hundreds of streams, which feed the rivers Pite, Lule and Ume. Several national parks have been created here, including Muddus 190 sq miles (491 km²), which contains the last primitive forest in Sweden. A wilderness of peat bogs, swamps and woodland, it is home to bears, lynx, white owls and lemmings. When their numbers in any one area become too large, the lemmings migrate, using tracks made by men or other animals.

Tracks are specially maintained for them in the park, but colonies of lemmings are fenced in from March to August to protect them from predators during the mating season. Stora Sjöfallet is a national park in the high mountains. Among its attractions is Sweden's largest reservoir, Akkavare. The trail from Porjus to the Norwegian border is one of the most beautiful in the country: 93 miles (150 km) long, it crosses several lakes, where rowing boats are provided for walkers to cross from shore to shore.

The Estonian lakes

One of the least-visited beauty spots of Europe, southern Estonia was known in former times as the 'Switzerland of the Baltic' because of its lovely undulating countryside of hills and lakes. It remains a delightful and out-of-the-way place today. The French philosopher Jean-Paul Sartre often came for the thermal waters at Lake Püha, and the Dalai Lama has also come to relax in its peaceful atmosphere. A giant oak grows on the lake shore, once used as a meeting place by locals, who consider it a sacred tree. Near Lake Püha is Otepää, a year-round holiday resort.

A hut, a rowing boat, a sunlit lake *Country life in Scandinavia at its simplest and most attractive.*

No licence required

You can fish for free along the coasts of Sweden, and in the five largest lakes: Vänern, Vättern, Mälaren, Hjälmaren and Storsjön. Everywhere else you need to buy a licence, but it doesn't cost much. Angling is popular in lakes and rivers, as well as in the *jokks,* or streams, that are found all over the country. There are very few towpaths, so people tramp about in boots or fish from boats. Char

is the commonest of the Swedish freshwater species. Related to the trout and salmon, it grows to 10-12 in (25-30 cm) in length and prefers cold clear waters. Pike, bream, trout and carp are also abundant – as is grayling, named *Thymallus thymallus* because it has a taste reminiscent of thyme. Perch, perhaps the most delicately flavoured of freshwater fish, is relatively rare.

Path to integration

The line of mountains that separates Norway from Sweden is the birthplace of dozens of rivers that flow into the Gulf of Bothnia. High in the mountains they are rocky, fast-moving torrents; lower down they grow fat and slow, often spreading into such wide expanses of water that they look like lakes. This is Swedish Lappland, about a quarter of the surface area of Sweden, with a mixed but scattered population of Lapps and Swedes. They tend to lead similar kinds of lives, intermarrying, going fishing, getting along well, a model of social harmony.

It has not always been so: the Lapps arrived 2000 years ago, while the first Swedes began to move in during the Middle Ages, attracted by the prospects for fur-trapping. Conflicts between the two groups for the same resources were frequent. In the 17th century iron ore was discovered and a mining industry began to grow. More recently, tourism and skiing have brought wealth and economic diversity to the whole of the region and the troubles of the past have been forgotten.

After the glaciers

Bathed by the warm ocean current of the Gulf Stream, Scandinavia has a milder climate than many people suppose. But its dramatic landscapes bear the scars left by the massive ice sheet that covered the whole area until 10 000 years ago.

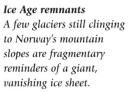

Ice Age remnants
A few glaciers still clinging to Norway's mountain slopes are fragmentary reminders of a giant, vanishing ice sheet.

At the start of the 17th century, fishermen on the Gulf of Both-nia were getting worried: they had noticed that the sea was retreating. Every four or five generations they had to build new harbours as the old ones became landlocked. They asked their priests for an explanation, and one of them came up with an incred-ible answer – the whole of Scandinavia was rising, together with its lakes, forests, mountains, coastlines and ports. The evidence for this theory – mussel shells collected on hillsides 165 ft (50 m) above sea level – did not convince the sceptical fishermen. Today we know that this theory is right: Scandinavia is rising, with the region around the Gulf of Bothnia moving particularly fast at a rate of 0.35 in (9 mm) a year. The reason is that the vast weight of the ancient ice sheet is no longer pressing it down.

Ghosts of the Ice Age

The glacial prehistory of Scandinavia can sometimes seem as titanic and strange as the old Norse legends that still scare chil-dren today. But if the stories of giant's footsteps are like fairy tales, there can be no doubting that there once were gigantic masses and forces here, which scraped smooth the plateaus, dug out the fiords, scoured the rocks, scooped out basins and heaped up the moraines that hold back the waters of thousands of lakes. To have had such an effect on the hard Scandinavian bedrock the layer of ice must have been more than 1 mile (1.6 km) thick. It must also have covered a huge area, because the scars it left over a period of 18 000 years can be found as far south as London and the plains of Germany.

Eight thousand years ago, as the first thaw was coming to an end, the ice sheet was still weighing down on the region with a mass of at least a million billion tons. Comparatively little of that ice remains today – just a few pale ghosts of that giant ancestor – although even these are some of the biggest areas of ice in Europe. On Spitsbergen, high in the Arctic Circle, a single tongue of ice named Monaco stretches 30 miles (48 km) from the principal ice cap down to the sea. It is twice the size of the largest glacier in the Alps.

In the south-east corner of Iceland is the Vatna glacier (Vatna-jökull), almost 0.6 miles (1 km) thick and a staggering 3300 sq miles (8540 km²) in extent. Vatna is not only the biggest glacier in Europe, but is as big as all the other European glaciers put together.

Norway's glaciers cover a total area of 1930 sq miles (5000 km²). The north-ern glaciers, which get little snow, tend to be small and quite close to the sea: as they slip down into the fiords they break up into small icebergs. The southern

Carved by glacier *The awesome erosive power of ice can be seen in fiords like this one, the Geirangerfiord, gouged by a glacier then filled by the sea.*

Climatic cycle

Since the end of the last Ice Age around 10 000 years ago, the world has undergone several changes of climate. The melting of the ice sheet accelerated 5000 years ago when global temperatures were 2°C (3.6°F) above present levels, only to slow down again during a mini ice age in the first 400 years of the Christian era. From the 9th to the 14th century the Earth warmed up again and the glaciers retreated once more. A second mini ice age that lasted from 1550 to 1850 interrupted the process, but the past 150 years have seen temperatures rise, with the ice melting further and sea levels creeping up. Liberated from the weight of so much frozen water, Scandinavia is rising, currently at a rate of 15-50 in (40-120 cm) every 100 years, gaining roughly the same area of land from the sea as it has from the melting ice – a few square miles in total.

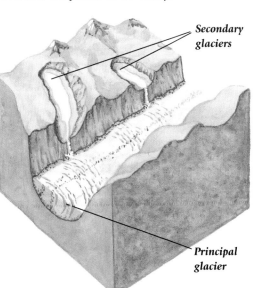

Pattern of erosion
Glaciers have scooped deep trenches and hollows in the mountains of Scandinavia. As they melt, the main glaciers leave long U-shaped valleys, while the subsidiary glaciers create hanging valleys above.

Secondary glaciers

Principal glacier

glaciers, which are regularly fed with snow but also exposed to warmer sunshine, are confined to the *fjeld*, or high central plateau. The largest of these, the Jostedalsbreen, covers some 300 sq miles (800 km²) and has 25 tongues.

Sweden and Finland have little permanent ice, apart from a few patches on mountain tops and in north-facing valleys. Traces of the Ice Age can be seen, however, in the countless lakes, peat bogs and swamps. Sweden has 90 000 lakes, chief among them the immense Vänern (2100 sq miles/5500 km²), the largest in Scandinavia.

Finland's lakes cover 10 per cent of the country, most of them in the south and east. The statistics alone are extraordinary: there are nearly 188 000 bodies of water over 200 sq miles (500 km²). Saimaa, the most extensive, covers 1700 sq miles (4400 km²), with a dense fretwork of water, islands and peninsulas.

Norway also has an enormous number of lakes, but its most noticeable legacy from the ice sheet is the fiords. Visitors from all over the world come to admire these natural wonders. Particular favourites are Sognefiord, north of Bergen, and Hardangerfiord to the south, with its brilliant summer flowers. Farther up the coast, Romsdalfiord and Lyngenfiord are ringed with sparkling, snow-capped peaks. Reisafiord, in the far north, is a magnificent spectacle in the summer midnight sun.

New forces in the landscape

The big glaciers are now confined to areas that are unaffected by the warm air and waters of the Gulf Stream – the Svalbard Islands in the Arctic Ocean, south-east Iceland, the Faeroes and the Scandinavian highlands. This means that over much of Northern Europe today glacial erosion plays only a minor part in the shaping of the land. Instead, ice and water are nature's sharpest tools. Ice splits rocks in winter, as water creeps into cracks and expands as it freezes.

The splinters and fragments of stone are carried along by running water as the melting snows turn into torrents and rivers. Although rainfall is not particularly high, these meltwaters are a powerful force, cutting, grinding and polishing

Mighty reflection   Iceland's Vatnajökull glacier is the largest remnant of Europe's ice sheet. It covers an area of about 3300 sq miles (8540 km²).

the rocky landscape previously scraped by glaciers. Cracks are widened into channels, hollows into gullies; valleys are deepened and new stream beds cut. Fresh links are formed between lakes and other watercourses, creating new channels.

The sea, too, is a great shaper of the land, pounding away at cliffs, flinging pebbles and sand at the shore and sweeping them along in an endless cycle of erosion and deposition. Thus the landscape is constantly changing – though the footsteps of the giants will always be there for those who know where to look.

Locked in rock   The Norwegian island of Spitsbergen (Pointed Mountain) was discovered in 1596 by the Dutch navigator Willem Barents. It is more than 50 per cent covered in permanent ice and contains rich deposits of fossils, which are keenly studied by palaeontologists.

Infinite forests

Viewed from the air, Northern Europe is like a huge green carpet with a brilliant blue pattern – the lakes and watercourses. The only exceptions are treeless Iceland, Denmark's farmlands and Norway's mountains.

Green and blue *Forests and water near Lake Inari in Finland typify Northern Europe.*

Roads that cross vast forests without passing a single house; signs that warn not of villages and schools, but elk tracks crossing your route: to the visitor used to a crowded city life, the silence of these immense spaces is a shock to the senses.

The advancing forest

Forests dominate the landscape in Sweden and Finland, and they are a notable feature in the Baltic States, too. When much of the rural population of Lithuania was deported to Stalin's Soviet Union in the late 1940s, huge areas were given over to forest, which now covers 40 per cent of the country. Elsewhere, unprofitable farms have been abandoned and the trees have moved in. In Sweden, forests now occupy twice the area they covered at the start of the 20th century. The trees, it seems, are reclaiming their ancient territory.

Most species of European broad-leaved trees grow in southern Scandinavia, which has mixed forests of oak, ash, lime and maple, as well as the more common conifers, pine and spruce. About 60 miles (100 km) north of Oslo and Stockholm the variety of broad-leaved species thins out considerably, giving way to the huge coniferous forests of the northern latitudes, although birch, rowan, aspen and willow can still be found in great numbers. At higher altitudes alpine birch is the only tree that will grow.

In southern Lithuania and Latvia, along the borders with Poland and Belarus, lie vast uninhabited stretches of marsh and virgin forest. These are wild and lonely places, home to beavers, otters and lynx – all species that are threatened or extinct elsewhere in Europe. There are black storks and great spotted woodpeckers, and rare orchids. Thanks to the combination of a 19th-century tsarist edict banning logging of much of the forest and a lack of interest by Soviet authorities in developing the economic potential of the area, it has remained untouched and contains a level of biodiversity that has long since vanished on the rest of the Continent of Europe.

Folklore and mystery

In Norse mythology, the Universe was held up by a great ash tree, Yggdrasil, with three roots – one in the underworld, one in the world of the gods, and one in the land of giants and elves. Three wells fed the roots: Urd (Fate), Mimir (Wisdom) and Hvergelmir (the source of all rivers). When the end of the world comes, Yggdrasil will be the source of new life.

Folklore calls the forest the kingdom of the wood goddess, who weaves nets of branches and moss to ensnare travellers, and sets obstacles in their path to lead them into swamps. Walking alone in the forest can be a frightening experience: with endless vistas of tree trunks and not a landmark in sight it is all too easy to get lost on forest paths. At first everything seems normal, but the further in you go the more anxious you become. Shadows become sinister, rocks seem to move, you get a feeling that you are being watched by thousands of eyes. The slightest sound makes you jump with fright. The locals say, 'Don't walk in the forest alone!' It is advice well worth heeding.

Sauna fuel *Birch is the commonest deciduous tree in Scandinavia. The twigs are tied together to make whips used in saunas.*

Autumnal beauty *In northern Scandinavia, trees struggle to adapt to the harsh climate. Forests are patchy and the trees quite stunted, although the colours are spectacular.*

In deepest Karelia

In the spring of 1828 a young pharmacist, Elias Lönnrot, set out on a walking tour of Finland. Disguised as a peasant, he collected ancient folk songs, incantations and spells. In Karelia he came upon a treasure – the *Kalevala* – an epic poem containing heroic and magical legends of the pre-Christian Finns. The epic tells of the creation of the world and the travels of the seer Väinämöinen, the smith Ilmarinen and the adventurer Lemminkäinen, and their loss and recovery of the *sampo*, a mill that produces salt, meal and gold, and is the source of happiness and prosperity. Lönnrot published the *Kalevala* in 1835, with an expanded version in 1849. A classic of world literature, it has been translated into 20 languages.

Managing the forest in new ways

A dead pine where a woodpecker has built its nest; an old birch trunk lying on the ground, blanketed with lichens and moss; a burnt forest clearing that swarms with new insect and plant life: these typical woodland scenes may look at first sight like neglect, but they are signs of a new 'hands off' approach to forest management, aimed at preserving a rich variety of plant and animal species.

Controlled forest fires are now a regular occurrence, and for good ecological reasons. Several insects and mushrooms actually depend on fires for survival, while certain seeds will not germinate below 40°C (104°F). Dead trees are often left to lie where they fall to provide nourishment for insects that feed off decaying wood. Copses and thickets that grow near water are left uncut because their leaves and insect populations are food for fish. Forest wetlands – bogs, marshes and swamps – are carefully protected, because these play an important role in maintaining the biodiversity of an area, providing habitats and refuge for a great variety of plant and animal species. Marshes are particularly useful as filters of nitrogen and heavy metals, and they play a valuable role in maintaining the level of the water table.

Home of the wild *Oulanka national park in Finland's Kuusamo region is a vast and beautiful wilderness still inhabited by wolves and bears.*

Balancing productivity and conservation

In the industrial age, man's ability to move in with chainsaws, lorries and lifting equipment, to drain swamps, clear forests and plant vast tracts of land with fast-growing tree species – all in the name of economic progress – have come close to destroying these precious environments. Giant logging operations, taking out 2000 acres (1000 ha) at a time, have wreaked havoc with wildlife. Many old woodlands have already been lost.

The destruction of forest environments reached its peak in the 1960s and 1970s. Only more recently has our growing awareness of biodiversity and the delicate balance of ecological systems led to greater public understanding, causing politicians and business leaders to put a brake on such careless and shortsighted policies of destruction. Owners of forests and logging companies now try to combine productivity with conservation and the bad old ways have at last begun to die out.

43

Life in the wild

Forests, tundra, mountains, lakes, rivers, marshes, sea coasts – all are habitats for a remarkable variety of animal species that include elks and reindeer, bears, wolverines, puffins, musk ox and lynx. Strict environmental laws protect these animals from the harmful activities of man.

Nocturnal hunter
The eagle owl has adapted well to the Arctic tundra and is believed to live for up to 70 years.

Despite its enormous antlers and long, clumsy legs, the elk is a surprisingly successful animal. Timid and shy in character despite its great size, this gentle, lumbering giant has thrived in the forests of Finland and Sweden in such numbers that it now has to be culled. Around 200 000 elks are shot each year. One reason for the elk's success is that its natural predators – wolves and bears – are in decline. Elk meat is good to eat, and is regarded as a delicacy by the Finns and Swedes. The northern latitudes, where tundra is the only vegetation, are the kingdom of the reindeer. A tough, patient animal domesticated by the Lapps, the reindeer migrates hundreds of miles each year, eating grass and willow shoots in summer, lichen in winter.

Wave watch *Puffins live in colonies on grassy clifftops and dive to catch fish in the sea below.*

Lemmings and predators

The mountains are lemming country. Small rodents with thick fur, they live in large communities and reproduce so quickly and efficiently that every three or four years their population outgrows its territory's capacity to support them. At this point instinct tells them to take to the road and they disperse in all directions in a mass exodus to new habitats. Thousands of lemmings take part in these migrations, and pick up new groups along the way. Foxes, crows and owls find them easy prey, but they press on, crossing streams, rivers and lakes despite being poor swimmers. Legend has it that lemmings 'commit suicide' by hurling themselves off cliffs into the sea. Although this is a myth, there is a small element of truth in it: they will stop at nothing to reach their destination. When they find a new home, their population has been severely reduced by the hazards of the journey: only the strongest and luckiest will have survived. The following spring they start breeding, and the great cycle of population increase, migration and death begins again.

Meanwhile the predators have not done so well. In the vast forests of northern Norway, Sweden and Finland some of the larger mammals that once roamed freely in Europe can still be found: brown bears, wolves, lynxes, wild boar and wolverines – pinemarten-like creatures with thick, silky fur and sharp teeth and claws. Driven away by human development, they find a refuge in these last bastions of wilderness, besieged citizens of a hostile world.

Seasonal colours *A young Arctic fox whose fur will turn white with the first winter snows.*

Phalanx of horns *Musk oxen survive the cold. They have been successfully introduced to Norway and even Spitsbergen.*

Solitary giant   The elk, or moose, is the largest member of the deer family, 5-6 ft (1.5-1.8 m) tall at the shoulder and weighing more than 1750 lb (800 kg). Its antlers can spread up to 6 ft (1.8 m). Elks sometimes form groups in winter.

Insulated
The Scandinavian lynx is protected from the bitter cold by a coat of thick winter fur.

The Matsalu reserve

One of many nature reserves in the Baltic States, Matsalu in Estonia is a wetland favoured as a breeding-ground by a variety of aquatic bird species. There are several different habitats spread across the entire estuary of the River Kasari and its neighbouring islands: reed-beds along the river banks; marshes near the river's mouth, grassy meadows and pasture-land on the island shores. During the great seasonal migrations, in April to May and again from August to October, as many as 35 000 birds rest here on their long journeys. These include thousands of swans, some 300 pairs of grey geese, and smaller numbers of mute swans and bitterns. More than 100 species have made their homes in the reserve, including marsh harriers, ducks, kittiwakes, coots and black-headed gulls.

Return to the source

From the first days of summer to the last days of autumn, millions of salmon and trout swim up the rivers of Sweden, Finland and Norway to spawn. For the preceding 18 months, they have lived in the sea, feeding intensively to build up a layer of fat. Now they set off on their arduous journey, fighting their way upstream, driven by instinct against powerful currents and over falls, never stopping till they reach their goal. Once there, the females lay between 8000 and 25 000 eggs, which the males then cover with a layer of sperm. After spawning, the fish are so drained of strength that most of them simply die of exhaustion. After hatching the young spend four or five years in rivers and lakes before swimming downstream to the sea. There they will live for another year or two, building up their strength and fat reserves before the long journey upstream to the spawning grounds.

Summer visitors, winter residents

In Denmark people say that the singing of skylarks is the first sign of spring. Cannier souls look out for flights of grey geese. Like many other north European birds, grey geese fly south for the winter, returning in spring and summer to breed. Their reappearance in northern skies is eagerly awaited by Scandinavians, weary of the long, dark, cold months. Other birds, such as the barnacle goose, prefer to nest in far northern locations such as Greenland, Spitsbergen and Franz Josef Land. In autumn they fly south to spend the winter in Denmark and southern Sweden, where the first shoots of spring provide nourishment.

Not all birds migrate: some have developed unusual techniques of survival. The ptarmigan, for instance, which lives

Fish hawks   Ospreys are magnificent-looking birds of prey that nest in Scandinavia. They seize fish from the water with their claws.

in the far north beyond the tree zone, has a white winter plumage that provides perfect camouflage in snow. When the thaw comes, the bird becomes conspicuous and is prey for foxes. The ptarmigan relies on the wind to lay bare ridges where it can find berries and shoots. If the weather is particularly harsh, it will bury itself in the snow and stay there for days on end.

Birds of the cliffs

The steep cliffs of the Faeroe Islands are inhabited by a very particular group of bird species. On the west coast of Stromø the different colonies live in clearly defined horizontal bands. The kittiwakes live on the bare rock, at the water's edge. Slightly above them, thousands of guillemots lay their eggs in the crevices and niches of the basalt rock-face. About 330 ft (100 m) above the sea, where scattered vegetation clings to the slightest crack or hollow, live the fulmars, a magnificent sight as they wheel and glide on stiff, outstretched wings.

The bird most typical of the Faeroe Islands is the puffin – easily identified by its large colourfully striped beak. It nests in long burrows, which it excavates under the turf on the clifftops. Brilliant swimmers, they dive into the sea and chase fish under water using their wings as fins. Puffins are now threatened by an introduced predator, the brown rat, which invades their tunnels and eats their eggs.

45

A world of archipelagoes

The coasts of Scandinavia are fringed with thousands of islands – large and small, bare and richly forested, mild and sunny in the south, battered by icy winds in the north.

When ships leave Stockholm, they have to weave through a maze of islands and peninsulas. Those closest to the port are occupied by the capital's suburbs; farther out the holiday homes begin. Then comes a scattering of tiny islands, each one smaller than the last, buffeted by the winds of the open sea. Soon the Åland Islands come into view – more than 6500 of them altogether. These are Finnish territory, but an independent province, with their own parliament and administration. The Åland Islands stretch all the way to Turku, like giant steppingstones placed across the sea to link the two cities. The islands vary from gentle green rustic havens to rugged grey knuckles of rock. Around them lies the Baltic, like a millpond on summer evenings when the sea is flooded with horizontal light – a scene of beauty and tranquillity.

Intensive cultivation
No opportunity is missed by Denmark's farmers, who use every inch of land – even on the islands.

Islands of sun and commerce

Öland and Gotland, two large Swedish islands lying south-east of Stockholm, are famous for their summer sunshine. Most of Öland is a rocky limestone steppe, a paradise for botanists, with some 30 species of indigenous orchid. The ruins of a magnificent 13th-century fortress stand guard over its only town, Borgholm.

Gotland is the largest island in the Baltic. Its undulating landscape is varied, with well-kept forests, traditionally farmed fields, steep cliffs and long sandy beaches. From the 12th to 14th century the capital, Visby, dominated the trade between Russia and western Europe, and later became a key port in the trading network of the Hanseatic League. It still retains its old ramparts and warehousing, and, above the cathedral, rope lofts.

Sand dunes and beaches

Only the bell-tower of the Church of St Lawrence is visible above the sand at Skagen, on the northern tip of the Jutland peninsula. The rest was swallowed up by dunes in the late 18th century. The North Sea's combination of long tides and violent storms has created a coast that is constantly changing shape, a total of 200 miles (350 km) of sandy beaches and shifting dunes, dotted with seaside resorts.

The Baltic States also have superb beaches, once polluted but now being cleaned up. The 19th-century Estonian resort of Haapsalu, south-west of Tallinn, is being restored to its former glory as a spa, with mud baths, cafés and grand hotels with balconies overlooking the sea. Founded in 1825, Haapsalu was fashionable with the cosmopolitan Russian upper class and artists such as the composer Tchaikovski.

The spectacular coasts of Møn and Bornholm

Denmark's Jutland peninsula (*Jylland* in Danish) is a northern extrusion of the coast of mainland Europe. The rest of Denmark consists of over 400 islands lying off the west and east coasts of Jutland. The largest of these are Zealand (*Sjaelland*) and Funen (*Fyn*). The islands are low-lying, mostly with fertile soils on a bed of chalk and limestone. Some, like North Zealand, are sandy.

The island of Møn is famous for its shoreline of white chalk cliffs, more than 330 ft (100 m) high, crowned picturesquely with woods. Bornholm, to the south-east, is a geological oddity: the most ancient part of Denmark, it is a mass of granite and gneiss forced up from the seabed in a prehistoric earthquake. Its unusual composition and the stormy seas that pound it have produced a deeply indented coastline, bristling with reefs and pitted with caves.

Black beach *A narrow strip of black volcanic sand on the Icelandic island of Dyrhólaey – a quiet reminder of the fact that the whole country was created by volcanic activity.*

Natural windbreak *North Jutland, where mile upon mile of dunes rise like a defensive wall against the winds and tides of the North Sea.*

Polar bears on Spitsbergen

The Spitsbergen islands, or Svalbard, 600 miles (960 km) from the North Pole, attract few visitors. Those that come tend to be explorers, scientists, naturalists and the occasional hardy traveller who delights in wild places. It is by no means the safest of destinations: temperatures can drop suddenly, and there is always the chance of an encounter with a polar bear, one of the most dangerous of all wild animals – guides always travel with a gun.

Females and cubs stay on the coast near their lairs, which they dig in the earth. Only the males venture onto the pack ice, hunting for seals which are their staple food. Polar bears are a protected species and so far they have survived well. As the polar ice continues to melt, however, the bears' habitat is shrinking: they may well follow the example of the Canadian bears on the Beaufort Sea, who have moved north to build lairs in snowdrifts.

Runde, a birdwatcher's paradise

Norway's coast, deeply indented by fiords, is bordered with long chains of islands whose green shapes stand out against the grey mountain background of the mainland. Birdwatchers come to the nature reserve of Runde, a little patch of land at the western end of the Ålesund archipelago, where over a million birds nest on the cliffs during the breeding season. More than 40 different species can be seen here: colonies of guillemots and fulmars, eiders and shags, razorbills, gannets and gulls, all under the beady eye of falcons and eagles on the lookout for easy prey.

Lofotens' dangerous currents

Some 125 miles (200 km) north of the Arctic Circle, along Norway's north-west coast, lies an archipelago of 80 mountainous islands, the Lofotens. Tiny fishermen's huts, painted bright red, have been built in sheltered creeks, away from the fury of winter winds. Inhabited since the 12th century, the islands are a rich cod-fishing area, where crowds of up to 30 000 fishermen used to gather at the height of the season. Despite their polar latitude, the presence of the Gulf Stream softens the climate. The sea rarely freezes and temperatures in summer can be up to 20°C (68°F).

Fishing grounds *Well inside the Arctic Circle, the Lofoten Islands enjoy a mild climate thanks to the warm waters of the Gulf Stream. The fishermen's huts stand out against the snowy backdrop.*

Strong ocean currents sweep around the islands, reaching alarming speeds in narrows and gaps, such as the channel that separates Moskenes and Vaeroy at the southern end – the famous 'maelstrom' described by Jules Verne and Edgar Allan

Windswept grasslands *Estonia's largest island, Saaremaa, is more than 1000 sq miles (2600 km²) in area. Its flat, grassy plains were once graced with dozens of windmills.*

Poe. Sometimes, when the tides are strong, such vicious whirlpools are created that ships are forbidden to pass. Farther south, the funnel-shaped gap between Saltfiord and Skerlafiord is particularly fearsome, with water running through at a rate of 48 ft (14.5 m) per second, equivalent to 32 mph (52 km/h), or 28 knots.

The island of Grimsey, situated right on the Arctic Circle, also benefits from the Gulf Stream, although snow is not uncommon, even in midsummer. Its 155 inhabitants live mainly by fishing. They also farm and collect eggs from the vast colonies of sea birds that nest along the shores.

Lands of endless day or night

The Arctic Circle is located at latitude 66°33'N. But there is no need to go so far to see the wonders of the aurora borealis, or to feel the strange gloom of the long Arctic winter night.

Oslo, Stockholm, Helsinki, Tallinn: four Nordic capitals which lie at 60°N, close to the Arctic Circle. About a quarter of Scandinavia lies north of the Arctic Circle, and the whole region experiences the typical polar extremes of light and dark: midnight sun in summer; endless night in winter.

It is 2 o'clock on a December afternoon in Oslo: dawn has just broken yet already the street lamps are coming on for the night. Christmas is approaching and the darkness twinkles with festive lights. In the countryside the night is blacker, but the moon's rays reflected on the snow spread a ghostly silver radiance. Beyond the Arctic Circle the sun never appears above the horizon in January and February: for eight weeks there is nothing but a bluish twilight, which seems to accentuate the shimmering whiteness of the snow.

The magic of the northern lights

Yellow, green, violet or red, the northern lights blaze like celestial fireworks in the winter sky. They are different every time, forming luminous arches, scrolls, folded crimson draperies with jets of yellow fire, or pale pools of light that glow and fade like a gigantic, beating pulse. Sometimes storms high in the atmosphere fill the heavens with an astonishing array of colours; more often there is just a soft, glowing incandescence. Some people claim they can hear a kind of crackling or whistling when the lights appear, but not everyone agrees about this.

Autumn and winter are the seasons for aurora borealis, although you have to watch the sky patiently, because the display only lasts for ten minutes. It can be seen in the northern parts of the Nordic countries; in the town of Kiruna, northern Sweden, you can see it practically every day.

Particle fires

Once upon a time, the appearance of the aurora borealis was taken to be an evil omen, especially when the lights were tinged with red. Certain tribes believed that the Earth, a flat disc with water around it, was hooped with a great circle of fire that sometimes burned so brightly its reflections could be seen glowing and dancing in the sky. Others said there were foxes in the heavens, running across the great northern spaces with sparks showering from their burning fur.

The aurora appears above the South Pole and the North Pole. The phenomenon is not totally understood, but we know that it is generated 60-150 miles (100-250 km) above the surface of the Earth. Electrically charged particles carried by solar winds are attracted to the two poles. As they approach they collide with atoms of oxygen and nitrogen. This knocks away their electrons, leaving charged ions.

Midnight sun and moonlit days

In summer, the farther north you travel, the longer the days become. Up by the North Cape, the sun does not set from the end of May to the end of July. At midnight, it seems to roll along the horizon before rising for a new day. Two months of summer pass without night ever falling – in effect, an eight-week day. Winter is the opposite: two months of permanent darkness, except on nights when the full moon, shining on a snowy white landscape, creates a ghostly kind of 'day' (above).

Celestial fireworks The fantastic effects of the northern lights (right) appear to occur quite near the horizon, but in fact they originate in the highest layers of the atmosphere (below). Billions of charged ions radiating red, blue and green light seem to ripple and sparkle with living fire.

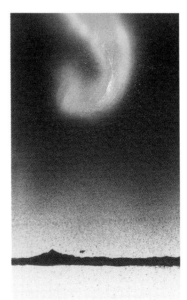

Ethereal landscape Snow, ice, wind and sun combine to create a strange, dreamlike light on Spitsbergen.

White nights

The sun sets quickly in countries near the Equator; near the poles in summer, it sinks slowly, approaching the horizon at a shallow angle. When it does finally set, it seems to rest just over the edge of the world in a long twilight-dawn, lighting the landscape from below. A white, shimmering glow seems to radiate from the Earth, and the whole natural world becomes a stage set, as if ready for elves and goblins to appear. Along the seashore, the wind drops: the Baltic is as calm as a millpond, its surface pale and opalescent, like watered silk.

In February, daylight starts to return. As soon as the sun first appears, around midday, everyone goes out of doors to sit on benches, heads raised to catch the welcome rays. The first swallow, a mulberry tree coming into leaf – every possible sign of spring is endlessly discussed. And when summer comes, people are determined to make the most of the sun: you will rarely see anyone heading for the shade, even on the hottest day.

The white nights of high summer can make sleep difficult, even in southern Scandinavia. If you go to bed late, you risk being kept awake by early morning birdsong. In fact people sleep less in summer, often making use of the long light evenings to spend time with friends, especially in the far north where distances between neighbours can be great. People react to the midnight sun in different ways. Some suffer from depression, while others get strangely high. For most it is just a fact of life.

But if there is a bad summer, or a few days of cloud and rain, the travel agents' phones start ringing and holidays in the Mediterranean suddenly sell like hot cakes. After a sunless winter, a gloomy summer is just too much to take.

Explosion of colour   After a hard winter, summer comes in with a glorious array of blossoms.

Feeling down? Time for a light cap

Winter or summer? The contrast between the two is so stark that Scandinavians are divided in their preferences. Some like the white nights of summer; others prefer the winter darkness, wrapping them like a warm coat, letting them sleep long hours and recharge their energy. But the absence of light can cause depression, which may sometimes be severe. In recognition of this, doctors have developed a new cure: light therapy. By wearing a cap equipped with a powerful lamp for just half an hour a day, patients can be relieved of their symptoms. There is even a café in Helsinki that provides its customers with light caps, so that they can cheer themselves up while having a drink.

CHAPTER 2

People AND Resources

Since the first settlers moved into Scandinavia in the wake of the retreating glaciers, three resources have provided the raw materials for life: water for fishing, trees for forestry and reindeer for hides and meat. In later times, other resources were found: iron – the foundation of the Swedish steel industry – as well as coal, oil and natural gas from beneath the seabed. Although Denmark and parts of the Baltic States possess excellent farmland, agriculture has never been a source of wealth for the other countries. The peoples of Northern Europe have always gone abroad to make money, through trade, technology, design and high-quality engineering. Cut off from this glittering success story for half a century, the Baltic nations have a long way to catch up, but the hope and determination are there. A free, democratic Baltic, able to draw on its commercial past, with the option of European Union membership, is an inspiring vision of the future to a new generation.

The cod catch in Norway's Lofoten Islands is hung up to dry, unsalted, on enormous wooden frames.

Reaping the silvery harvest of the sea

In terms of tonnage of fish caught, Norway ranks among the top ten countries in the world. Its waters are some of the richest fishing grounds on Earth. Cod, herring, hake, whiting and haddock are plentiful, and fish farms are booming.

Fishing has always been a way of life for the communities that are scattered along Norway's 13 000 miles (21 000 km) of coastline. The temperate maritime climate, as well as an unfailing source of food, drew the earliest settlers to these places at the end of the last Ice Age. Today there are 21 300 Norwegian trawlermen, nearly 13 000 workers in canning and processing factories, and more than 3700 employed on fish farms. The fishing industry provides jobs in other sectors, too, including transport, boatbuilding, and the manufacture of nets, clothing and safety equipment. Norway is Europe's leading exporter of fish, with foreign sales amounting to £2.3 billion ($3.4 billion) per year. Next comes Denmark, with annual exports worth £1.39 billion ($1.9 billion). The vast majority of the Danish catch is not meant for human consumption – a great percentage goes towards animal feed, particularly for the country's mink farms.

Today's catch
A Norwegian trawler crew winch in their net.

Protecting a vital resource

Iceland has no natural sources of fossil fuels or metal ores and relies heavily on imports. Its balance of payments is made up by selling vast quantities of fish, which account for around 65 per cent of its annual exports. Off the coasts of Iceland and the Faeroe Islands, the warm waters of the Gulf Stream meet the cold currents from the Arctic Ocean, forming an ideal environment for many species of fish. Until the early 1980s, Icelandic and Faeroese fishermen had to share these teeming waters with the trawler fleets of other European nations, all constantly growing in size and technical sophistication, with aids such as echo sounders making the task of locating shoals of fish easier than ever before. Faced with the dangers of over-fishing, the governments of Iceland and the Faeroes persuaded the United Nations to grant them an extension of their territorial waters. An

Fishing quotas

Once accessible to all, Norway's vast and highly productive fishing grounds have been subject to quotas and licences for almost 30 years. These regulations were introduced in the 1970s to prevent overfishing, an ever-present danger since the end of the Second World War, with trawlers becoming increasingly sophisticated and efficient. The migration of shoals between territorial and international waters, and the pressure of foreign fleets, made it necessary to establish international agreements for the maintenance of fish stocks.

economic exclusion zone was then created for 200 nautical miles around the coasts of both countries, preventing many other nations from fishing in their waters.

In the old days, fish was salted or dried as soon as it was caught. One of Iceland's leading exports until the 1950s was *klipfisk* – cod gutted and salted on board the trawlers, then, once ashore, washed and hung out to dry on wooden frames for between 2 and 15 days, depending on the weather. This was laborious work. Every evening the fish was collected, stacked and covered. After a final salting it was packed and exported, mainly to the Catholic countries of Southern Europe, where the Church imposed numerous meatless days. Today, only about half the catch is dried in the traditional way: the rest is transported to large warehouses where it is salted, packed and sent to Spain and Portugal.

When the boats come in

At the start of spring, in the Lofoten Islands off the north coast of Norway, a remarkable sight can be seen: a maze of tall wooden drying frames hung with hundreds of thousands of cod. Preparations begin in January, as fishing boats gather in vast numbers

Pen patrol *In Finland, as in Norway, farmed fish provides a valuable source of income while protecting natural fish stocks.*

Ice drill *Fishing through a hole in the ice in Swedish Lappland. Fish are attracted by the light.*

Hanging out *Gutted cod is hung on wooden racks to dry in the wind on the Lofoten Islands.*

Cottage industry *Smoked fish is popular in Latvia and Lithuania. Here, near Riga, it is still smoked in the traditional way.*

to keep alive an ancient tradition: the *lofotfiske*, or Lofoten fishing. The tradition goes back to the winter of 874, when the great chief Torul Kvedulfson launched a fishing campaign at Vagan, one of the towns in the Lofoten archipelago. He had the catch salted, and in the months that followed a ship was made ready to transport the entire catch to England for sale. Ever since then, the Lofoten islanders have made good use of their abundant Arctic cod, or *skrei*. The fish migrate from the Barents Sea at the end of January, joining the coastal cod in the warmer waters of the Gulf Stream around Norway. From January to March each year, thousands of tons of cod are landed in the Lofoten ports.

Way of the future

Over the past 20 years fish farming has become big business, especially in Norway and the Faeroe Islands. Trout and Atlantic salmon are the main species farmed, but Arctic char is also becoming popular. Researchers are working hard to extend the range of fish that can be farmed to include halibut, sea bass and scallops. Norway today produces more farmed fish than meat, and if fish farming continues to develop at the present rate it is likely to become one of the country's key industries. Between Hvaler in the south-east and Finnmark in the far north there are more than 3000 licensed fish farms.

Fish farming is a great deal more predictable than traditional fishing, and offers a more reliable return on investment. So successful is it, that the government has had to place limits on the industry to prevent supply outstripping demand. In 1996 Norway signed an agreement with the European Union, guaranteeing access to European markets for Norwegian salmon, but also fixing minimum prices and a ceiling for exports.

Making the most of a resource

On the Lofoten Islands, which lie off the north coast of Norway in the Arctic Circle, farming is practically impossible. The locals therefore take everything they can from their major resource – the cod. They waste nothing: every part of the fish is used except the intestines. The heads are eaten boiled or dried, or exported to African countries, where they are an important ingredient in cooking. Cod tongues are highly prized by the islanders, as are the roes, which are sent to factories on the mainland for canning and cod liver is processed to extract its highly nutritious oil, a valuable source of vitamins.

The reindeer civilisation

The Sami or Lapps are the last Europeans to live by herding reindeer, and in the mountain areas of Scandinavia's far north, the size of a family's reindeer herd is the main indicator of its wealth.

First stage *After skinning, reindeer hides are stretched out to dry in the sun.*

The cold air fills with steam and dust as the reindeer stamp and scrape the ground with their hooves. The lasso whistles and swoops, circling the neck of the chosen animal with deadly accuracy. The reindeer struggles and bucks, but there is no escape: she has been picked out by a breeder, who leads her off to a separate corral. So it goes on for days – thousands of reindeer are brought together each winter in a vast enclosure, then selected by individual owners for their herds.

Herding today *The Sami use the latest labour-saving technology, including snowmobiles, to herd their reindeer.*

Traditionally, the Sami have used reindeer as draught and pack animals, and as a source of food. They also make tools from the antlers, and tents, clothes and footwear from their hides. Over the years, methods of herding have changed enormously. First, the Sami domesticated only a few reindeer, which they used as lures to attract wild reindeer during the hunting season. Then in the 17th century they started gathering large herds and leading a nomadic life.

Not all Sami are nomads, however. Those who live on the Arctic coast are fishermen and farmers. (The Norse sagas speak of them as builders of fast and excellent ships.) The forest-dwelling Sami of northern Sweden and Finland have never been true nomads: they move only small distances with their herds.

A life dictated by the herd

Most reindeer herdsmen live in the mountains. They follow the herds in their annual migrations through the remotest regions of Norwegian, Finnish and Swedish Lappland. The timetable of their lives is ruled by the movement of reindeer. In winter, the animals seek sheltered pastures in forested valleys; in summer they climb to the tundra of the high plateaus, where the air is too cold for the mosquitoes and ticks that torment them. This seasonal migration, known as the great *rajd*, once involved whole families: it would take 40 reindeer to pull a family with its tent and belongings. Today, technology has taken over, and with the aid of snowmobiles, portable phones and even helicopters, a handful of men can manage an enormous herd. Their families still follow them, but they now live in separate summer and winter homes.

More than half of the Sami live in Swedish Lappland, which covers about 35 per cent of the country. Reindeer herding is restricted to them, and they must all by law belong to cooperatives. They own about 750 000 reindeer. Sami herdsmen also have special hunting and fishing rights that are exclusive to their people.

Annual round-up Every summer the Sami gather the herd for marking – a big event in each community, as well as tough physical work.

Reindeer cheese and meat

Reindeer are seldom kept for dairy produce these days, since the females (*vaja*) give little milk. Reindeer cheese, once a great favourite, is now hard to find. The meat, however, is still available and much appreciated – it is especially delicious smoked. The grass and lichens that reindeer eat were contaminated by the nuclear accident at Chernobyl in 1986, which was a disaster for the Sami. Reindeer meat was banned from sale for several years and health warnings were issued over mushrooms and berries growing in the affected areas.

Wooden houses of the future

The walls of a traditional house in Scandinavia are made either of planks laid vertically, as in Sweden or Norway, or logs laid horizontally, as in Finland and the Baltic States. The preference for wooden construction is because wood breathes and is less prone to holding the damp than stone. Times change, however, and in recent years timber construction has gone into decline – partly for reasons of cost, partly because of the fire risk. In Finland, only single homes can now be built of wood, although the government has recently backed a project in the town of Oulu to build special timber houses, whose flexible structure makes them ideal for export to earthquake zones. Meanwhile, the new Sibelius concert hall at Lahti is the world's first to be built entirely of wood. A mixture of pine, birch and poplar has been used, and its acoustics are said to be near-perfect.

Timber: the growth industry

The forests of Scandinavia are both a magnificent natural resource and a mainstay of the economy. Timber has always been the building material of choice, and it is one of the region's biggest exports.

Since earliest times wood has been used to build houses and boats as well as furniture, tools, weapons and countless everyday objects. In the 16th century, Norway was Western Europe's largest supplier of timber for construction. When its coastal forests began to be depleted, Finland and Sweden were quick to take up the trade with countries farther south.

From forest to mill

During the spring floods, the great rivers of Scandinavia became transportation networks, as felled timber was floated downstream from inland forests to the coast. The raftsmen who managed the operation were tough professionals, with all the prestige and rugged glamour that comes with a dangerous job. Today, the raftsmen have all but vanished: most felled timber is transported by road and rail, destined for the sawmills and pulp factories dotted along the northern coast of Sweden, around the Finnish lakes and along the Finnish coast.

Forestry provides timber for construction and joinery, as well as pulp for making paper and cardboard, cellulose, and a number of chemical products. The industry has grown at an average rate of

4.5 per cent a year since the start of the 19th century. Most Swedish and Finnish timber is destined for export. Finland, which is 75 per cent covered in forests, is the world's second largest exporter of paper and cardboard after Canada. In Sweden, paper products make up 14 per cent of the country's income from foreign sales.

Paper giants

The timber industry needs high investment, and with competition from North America, the Scandinavians have grouped together for strength. The Swedish company Stora ('the Great') and Finland-based Enso have merged to form one of the world leaders in the sector, with a turnover of 10 billion euros (£6.2 billion) and a total of 40 000 employees in 40 countries. Norway's forests are less accessible and difficult to exploit, so its timber industry is less competitive. In the Baltic States, timber exports have boomed since independence. Their main markets are Sweden and Finland, who buy birch wood pulp for paper-making.

Axe work Splitting low-grade timber for fuel in a Baltic sawmill.

Where farming comes first

Denmark's agricultural wealth is due to two factors: good land and a mild climate. In summer the average temperature is around 16°C (61°F). In winter it rarely drops below zero.

For centuries, farming has been the foundation of the Danish economy. It still plays a big part, socially and financially, although the number of farms is now down to 6000.

In the middle of the 19th century, 78 per cent of the population lived in the country, most of them working as farm labourers. Today, while 60.7 per cent of the land is used for agriculture, less than one per cent of the active population work in the farming sector: 25 600 people out of a total workforce of 2.8 million.

The Danes produce enough food each year to feed 15 million people. Cereals are the main product, with 60 per cent of arable land devoted to crops such as winter wheat and spring barley. Farming has become a specialised business: whereas 30 years ago most farmers would keep a few cows, pigs, poultry and horses, today they concentrate on a single crop or animal. The old family pig farms have given way to large complexes of battery sheds. These are so profitable that just 25 per cent of pig farmers are responsible for 80 per cent of the country's pork production. The government keeps a close eye on the major producers, however, with strict legislation and licensing regulations. Dairy farming is highly productive, too: 700 000 dairy cows give a total of 4.5 million tons of milk a year. Denmark exports 80 per cent of this in the form of cheese, butter and powdered milk.

they own. In the winter 65 per cent of arable land must be laid down to green crops to limit nitrogen pollution. All use of pesticides, herbicides and fertilisers, whether natural or synthetic, have to be justified, and a diary of crop rotations must be kept.

With the rise of environmental consciousness, a vigorous debate has sprung up throughout the countryside and elsewhere about alternative farming methods. Farmers, the media, and the population in general are all worried by increased pollution and the related ecological hazards. Consumers are showing that they are prepared to pay higher prices for organic produce, and suppliers are seeking to fulfil this growing demand by switching to greener, more traditional methods of farming.

Strength in numbers

Over the past century a strong cooperative tradition has grown up among Danish farmers. By grouping together to run the business side professionally, they can buy in bulk and market their goods more effectively. The members have to sell their entire production to the cooperative, which buys at the best market price and then takes care of processing, conservation, packaging, marketing, distribution and sales.

Environmental concerns

Strict laws protect the environment. Cattle farmers are obliged to have an area of pasture proportionate to the number of animals

Pick of the crop   The Germans introduced the potato to Lithuania and other Baltic lands, where it quickly became a staple food.

Favourite fruit

Apples, pears, strawberries, plums and other fruit grow well in the Danish sun, but the most popular fruit of all is the morello cherry – used for jam, syrups, juices and a delicious liqueur, *kirsebaerlikoer*.

World players on the industrial scene

Scandinavian businesses have responded in their own way to the challenge of global competition: despite high salaries and taxation, they achieve world-leader status through innovation, quality and design.

__Quality comes first__ Saab is renowned for its high-tech, high-quality construction.

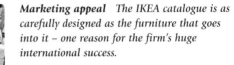

__Marketing appeal__ The IKEA catalogue is as carefully designed as the furniture that goes into it – one reason for the firm's huge international success.

For a perfect example of the Scandinavian approach to business, you need look no further than Bang & Olufsen, Denmark's leading hi-fi and television manufacturer. In a highly competitive world market, where prices have dropped steadily over the past 20 years, Bang & Olufsen have continued their unstoppable rise – with products costing three times as much as the competition. Their secret is cutting-edge technology, a reputation for quality, and a cool, sophisticated design that appeals to a discriminating clientele. Similar principles are applied to cars by Volvo and Saab of Sweden: no cost is spared, no technology ignored, in the pursuit of safety and reliability. Design is valued too: Volvo has recently made a successful effort to break away from its image as provider of executive family buses – in recent models they have even abandoned the famous rectangular lines.

Strategies for success

Most Scandinavian businesses are small-to-medium size and employ a specialised, highly trained workforce. They succeed by identifying the most favourable markets for their products. A spectacular example is TetraPak. In 1953, this tiny Swedish firm started producing plasticised cardboard containers. It is now the foremost manufacturer of food and drink packaging in the world,

and has recently merged with Alfa-Laval, the global leader in dairy technology. Meanwhile Nokia, the Finnish mobile telephone manufacturer, battles for top position in the world market with Ericsson of Sweden.

Success is achieved in a variety of sectors. Furniture specialist IKEA has established itself worldwide by offering Swedish design at budget prices. Norway's Statoil is the world's biggest exporter of light petroleum products outside OPEC. Maersk of Denmark is the world's most successful transportation and delivery company. As for Lego – there are few more famous household names in toys. The Danes seem to have the trick of inventing and producing just about anything – whether it be electronic components for the Ariane rocket, voice-commanded postal sorting machines, or ready-to-run cement factories for export anywhere in the world.

The Baltic challenge

Like other nations of the former Eastern Bloc, Estonia, Latvia and Lithuania underwent a crisis following the collapse of the Soviet Union in 1991. Over the next five years, the disappearance of this powerful 'big brother' and its centrally planned socialist economy meant the meltdown of their markets and industries. But the Baltic States had a few special advantages: a highly developed electronics sector, a low-paid yet able workforce, and some unusually dynamic

companies. There were also historic trading links with Scandinavia and Germany that had never been completely severed during the communist years. As a result of these factors, and a total determination to succeed, their economies recovered with remarkable speed, and several major European manufacturers are today building factories in the region.

__Talk on the move__ Nokia's head office in Finland is at the leading edge of mobile telephone design. State-of-the-art technology and a sound commercial sense are hallmarks of Scandinavian business.

Riches below the seabed

For over a quarter of a century, oil from the Norwegian sector of the North Sea has provided the country with a vast source of wealth – and a cushion against recession.

Oil was discovered off the coast of Norway at the end of the 1960s, but it was not, at the time, worth trying to extract it. Events in the Middle East changed the situation abruptly. The Yom Kippur War broke out between Israel and its Arab neighbours in October 1973. When the Western countries supported Israel, the Arab-dominated Organisation of Petroleum Exporting Countries (OPEC) raised the price of crude oil by 70 per cent in retaliation. In December, they increased the price a further 130 per cent. The Norwegians immediately saw their opportunity and stepped up exploratory work in the North Sea.

As oil prices climbed – from $3 a barrel in 1973 to $30 in 1980 – it was clear that the gamble had paid off. Today, Norway is the world's sixth largest oil producer and, after Saudi Arabia, its second largest exporter. It has 36 oilfields in the Norwegian Sea and the North Sea, with 25 more under consideration or development – they are predicted to remain productive for years to come.

Norway, a special case

Unlike most other oil-rich countries, Norway has not allowed the benefits of its natural wealth to flow to a privileged few. True to the Scandinavian ideal of equality, the government has distributed the profits fairly to all members of society. Most of the oil companies, including the two biggest, Statoil and Norsk Hydro, are state-owned. Both their profits and tax contributions have been ploughed back into spending on schools, universities, hospitals and other public services. As a result, while other Scandinavian countries have suffered high unemployment (it reached 20 per cent in Finland at one point) and a drop in living standards and social security, Norway has been relatively untouched. With typical prudence, the Norwegians have also placed a part of their oil revenues in a special fund, which topped 100 billion dollars in 2003. The country's present rate of

Arctic Ocean

Arctic Circle

Norwegian Sea

SWEDEN

Statfjord/ Gullfaks

Troll

Frigg

Sleipner

Ekofisk

DENMARK

NORWAY

Gulf of Bothnia

Oil

Natural gas

Oil town *This one-time fishing port of Stavanger is now the centre of Norway's oil industry.*

High technology

In the early years of offshore exploration Norway depended heavily on expertise from abroad, but quickly realised the need to train its own technicians and develop its own solutions to the problems of drilling beneath the seabed. The jewels in its crown are the Condeep platforms, gigantic steel and concrete structures that drill for oil and gas in the deep waters of the Outer Continental Shelf, then pipe them directly to clients in Belgium and the UK.

Well of prosperity One of the refineries belonging to the Norwegian state oil company, Statoil. A large share of its profits is ploughed into schools and hospitals.

Norway's, the supply is sufficient for all the nation's domestic needs and provides some valuable export income, too.

Denmark and Britain were locked in a bitter dispute for more than 20 years over oil-exploration rights in the territorial waters of the Faeroe Islands. Finally, in 1998, the two governments managed to hammer out an agreement and international drilling teams started boring in the Faeroes oilfields in 2001. Although the Faeroese

unemployment is 3 per cent, the lowest in Europe after Luxembourg.

The flow of oil from the North Sea fields may fluctuate over the next decade or so, but the enormous offshore reserves of natural gas (which is used to fulfill the needs of Germany, France, Belgium and other countries) are likely to make up for any drop in oil revenues. Norway is currently riding high economically, although some analysts fear that it may be over-dependent on oil and may have failed to develop its other industries adequately.

lack the technology and know-how to exploit the reserves themselves, the opportunity to provide service industries and collect royalties on the oil has the potential to rescue an ailing economy that at present is based almost exclusively on fishing. Older islanders fear that it will lead to another bonanza for foreigners, with few local benefits, but young people see the promise of a brighter future. There is even a chance that oil revenues will be enough for the Faeroe Islands to achieve complete independence, both economic and political, from Denmark.

An oil Eldorado

The sea has always been kind to the people of Stavanger. Situated on the south-east coast of Norway, with a North Sea harbour that is ice-free 365 days a year, it was once a great fishing port. When the fishing industry declined, oil came to the rescue. Today Stavanger is a perfect example of an oil boom-town.

Offshore drilling technology had been perfected in the 1960s, as the big oil companies realised that there were enormous reserves to be tapped under the world's seabeds. When oil and gas exploration began in the North Sea in 1971, Stavanger was chosen as the centre of operations and the base for service industries. Prosperity and jobs quickly followed. Thirty years on, practically everyone in the town has reaped the benefits. Speak to any child and the chances are they will tell you, 'My daddy's in oil'.

The other players

The remaining North Sea countries – Denmark, Britain and the Faeroe Islands – quickly joined the oil rush that Norway began. As a result, the question of limits to territorial waters became a subject of fierce debate. Once oil-exploration rights were settled in 1972, Denmark set about prospecting. Its first drilling rig came online in 1984, and by 2001 the country had 13 offshore wells, controlled by Maersk Oil in association with a consortium of international companies. Although the Danish oilfields produce only a fraction of

Prospecting the Arctic

So far, exploration in the Norwegian zone of the Barents Sea has proved fruitless, but large reserves of natural gas have been found in the Russian zone. The two countries formalized cooperation in oil production in order to exploit these and other hydrocarbon deposits in the area. Meanwhile Norway is developing the Snøhvit project in the Tromsø oilfield, where there are reserves of around 420 billion cu yds (320 billion m³) of gas. When this starts to flow in a few years' time, it will be the first offshore well in the Arctic Circle.

Monster of the deep
The Troll platform, here pictured under construction, can drill to a depth of 994 ft (303 m). Its flare burns 328 ft (100 m) above the waves.

Know the drill Exploring for and recovering oil from the seabed requires high levels of engineering know-how. The Norwegians are world leaders.

Toy town

It is a Scandinavian idea that has crossed all borders and made millions for its creators. Lego's interlocking plastic bricks allow children to create whatever they can imagine – they are the building blocks of a fantasy world.

I n 1932, a carpenter called Ole Kirk Christiansen set up shop in the small Danish village of Billund, where he made ironing boards, stepladders and wooden toys. He called his company Lego, a contraction of the words *Leg godt* , 'play well'. He later discovered that *lego* means 'I read' or 'I assemble' in Latin. It seemed a lucky choice of name.

From carpenter's workshop to world empire

Ole Kirk Christiansen bought an injection mould in the late 1940s and produced his first plastic building bricks for children. These remained his most successful product for 20 years. Then came a new idea: a range of self-assembly vehicles and scenes (airports, harbours, police stations, etc). These ingenious toys made Lego's international reputation, selling 18 to 19 million boxes a year worldwide. A range of bigger bricks for toddlers was marketed as Duplo, extending the market even further.

In 1969, Lego opened a theme park at Billund, called Legoland. In its first year, there were 625 000 visitors. Legoland had a farm, a Wild West town, and famous tourist attractions such as the Eiffel Tower and Mount Rushmore built with amazing ingenuity out of Lego bricks. Since then the Billund theme park has drawn a further 30 million visitors, and spawned new Legolands in England and California, with a third to open shortly in Germany.

The company's chief executive today, Kjeld Kirk Christiansen, is the grandson of the founder. With 10 000 employees in 50 factories spread across 30 countries, Lego is one of the world's biggest toy manufacturers and among the wealthiest of Denmark's companies. A constant effort to invent new products led to the creation of space shuttles and underwater towns in the 1990s, but even these could not satisfy their young customers' demand for

Big game *Legoland, built in 1969, is one of Denmark's most popular tourist attractions. The nearby Lego factory (right) uses ultramodern machines and production processes created by Lego's own designers.*

the latest technology. Lego's response was the Mindstorm collection, which allows children to build their own programmable robots and vehicles, complete with mini-computers. This series, together with its multimedia games on CD-Rom, has taken Lego to new heights of success.

As a model of innovation and research, Lego has financed a Professorship at the renowned Massachusetts Institute of Technology (MIT), where Michael Resnik is the world's first Professor of Lego. In 1999, the Lego brick was voted best toy of the 20th century, beating Action Man, Barbie and even that old nursery favourite, the teddy bear.

A family and its town

T he Kirk Christiansen family has created one of Denmark's largest fortunes with their plastic bricks, but they remain true to their Jutland traditions by living very simply in Billund. Lego dominates the economic life of this ancient village, now a town of 4000 inhabitants with its own airport (the second largest in the country, after Copenhagen), built for the numerous charter flights bringing visitors to Legoland.

The benefits and costs of economic regeneration

Following the collapse of the Soviet Union in 1991, Estonia, Latvia and Lithuania were forced to adapt quickly to the demands of a free-market economy. After a shaky start, these young independent republics are now growing faster than any other economies in Europe.

Source of concern *The nuclear power station at Ignalina in Lithuania lacks proper safety systems.*

In the Soviet era, the Baltic States lived in a time warp, with sleepy industrial and agricultural economies that had suddenly, in 1991, to wake up to the realities of the modern world. Instead of buying raw materials at subsidised rates, businesses and industries in the Baltic States suddenly found themselves paying full market prices. Guaranteed export sales gave way to fierce global competition. The change was traumatic: industrial production declined, while unemployment and inflation soared.

Despite this crippling heritage from their Soviet past, the Baltic States have turned themselves around remarkably quickly. Services and business, the so-called 'tertiary sector', have grown particularly fast, accounting for 69 per cent of GDP by 1999. Today, analysts say, the region is bursting with promise. In 2000 the fastest growing economy in Europe was Estonia, with a growth rate of 7 per cent.

Energy for sale

Estonia's main industry is generating electricity. Most of its power stations are fuelled by oil shales, the country's main mineral resource. Oil shale is a sedimentary rock that produces oil and gas when crushed and heated to a high temperature – a process that carries a high environmental cost. Two oil-fired generating stations near Narva supply electricity for Estonia's Baltic neighbours and the north-western provinces of Russia. The power station at Ellamaa is unusual in that it burns peat. Gas from processed oil shales is supplied to Russia along a pipeline from Kohtla-Järve to St Petersburg. A key concern for the future is to expand the industry while minimising environmental damage.

Heavy industry

The main employers in the industrial or 'secondary' sector are steel and heavy engineering. Typical products include mining equipment, oil-refining installations, pipelines for transporting oil and gas, as well as heavy machinery for earth-moving and agriculture. The manufacturing sector, on the other hand, specialises in precision instruments and electronic apparatus. As well as providing fuel for power stations, processed oil

Highly skilled *Staff working at a Latvian radio factory. All that is needed now is more up-to-date technology.*

Threats to the environment

Heavy industry and power generation in the Baltic States have had unfortunate consequences. Ecologists are worried by pollution of groundwater, toxic waste from oil-shale processing, and emissions of sulphur dioxide from power stations and phosphorus mines. The region's nuclear sites are also causing concern. Lithuania's Ignalina power station has a similar design to Chernobyl, which exploded catastrophically in 1986, and is now under strict observation.

Goodbye to all that *Kunda, in northern Estonia, is an old-style industrial enclave that struggles to shake off its polluting past. The town's huge cement works still belch clouds of unhealthy dust into the surrounding air.*

shales supply the chemical industries based in Tallinn and Kohtla-Järve with a range of by-products that include adhesives, resins, tannins, formaldehyde, benzene, paints and detergents.

Despite their economic turnaround, the Baltic States continue to have an uneasy relationship with Russia, which is wary of their ambition to join the European Union. The balance of interests is delicately poised, however. The continuing economic success of the Baltic States is likely to depend on creating a better climate of understanding with Russia, as their great selling point for Western investors is as a gateway to the huge Russian market.

Supporters Norwegian, Danish and Swedish flags are waved in a pro-European demonstration. Feelings both for and against Europe run high in Scandinavia.

A new unity?

For much of their long history, the countries around the Baltic Sea have had stormy relationships with each other. Between 1940 and 1990 they were divided into two camps: the dynamic, forward-looking democracies of Scandinavia on the one hand, and a set of increasingly decrepit Soviet satellites on the other. Since 1991 and the fall of the communist system, a new spirit of Baltic unity has been in the air. Yet the economic divide remains: GNP per inhabitant is ten times higher in the west than the east. The solution seems to be rapid integration of the Baltic States into the global economy so that they can close the prosperity gap between themselves and their neighbours.

The European question

Scandinavians have always felt slightly separate from the rest of Europe. Although each country has its own policy, they all approach European integration with a mixture of level-headedness and scepticism.

Denmark joined the European Community in 1973, and has kept a cool and reserved stance ever since. In a 1992 national referendum, the Danes voted against the Maastricht Treaty. While accepting some of its provisions a year later, they still rejected the principle of a single currency and a common defence policy. On September 28, 2000, this was reinforced when the Danes rejected the adoption of the euro in a national referendum.

Norway joined the European Free Trade Area in 1959, but has twice refused to join the EU after holding referendums on the issue – once in 1972, and again in 1994. With oil revenues still pouring in, the Norwegians undoubtedly feel able to stand alone.

Although Iceland and the Faeroe Islands are not in the EU, they have special trade agreements with member countries, particularly over fishing, their single most important export. Sweden and Finland applied for EU membership after the collapse of the Soviet Union and were accepted in 1995. In the same year, Estonia, Latvia and Lithuania applied to join, and the date for their admission is set for May 1st 2004.

Explanations and hesitations

The reluctance of Scandinavians to integrate fully in Europe is not easy to explain. Most of their commercial partners are members of the

EU, so it would seem logical to join. The explanation may well be historical, going back to a time when religious differences between Lutheran Scandinavia and a predominantly Catholic Europe placed them on opposite sides of a cultural gulf. Equally, an ancient dislike of German influence may play a part; or it could be a fear of being sucked into the European bureaucracy. Scandinavians believe in total transparency in public services, and the arcane institutions, offices and pronouncements of the Brussels/Strasbourg machine do not give them confidence. There is also a distrust of any political system based on the American federal model, as the European Union is. The struggle for independence was long and hard, and they are not keen to sacrifice it unthinkingly.

Yet, despite the reluctance, public opinion has been changing. Denmark is softening, perhaps Norway, too, in the realisation that they must either form their own group or join the EU if they want collective strength on the world stage. Denmark has a special role to play as a stepping-stone between Scandinavia and Europe, and Finland advocates creating a regional unit within the EU in order to give the community a new 'Nordic dimension'.

Day of decision On November 24, 1994, the Norwegians said 'No' to joining the European Union. Despite this they have special links with the member countries.

A wealth of resources

Coal, iron, copper, zinc, lead . . . Northern Europe is rich in mineral deposits. Natural energy is exploited, too, with wind power, waterpower and geothermal sources all being harnessed on a growing scale.

Harnessing heat
Iceland makes varied use of geothermal resources.

In the 17th century, Scandinavia's economic power depended on iron, which came principally from one source, Bergslagen in central Sweden. Today the main iron mines are in Lappland, at Gällivare-Malmberget ('mountain of ore') – the largest in Europe, with an annual production of 6 million tons. Although iron ore is abundant here, much of it contains excessive amounts of phosphorus. A new seam with better ore, 3000 ft (1000 m) below ground level, was opened in 2001.

Iron in the far North

The iron mine at Kiruna, 91 miles (148 km) north of the Arctic Circle, is the largest underground operation in the world. It measures 2.5 miles (4 km) long by 262 ft (80 m) wide, and is 2296 ft (700 m) deep – and likely to go down as far as 6500 ft (2000 m) before the seam is exhausted.

Mining in these latitudes has always been a tough business. In the 18th century, ore was transported by boat, or in winter by reindeer sleds across the ice. A railway connecting Kiruna to Narvik, an ice-free port in Norway, was opened in 1902. The line, which is the most northerly in the world, is famous for its majestic landscapes and fine engineering. Even the train is unique, with massively powerful brakes for its steep descent into the town.

The power of nature

The Norwegians use more electricity per head than any other nation in the world. This is a privilege they can well afford, as they have an endless, nonpolluting supply from nature in the form of hydroelectric power. Europe's leader in the hydroelectric field, Norway has a large number of waterfalls. The main ones used as energy sources are at Nore, Hol and Rjukan, in the interior of the country. Rjukan was the site of the German heavy water factory in the Second World War: resistance fighters managed to blow it up in a series of daring raids, setting back Nazi attempts to build an atomic bomb.

Iceland produces 95 per cent of its energy through hydroelectric power. There are also many geothermal springs, which are the result of rainwater soaking into the ground and making contact with hot volcanic lava. The hot water is used to heat buildings in Reykjavik, as well as the numerous greenhouses where exotic flowers and out-of-season vegetables are grown.

Harnessing the winds

Lacking other natural sources of energy, Denmark has turned to the wind. With its low-lying islands and North Sea coasts, Denmark, like Holland, provides an ideal landscape for the tall white masts mounted with giant rotor blades that convert the wind's energy into electricity. The world's first wind-powered electric generator, an adaptation of the windmill, was built in Denmark in 1890. Today's wind turbines can generate current of up to 500 kilowatts.

Rich seams
Inside the iron mines at Kiruna.

Iron town *Kiruna, in the far north of Sweden, is a huge iron-mining centre. Several scientific research projects are also based here, well inside the Arctic Circle.*

Spitsbergen coal

The Spitsbergen archipelago, located at 80°N, was granted to Norway by the Treaty of Paris in 1920, although other nations were permitted to extract coal. In fact, none but the Norwegians and Russians could face the extreme climate. Today there is just one coal mine still operating, at Longyearbyen. A Russian community continues to live in Barentsburg, a town near the disused mines where they once worked.

CHAPTER 3

LIVING IN THE CITIES

M ost big cities in Scandinavia are ports. Arrivals and departures, whether of trawlers, yachts or passenger ships, add a special air of excitement. Along the canals of Copenhagen, in the fiord of Oslo, or around the island labyrinths of Stockholm and Helsinki, the pleasures of living by the sea have retained their appeal. Once ashore, the traveller soon discovers that cars are kept under strict control: vast pedestrian areas, respectful cyclists, plus the people's sense of civic duty, contribute to a relaxed and civilised atmosphere and make it easy to understand why the Scandinavians are said to be the world's experts at city living. Parks and museums; quays that keep old mercantile traditions alive; open spaces for sunbathing, strolling and swimming; narrow medieval streets and wide neoclassical avenues; simple wooden houses and grand Baroque palaces: every city has its special character, but all share a happy blend of past and present.

Numerous public statues are a feature of Helsinki. This one is called 'The Three Blacksmiths'.

The key to urban success

In a region where the route to economic and military expansion has traditionally lain over the waves, settlements by the sea have always had a head start, although chance too can play a part.

Baltic wharf *A cargo ship tied up at Riga, the Latvian capital, is a busy port on the Western Dvina river, 9 miles (15 km) from the Baltic Sea.*

Gothenburg (Göteborg) is Sweden's second largest city. It is also Scandinavia's busiest port, centrally located between Oslo, Stockholm and Copenhagen: 14 000 ships come in and out each year. Gothenburg owes its importance to its position at the mouth of the Göta älv river, used since Viking days as a means of communication with the country's interior. The city was founded in 1603 and quickly became cosmopolitan, with a busy trade in herring, grain, iron ore and wood. In 1800 the Trollhättan Canal was completed, linking the port with Lake Vänern to the north. This led to further growth and a thriving city that today has 800 000 inhabitants.

From fishing to ferries

Esbjerg, on the west coast of Jutland, is Denmark's biggest port and provides the only direct car-ferry link with Britain. Its prosperity is relatively recent, however, dating from the year 1866 when Denmark lost the province of Schleswig, and with it every North Sea port it possessed. Looking for a suitable site to develop, the Danish government picked

Island city *Ålesund, in Norway, was once a fishing village. Today the city spreads over several islands connected by bridges and tunnels.*

Old world charm *Smögen, an active fishing port, is one of many colourful old towns in Sweden's Bohuslän region, north of Gothenburg.*

Narvik's good fortune

A port needs to be free from ice throughout the year to be commercially viable. Hidden away at the far end of Ofotfiord on Norway's north coast, Narvik's deep green waters remain open to ships right through the year – in contrast to Sweden's ports on the Gulf of Bothnia. This is why the ore from Kiruna, Sweden's huge iron-ore mine, is shipped through Narvik. Since the railway was built in the late 19th century, Narvik has grown from a tiny village of just 50 inhabitants to a busy town of 19 000.

Esbjerg, which in those days consisted of just two farmsteads. It quickly grew to its present size of 73 000 inhabitants as a centre of North Sea fishing as well as an export outlet for Denmark's rich farming produce. Today, Esbjerg is the biggest fishing port in the country, with some 6 miles (10 km) of quays.

All over Scandinavia there are fishing villages dotted along the coasts, particularly around the Baltic. Once the fish was sold locally, but now it tends to be sent off for canning and processing in large ports such as Esbjerg.

On the Gulf of Bothnia

When trees are felled in Finland's vast forests, the logs are transported by road or rail. They are collected for export at ports such as Oulu, ideally placed at the mouth of the River Oulujoki, which flows east to west through the country's richest timber region.

Another major port is Vaasa, which lies directly opposite the Swedish port of Umea at the narrowest part of the Gulf of Bothnia. This is a region of constant change: the land is tilting upwards at unusual speed here, so several ports on the Gulf have either had to move to keep up with the retreating sea, or reconcile themselves to becoming landlocked. Pori, which was originally founded on the Kokemäenjoki estuary, is now 6 miles (10 km) inland thanks to silt deposits from the river. The new port of Mäntyluoto has been built on the coast to take its place.

Feeding the birds *A favourite place for family strolls is Lake Tjörnin, where a crowd of hungry ducks and geese is guaranteed to turn up if you bring some bread.*

Swim to get warm

Once the weather gets really cold, there is nothing quite like an open-air swim. Reykjavik boasts five geyser-fed outdoor pools, where bathers can swim in comfort while the air freezes above them. The main pools are ringed with Jacuzzis and hot tubs where the temperature can reach a delicious 45°C (113°F). With such luxurious facilities, it is not surprising that swimming is a national sport in Iceland. Skiing is a favourite activity, too, with slopes just 30 minutes' drive from the capital.

Summer or winter, Reykjavik aims to be cool

The world's northernmost capital city, Reykjavik is home to 110 000 people – over one-third of Iceland's population. Until recently noted for brightly painted houses and spacious parks, the city is also gaining a reputation as a clubbing capital.

In Icelandic, Reykjavik means 'smoky bay'. This was the name given to the place by Viking chief Ingolfur Arnarson when he saw vapour rising from its hot springs. Iceland was the last part of Europe to be settled by humans. Its first inhabitants, who arrived in around AD 870, were a handful of Irish monks, followed by a band of Viking outlaws from Norway who were looking for a place to live outside the jurisdiction of their king.

The old city centre of Reykjavik, with its markets, bustling street-life and traditional wooden houses, lies between Lake Tjörnin and the harbour. At its heart is the National Museum of Iceland and the Arni Magnusson Institute, dedicated to the history of that uniquely Scandinavian form of storytelling, the saga. Manuscripts of the Norse epics can be seen here, including the *Landnámabók* and *Burnt Njal's Saga*, which the Danish government presented to Iceland when the country achieved its independence.

Painter's palette *Reykjavik's traditional wooden houses are brightly painted.*

Conferences and all-night parties

In the year 2000, Reykjavik was one of nine officially designated European Cities of Culture. 'Nature and culture' was its slogan for the occasion. In the same year, Iceland celebrated 1000 years of Christianity and the discovery of America by the explorer Leif Ericsson. It also hosted the International Women's Conference, chaired by Hillary Rodham Clinton.

Painters, musicians and other artists flock to Reykjavik, with its fizzing arts scene and a packed calendar of concerts, exhibitions and festivals. In recent years the city has become a centre of youth culture, too, with planeloads of visitors arriving every Friday to spend the weekend partying, clubbing and having fun. Reykjavik's place on the fashion map of Europe is largely due to the singer Björk. And where one goes, others follow: a big name in British pop music, Damon Albarn, owns a nightclub here. Rules on alcohol consumption, once exceptionally strict, have been relaxed recently, and clubs now stay open until 3 am on weekends.

Not that the party ends there: the sleepless clubbers move on to empty warehouses for the rest of the night's entertainment. A word on the street is enough to get you into this *runtur,* or crawl, round the happening places of nocturnal Reykjavik. The only thing to watch out for on these dark odysseys of pleasure is a local schnapps, *Svarta ded.* The name means 'black death' – said by those who have tried it to be a very accurate description of its effects.

Basking in history The old harbour of Nyhavn is a hub of social life for tourists and locals alike. Bars, cafés, restaurants and shops line the 300-year-old quays, which once resounded to the brawling and shouting of drunken sailors. History is everywhere in Copenhagen, yet the atmosphere is young, contemporary and open. Half-timbered houses (below) add colour and charm to a fascinating city.

Denmark's seductive capital

With its quays, canals and sailing ships, Copenhagen has the spacious feel of a great port. Rich in palaces and museums, the city also has its wild side, with cafés, bars and relaxed outdoor places – a reminder that this is the most southern of the region's capitals.

The name says it all: København, or 'merchant's port'. It was through commerce and the sea that this, the largest city in Scandinavia, rose to prominence. At the close of the Viking period, Copenhagen was a small herring-fishing town on the eastern tip of the island of Sjaelland. In 1167 King Valdemar the Great gave it as a gift to his ambitious half-brother Absalon, Bishop of Roskilde, who built a fortress on the islet of Slotsholmen. The town soon prospered: strategically sited on the straits of Øresund, it was easy to control the passage of shipping through the narrows, and to make a great deal of money by doing so. Its position at the centre of the Danish kingdom, which until the middle of the 18th century included the southern provinces of Sweden, made Copenhagen the obvious choice of capital in 1445.

The golden age of Christian IV

Copenhagen's air of grandeur owes much to Christian IV, who ruled from 1588 to 1648 and commissioned many of the city's most magnificent monuments. On each of these, this extravagant builder-king had a monogram set into the brickwork: RGF. This stood for

Royal fantasy Rosenborg is one of many fine 17th-century buildings in Copenhagen commissioned by Christian IV.

the royal motto, *Regina Firma Pietas* (piety is sovereign). His less respectful subjects claimed the true meaning to be *Riget Fattes Penge* (the kingdom is short of cash).

Real money was being made, however, in the Børsen, Stock Exchange, which Christian built in a fantastic Dutch Renaissance style, with a spire of three tangled dragons' tails. Nearby is Europe's first astronomical observatory, the Rundetårn (Round Tower). Built for the use of astronomers at the university, it has a spiral ramp up to a viewing platform with a spectacular panorama across the city. From here you can see the surrounding lakes and ramparts, also built by Christian IV, now converted to a series of public gardens.

Castle of Roses

Christian felt the medieval city of Copenhagen was too small, so he decided to make it bigger. To the north he created a royal garden, in the middle of which, in 1634, he built a new residence, Rosenborg, the Castle of Roses, a dream palace in red brick and white tufa which he helped to design. The palace amply expresses Christian's personality, especially his love of beauty, novelty and whimsy. Keen as he was on the latest comforts, he had running water piped to all the bathrooms, a real luxury at the time.

Today, Rosenborg houses a Royal Museum, where the magnificent Danish crown jewels can be seen alongside more bizarre exhibits such as the bloodstained shirt worn by the king in the Battle of Kolberger Heide, where he lost an eye. On display nearby are pieces of shrapnel removed by surgeons from the royal body.

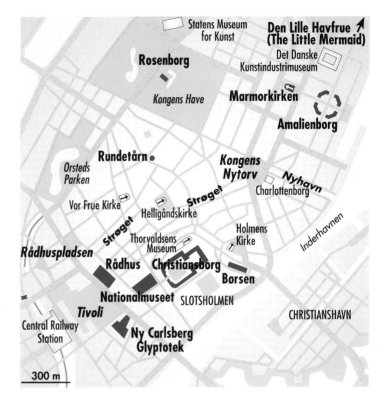

Red brick, green roofs

A series of fires ravaged Copenhagen in the 18th century. This had at least one lucky consequence: it meant that the city was rebuilt in a harmonious style. Today Copenhagen presents an elegant mix of Baroque, neoclassical and modern buildings. The visitor's eye wanders with no sense of shock from 17th-century red-brick houses with green copper roofs to the stainless steel and glass of the late 20th century. The best way to appreciate the city's architectural beauty is on foot. Although Copenhagen is a big place, with 2 million inhabitants, the finest buildings and the best museums are concentrated in the relatively small historic centre.

Strøget is the longest pedestrian precinct in the world: it is a series of streets and squares that runs from the colourful old port of Nyhavn to the sombre 19th-century Rådhus (City Hall). On the way it passes the Royal Theatre and the resplendent Hotel D'Angleterre, converted from a 17th-century manor house. Nearby is the Ny Carlsberg Glyptotek, with its tropical glasshouse and superb art collection, including Etruscan paintings, Greek and Roman sculpture, and works by the leading French Impressionists.

Fine day for a walk Copenhagen's pedestrian zone is one of the largest in the world. On summer days the streets are buzzing, and in winter, as the New Year festivities approach, the lights and atmosphere of celebration are truly magical.

Shopping around

Swarming with buskers, strollers and postcard-vendors, the pedestrian zone of Strøget is a shoppers' paradise. Here you will find shops selling Danish arts and crafts; Royal Copenhagen, a temple of china, crystal and glassware; department stores like Illum and Magasin; and designer shops as smart and exclusive as any in Paris, London or New York. Be warned, though: the prices are high, with 25 per cent VAT. Bargain hunters may prefer the Saturday morning fleamarkets, or the Larsjørnsstraede, renowned for their organic foodstores, bookshops, cafés and secondhand clothes shops.

Changing of the guard

Christianborg Castle, today the home of the Danish Parliament and the foreign ministry, was once the residence of the Danish royal family. In 1794 it suffered a major fire, and King Frederick IV moved his household to Amalienborg. This simple yet splendid group of four buildings had been given by Frederick to a number of noble families, but he bought the place back for his own use. When Christianborg was finally restored, the king preferred to stay at Amalienborg, which has remained the royal home ever since.

The queen now lives in the south-east wing, using the south-west wing for state receptions. Every day at noon, when she is in residence, people gather to watch the changing of the guard, a picturesque ceremony that takes place against the backdrop of the Amalienborg and the Marmorkirken, in one of Europe's most stately squares.

Tivoli funfair

In the heart of Copenhagen, facing the City Hall, is Denmark's largest amusement park. Created in 1843 by the architect Georg Carstensen, the world-famous Tivoli gardens are visited by 4 million people each year. Among the attractions on its 20 acre (10 ha) site are a Chinese pavilion, a Moorish palace, 24 restaurants, 400 000 flowers, and a lively funfair. The last has all the usual favourites and plenty of surprises, too, including a flying trumpet inspired by Hans Christian Andersen.

In the Italian theatre, pantomimes delight crowds of children and adults alike throughout the summer. As soon

Free thinkers welcome *A painted house in Christiania, an alternative commune within the city that keeps alive the spirit of the 1960s.*

Pleasure gardens *At Tivoli you can find everything from bumper cars to quiet lakeside restaurants.*

as dusk falls, 100 000 lanterns are lit and a fairy atmosphere is created, with sounds of jazz or classical music floating by from concerts in the park.

The Tivoli's first musical director was H.C. Lumbye (1810-74), Scandinavia's finest composer of salon music, who wrote more than 700 waltzes, polkas and other dance tunes for the orchestra here during a 30-year career. The world's most celebrated virtuosos have performed at the Tivoli auditorium, from Artur Rubinstein to Mstislav Rostropovich, while more popular shows, including variety acts and rock concerts, are performed on an open-air stage.

The Tivoli 'concept' has now been exported to Japan, where a replica under Danish ownership and management has been open since 1997. The spirit and beauty of the original has been lovingly reproduced in all its detail, with miniature lakes, thousands of flowers, and a relaxed atmosphere.

Sailing ships and cafés

The Nyhavn Canal was cut in the north of the old town in the late 17th century to improve access for cargo ships. Along its quays were warehouses, merchants' homes and waterside bars catering to the rougher end of the market: 'a bit of a port, and a harbour for every vice' as the writer Céline put it. Beer flowed endlessly and fights were frequent, although peaceful citizens lived here, too, among them Hans Christian Andersen, at Nos. 20, 67 and 18.

Today, with its smart houses and sailing ships, Nyhavn is the city's trendiest district. A few odd tattoo shops have remained, but the old sailors' bars have been transformed into chic restaurants, art galleries and advertising agencies. In summer, the café tables spill out into the street. They are always full, especially at *hygge* (cosy) time, when the locals get together to relax and chat. The Danes are the most European of all Scandinavians: reserved when you first meet them, they quickly become warm, open and easy to talk to.

Kingdom of the bicycle

Quiet days *A tranquil square where only cyclists and walkers can go, and a favourite place to meet for coffee or lunch.*

In the 1950s, the traffic jams were so bad it was thought that the city would suffocate. Since then Copenhagen, home to a quarter of Denmark's population, has become a haven for pedestrians and cyclists, with one of the world's largest car-free zones. There is even a system of free bicycle loans: neatly ranged in 150 stands around the city, these bright yellow bikes are available for anyone to use. Like a supermarket trolley, the bike is released by a coin-in-the-slot mechanism, with money back on return and an electronic tracking system to discourage thieves.

The Little Mermaid

In Copenhagen harbour, sitting quietly on her block of granite, the Little Mermaid (*Den Lille Havfrue*) looks out to sea. This bronze sculpture, which was inspired by one of Hans Christian Andersen's famous children's tales, was created by Edward Eriksen and presented to the city in 1913 by Carl Jacobsen, owner of the Carlsberg brewery. The mermaid became the symbol of Copenhagen, expressing the Danish people's restless passion for the sea. The tourists who flock to admire her are often surprised at her size: not a giant like the Statue of Liberty, but life-sized. This fits in with the Danish trait of keeping things in perspective, on a human scale.

Tórshavn, Queen of the Faeroes

The world's smallest capital, Tórshavn likes to be known as the 'Paris of the North'. This may seem a grandiose title for a city of just 16 000 inhabitants, but the architecture is impressive and the cultural life surprisingly rich.

It rains on average for 300 days each year in the Faeroe Islands. The wind is relentless, and little will grow on the islands but grass and moss. But the temperatures are generally mild and the landscape is superb, with some of the most beautiful and unspoilt scenery in the world.

Built around a bay on the island of Streymoy, Tórshavn seems to grow directly out of this rugged natural environment. It was founded in AD 800 and named after the Norse god Thor. The first settlers were Vikings on the run from their king. On the Tinganes peninsula they set up an assembly, the Løgting, whose members gathered once a year to make laws and settle disputes. Today the Faeroes parliament, which is self-governing under the Danish crown, is based on the same historic site.

A warren of medieval streets

Steps and narrow lanes wind between little peat-roofed houses, their fronts painted black with bitumen, their windows sparkling white. Tórshavn is one of the few medieval cities in the world that has never had a major fire. It may look like a film set – indeed it was used by Danish director Niels Malmroos for his film *Barbara* – but its houses are in fact the real thing, beautifully preserved originals. Around the medieval core, a newer city has grown, with excellent restaurants, hotels, galleries and shops. In this hardy but inspiring environment the arts flourish, particularly music, painting and sculpture.

The feast of St Olav

The best time to visit Tórshavn is at the end of July, when the weather is warm and the locals are celebrating the week-long festival of St Olav. This commemorates the Battle of Stiklestad, fought on July 29, 1030, at which the Norwegian king, Olav II, who brought Christianity to the islands, was killed. For many Faeroese, this is the most important day of the year: work stops, offices close, and there are concerts, exhibitions and boat-races around the islands.

Inspecting the catch   Fishing has always been the main industry in Tórshavn, and remains the foundation of its economy today.

Harbour view   Clean, simple lines and bright colours are typical of Tórshavn's traditional architecture. More than a third of the 43 000 islanders live in this small but lively city.

At midnight on July 28, thousands of people gather in the centre of the city to sing traditional songs and perform great ring-dances in honour of the heroes of Norse sagas such as Sigurd or Roland, nephew of Charlemagne.

Barbara, *femme fatale*

In 1997 Danish director Niels Malmroos shot the most expensive film in the history of Scandinavian cinema in Tórshavn. The story, based on the novel *Barbara* by Jørgen-Frantz Jacobsen (1900–38), is set in the 17th century and concerns a beautiful but unpredictable woman, Barbara, twice married to a priest and twice widowed. She comes to the Faeroes and quickly seduces a third clergyman, then leaves him for a younger man. The film was a great hit, especially with the 43 000 islanders, as many of them had worked on it, either as extras or indirectly through services to the film crew, who spent several months in Tórshavn.

Oslo: where the countryside comes to town

Deep in a magnificent fiord and surrounded by wooded hills, the Norwegian capital is a surprisingly rural place. Three-quarters of the urban area consists of forests, orchards and lakes: you could almost be in the country.

Despite a relatively modest population (just half a million), Oslo is the fifth largest city in the world in terms of physical size. It covers no less than 175 sq miles (450 km²), and the site is breathtaking. At the end of a fiord 60 miles (100 km) long, the site was used by the Vikings as a harbour for many years before Harald III Hårdråde founded it as a city in 1048. It became the capital of Norway at the end of the 13th century, when King Haakon V built the fortress of Akershus (Akershus Festning). Yet, despite its military importance, prosperity was slow to come, as the rich Baltic trade was controlled by the Hanseatic League and Norway lived in the shadow of its powerful neighbour, Denmark. In 1397, the three Scandinavian kingdoms were joined by the Union of Kalmar, led by the unifying vision of Margaret I, Queen of Denmark.

Ship to shore *Ferries, yachts and fishing boats in the port of Oslo, which lies at the heart of the city.*

Under Danish rule

In 1536, Norway became a province of Denmark. Its capital was renamed Christiania by King Christian IV, and it stayed under Danish sovereignty until 1814, when Denmark was ruined by its involvement in the Napoleonic wars. Throughout this time, Christiania was a backwater. In the early 19th century, Jean-Baptiste Bernadotte, the newly adopted King of Sweden, annexed Norway to his country and Christiania began to grow, both economically and physically. The first factories were built and a university was founded. In 1905, after six centuries of subordinate status, Norway regained its independence. This brought new life to its capital, which reclaimed the Viking name of Oslo in 1925.

Around the city centre

The journey by boat up the fiord is the best possible way to arrive in Oslo. Ferries from Denmark, England, Holland and Germany dock daily in the heart of the city, between the Akershus fortress and the town hall (Rådhus), an impressive red-brick building, officially opened in 1950 to celebrate Oslo's 900th birthday. Inside is the biggest mural in the world, depicting the history of Norway in scenes painted by the country's most celebrated artists. It is here that the Nobel peace prize is awarded in December each year.

Karl Johans Gate is the city's main thoroughfare, crowded with pubs and shops. It runs north-west from the central railway station to the royal palace (Det Kongelige Slott), passing the university and parliament (Stortinget) along the way. In the university's central hall is a series of murals by Edvard Munch, Norway's most brilliant, and most anguished, painter. The Munch Museum at Tøyen houses 18 000 of his prints and 1100 of his paintings, while his most famous picture, *The Scream* – an unforgettable image of mental agony – is on show in the Munch rooms at the national gallery (Nasjonalgalleriet). Karl Johans Gate ends at a statue of the Swedish king, Karl XIV Johan, who ordered the building of the road and the royal palace in the mid-19th century. His grand urban scheme still dominates the city centre today, though he did not live to see the palace finished, or the rather sad spectacle of its rooms filled with furniture from previous reigns.

Holmenkollen ski jump

Where else could you find a ski jump at the end of a metro line? At Holmenkollen, 6 miles (10 km) from the centre of Oslo, the world's first ski jump, 1476 ft (450 m) long, was built in 1892. Modernised for the Winter Olympics of 1952, it is still used for international competitions. In winter a popular cross-country skiing race is held in the area, with its finish at the foot of the jump. Holmenkollen is also a favourite spot in summer, as its restaurant offers dizzying views. Nearby is the Skiing Museum, where you can see the Ovebro ski, which is 2500 years old.

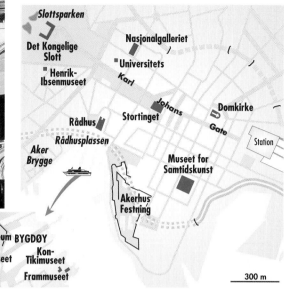

Royal prospect   Karl Johans Gate, Oslo's grandest boulevard, leads up to the Royal Palace and its extensive gardens.

Love of the sea

The other great shopping area of Oslo is Aker Brygge, where the quays are crowded with first-class restaurants, all with spectacular views of the fiord. Nearby the ferries run out to Bygdøy, where you can see the royal family's summer residence (a surprisingly ordinary house) and the Norsk Folkemuseum, a collection of 150 rural buildings from all over Norway.

There are also no fewer than three museums dedicated to the Norwegians' love of the sea: the Vikingskipsmuseet, with the best-preserved Viking longships; the Frammuseet, which is built around the vessel used by two great polar explorers, Fridtjof Nansen and Roald Amundsen; and the fascinating Kon-Tiki Museet, housing the balsa raft on which Thor Heyerdahl crossed the Pacific from Peru to Polynesia in 1947.

Dreaming beneath the trees

Nature is always close at hand in Oslo. The county of Akershus, which borders the fiord, is scattered with picturesque villages, forests and streams. It takes just a metro ride from the city centre to reach wild places where you can pick berries in the woods or watch the deer come out to feed as dusk falls. In the summer, Hovedøya and Lindøya, two of the 300 islands in the fiord, are popular for their splendid beaches, while in winter, with temperatures plummeting to -15°C (5°F), the inhabitants of Oslo love to ski, even after a hard day at the office: at night the slopes around the capital are lit up like city boulevards.

Fortification   The medieval fortress of Akerhus Castle, was enlarged and modified by King Christian IV in the 17th century.

Independence Day

On May 17, 1814, the Danish governor, the future King Christian VIII, gave Norway its freedom by signing what was called 'the most liberal constitution in the world'. Even though a Swedish invasion soon put an end to the dream of freedom, the day is still celebrated as a national holiday. It coincides with the end of the school-leaving exams, so the celebration is heartfelt by all generations. Norwegians relax on May 17 as on no other day of the year. For a sense of its significance, one need only look at the journals of the explorer Roald Amundsen, who never failed to give a party for his team on that day – no matter how frozen, hungry or exhausted they were in the wastes of Antarctica or the North Pole!

Sing its praises
The opera restaurant, dating from 1787, is Stockholm's grandest place to dine, with exquisite food served in traditional style.

A place to relax One of the city's most popular parks is the Kungsträdgården, with its skating rink, cafés, restaurants, children's theatre (right) and amusements. It was once the royal kitchen garden.

Rooms with a view A clifftop position along the city's southern shore gives life in Södermalm a special quality. It is the only part of Stockholm that is at all elevated. Once a worker's district, it has now become one of the most sought-after and expensive places to live.

Cavern railway Solna Centrum, a futuristic station on the T-bana, Stockholm's efficient underground system.

All aboard
Ferries come right into the city centre, connecting it with dozens of islands in the archipelago and beyond.

VIKING LINE

Hostel on the water The Af Chapman, moored in front of Skeppsholmen Island, is one of Stockholm's most famous sights. The sailing ship is now used as a youth hostel, offering cheap and distinctive accommodation right in the city centre. It is usually booked up weeks in advance.

Urban anonymous *Sergels Torg is a modern area of the city, all reinforced concrete and glass. The impersonal style of this shopping precinct is not popular with the local inhabitants.*

Landmark *The distinctive square tower of the cathedral (Storkyrkan) rises high above the surrounding buildings on the island of Gamla Stan.*

City of many islands

From the rocky elevation of Södermalm, you can see the whole city laid out before you. Quays, bridges, palaces, parks, churches – and boats everywhere. Like a northern Venice, Stockholm occupies a unique site in a maze of waterways and islands. Founded in 1250 on an island where the waters of Lake Mälaren flow into the Baltic Sea, the oldest part of Stockholm, Gamla Stan, has a distinctly medieval feel, despite the Baroque castle that crowns the site. From here you can set off along the meandering quays and enjoy endlessly changing views.

Stockholm is a city of pastel colours. Ever since the 'Swedish Grace' style of the 1920s saw architects and craftsmen working closely together, Swedish design has specialised in clean lines and light colours.

Stockholmers love the quality of life offered by their environment. Steamers leave from the town centre for hundreds of destinations around the archipelago. To the west are castles and historic sites in the enchanted setting of Lake Mälaren. To the east is the sea and the Baltic islands, with sandy beaches and rocky shores. Whether swimming and bicycling in summer, or ice-skating in winter, the people of Stockholm enjoy opportunities for outdoor living that few other cities can match.

Royal guards In their grey-blue uniforms, the guards outside the royal palace are a reminder of a proud military past.

Stockholm

1. Sigtuna, the first capital of Christian Sweden, is a charming old town of narrow streets and coloured wooden houses 18 miles (30 km) from Stockholm.

2. Vaxholm is one of a chain of forts that once defended the approaches to the Swedish capital.

3. A view over the Djurgården, Stockholm's pleasure island, from the top of the television tower.

4. Statues by the sculptor Carl Milles (1875-1955) in the garden of his house on Lidingö Island, a popular attraction in summer.

5. On sunny days, Stockholmers head for the nearest beaches. This one is on the lawns of the Mälarstrand, in front of the City Hall.

6. The Globen sports arena, designed by Svante Berg, is the world's tallest spherical building. This covered stadium in the south of the city hosts sporting events and musical extravaganzas.

7. The island of Fjärderholmarna in the Stockholm archipelago, with its houses on the water and parking right outside the door.

8. Cruising among the islands is one of Stockholm's chief pleasures. Here visitors enjoy a view of Drottningholm, a castle lived in by the Swedish royal family.

9. Rålambshov park is a favourite destination for a summer bike ride.

2

3

4

5

6

Saved from the deep The 17th-century warship Vasa (above), salvaged in 1961, is now restored.

Ornamentation Begun in the 13th century, Stockholm cathedral (right) has a sumptuous Baroque interior.

Renaissance style Completed in 1760, the royal palace is also a museum, housing the Swedish crown jewels.

Northern light Winter sunshine adds a special beauty to the buildings on the island of Riddarholmen. When the temperature drops really low the waters freeze and the city becomes a giant open-air skating rink.

Pedestrian zone The heart of old Stockholm, on the island of Gamla Stan, is a place of quiet cobbled lanes where visitors stroll among shops, art galleries and bars. After dark the two main streets become a vibrant centre of nightlife.

City beaches In summer one of the pleasures of Stockholm is swimming from the island beaches. This is Långholmen, which has lovely views of the old city.

Monumental Stockholm In the foreground, the parliament building (Riksdagshuset), skilfully extended and rebuilt in 1970. To the right the royal palace, and in the distance the Vasa Museum.

Harmony of colours Stepped gable houses, typical of Hanseatic ports, look down on the main square of Gamla Stan, Stortorget, where public benches and cafés offer welcome relief to footsore tourists.

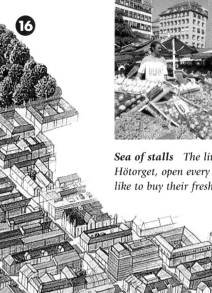

Sea of stalls The lively street market of Hötorget, open every day, is where Stockholmers like to buy their fresh fruit and vegetables.

1. Gamla Stan Island
2. Royal Palace (Kungliga Slottet)
3. Cathedral (Storkyrkan)
4. German Church (Tyska Kyrkan)
5. Parliament (Riksdagshuset)
6. House of Nobles (Riddarhuset)
7. Riddarholmen Island
8. City Hall (Stadshuset)
9. Sergels Torg
10. Opera (Operan)
11. Kungsträdgården
12. Nationalmuseum
13. Af Chapman
14. Museum of the Orient (Östasiatiska museet)
15. Skeppsholmen Island
16. Humlegården
17. Royal Theatre (Kungliga dramatiska teatern)
18. Strandvägen
19. Vasa Museum (Vasamuseet)
20. Nordic Museum (Nordiska museet)
21. Djurgården
22. Skansen
23. Gröna Lunds Tivoli
24. Beckholmen

Traditional crafts A silversmith at work in the Skansen folk museum, one of the first of its kind in the world. As well as practising craftsmen, there are ancient dwellings and artefacts from all around the country, and activities such as communal singing and traditional games for visitors to try for themselves.

Quay location Strandvägen is Stockholm's most famous quay, with luxury shops, hotels and restaurants.

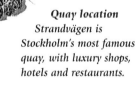

Children's paradise Gröna Lunds Tivoli, an amusement park, is a favourite place for young Stockholmers.

Snow at Skansen Winter brings hard work for the city's snow-clearing teams as roads and pavements are made safe for the public.

Helsinki: the city that came in from the cold

Old Helsinki, built by the tsars, has a distinctly Russian feel – a proxy Moscow in a string of Cold War spy films. But around every corner there are glittering 20th-century buildings which testify to the Finnish capital's contemporary, cosmopolitan character.

At first sight it seems a cold, unwelcoming place, with its long, straight avenues and wintry climate. The mean annual temperature is 5.4°C (41°F) – about the same as the salad compartment in a refrigerator – and but for a busy ice-breaker the water in the harbour would be frozen solid for four months of the year. In summer, though, the city blossoms into life and July temperatures can reach up to 30°C (86°F). Café and restaurant tables are set out on the pavements, and the streets come alive with cyclists and strollers. The sea is perfect for bathing – a comfortable 20-22°C (68-72°F) – and there are plenty of good beaches around the city. Some you can reach by bike, others, such as Pihlajasaari, Seurasaari and Suomenlinna, are hidden on the islands, a waterbus ride away. There are five ports, controlling the vast majority of international shipping to and from Finland.

A young capital

In 1550 Gustav Vasa, King of Sweden, founded a city at the mouth of the River Vantaa.

Peninsular city   Helsinki is founded on maritime trade. Built on a peninsula, with five ports and 315 islands, its life is still closely bound up with the sea.

Downtown Helsinki   A view of Mannerheimintie, one of the main streets of the city centre with a typical mix of neoclassical and 20th-century buildings.

He intended it to rival Tallinn, the Hanseatic port on the far side of the Gulf of Finland. Trade was sluggish, however, and for two centuries Helsinki remained a backwater in comparison to the capital, Turku. Helsinki owes its growth to the Wars of the North between Russia and Sweden in the first half of the 18th century. The Russians occupied the city from 1700 to 1721, then again in 1742-3. The Swedes responded by building a fortress on the island of Suomenlinna to protect their eastern frontier. This led to a boom in Helsinki's fortunes as its maritime trade and activities began to flourish.

In 1808 Finland became part of the Russian empire, with the status of an independent Grand Duchy, and in the same year a massive fire ravaged Helsinki. Reconstruction of the city, and the tsar's wish to have the Finnish administration closer to St Petersburg, led to its proclamation as the capital in 1812. In 1819, the Senate moved from Turku to Helsinki, followed in 1828 by the university. Since the end of the 19th century, much of the country's industry has been concentrated there, too.

The sound of music   Helsinki is one of Europe's liveliest centres of music, with a keen concert-going public well served by numerous auditoria, including the Finlandiatalo by Alvar Aalto, the new opera house (built in 1993), and the Philharmonic Orchestra, here rehearsing.

On January 4, 1918, the revolutionary government of Russia recognised the sovereignty of Finland, but a civil war between pro-Russian and pro-Finnish forces raged through the streets of Helsinki for five months. The Finnish republic was finally established in June 1919. Over the course of the 20th century the city's population grew from 100 000 to 525 000 – around 10 per cent of the national total. In 2000 Helsinki celebrated its 450th birthday, and was designated one of nine European Cities of Culture.

Architects of the tsar

The centre of Helsinki is built in an elegant neoclassical style. This it owes to the fire of 1808, and the reconstruction that followed under the supervision of two architects: Johan Albrecht Ehrenström and the German-born Carl Ludwig Engel. They designed the Senate (Valtioneuvosto), the first official building in the Empire style, which was completed in 1832. The Lutheran cathedral (Tuomiokirkko), a magnificent white building with a green copper dome, was inaugurated 20 years later. The Orthodox Church of the Holy Trinity, designed by Engel, stands close by. The finest legacy of Russian rule, however, is the Ouspensky Cathedral (Uspenskin-Katedraali) with its bristling gold turrets and domes on the island of Katajanokka.

In Market Square (Kauppatori) is the presidential palace (Presidentinlinna), which was donated by a wealthy businessman. Every morning the square bustles with activity, as stalls are set up to sell fruit, smoked fish, flowers and wild berries.

Market day   The vegetable market is a popular spot for the health-conscious Finns, who like to buy their produce direct from market-gardeners.

Between East and West

During the second half of the Cold War, Helsinki was the capital of *détente*, the attempt to reduce military and diplomatic tension between the communist East and capitalist West. In 1970, the city hosted the Strategic Arms Limitation Talks (SALT) between the USSR and USA. Then in 1975 came the conference on security and cooperation in Europe (CSCE),that culminated in the signing of the famous Helsinki Accords on human rights and bilateral relations. In 1990 a meeting of symbolic importance took place between the presidents of the USA and the USSR, George Bush and Mikhail Gorbachev.

A passion for art

The work of Akseli Gallen-Kallela (1865-1931), Finland's great figurative artist, can be seen at the Ateneum, a neo-classical building that houses the National Museum of Art. His paintings include portraits, scenes from everyday life, and mythical subjects from the *Kalevala*, such as *The Forging of the Sampo* and *Kullervo's Curse*.

While art from the 18th to the mid-20th century is exhibited at the Ateneum, more contemporary works by hundreds of modern artists such as rock musician Brian Eno are displayed at the Kiasma, a building completed in 1998 to a design by Steven Holl. The Kiasma uses every technique available to help visitors enjoy the experience of contemporary art, including interactive screens and computer rooms with artworks on CD-Rom.

Let there be light   Glass and steel are hallmarks of the modern style.

A feast of modern architecture

The rapid urbanisation of Helsinki in the 20th century attracted many gifted architects to the city. The Art Nouveau style can be seen in the main railway station (Rautatieasema), designed by Eliel Saarinen in 1904. This is ornamented with sculptures by Emil Wikström in the National Romantic style, which flourished in the final years of Russian rule.

The new parliament (Eduskuntatalo), built of red granite in 1931, is a superb example of Functionalism. In the years following the Second World War, a new exuberance was found by Finnish architects, chief among them the legendary Alvar Aalto. His House of Culture, university library (Yliopiston Kirjasto) and social security building are all acknowledged masterpieces. Perhaps greatest of all is the Finlandia Hall (Finlandiatalo) on the bay of Töölönlahti, inaugurated in 1971. This winged white concert hall is the perfect place to hear a performance of *Finlandia*, the powerfully moving anthem to his country by Jean Sibelius.

Bridges over the sea

In Scandinavia, where the landscape is intersected by a labyrinth of waterways and islands, bridges are a crucial part of the communications network. Thanks to some far-sighted investment and superb engineering, it is now possible to travel by road from one end of Scandinavia to the other.

Planning on a grand scale

The bridge that links Copenhagen and Malmö across the straits of Øresund is one of the largest civil engineering projects of modern times. The company in charge of the work, Øresund-konsortiet, employed 5500 people during the busiest period of construction in 1998. The Swedish and Danish governments imposed strict environmental rules: only 5 per cent of the material dredged from the bottom could be dumped back into the sea, and the structure of the bridge had to be designed in such a way that it would not affect the natural flow of the current towards the Baltic. The total budget was enormous: 14.8 billion Danish Krone (£1.3 billion). In order to recoup their investment, the project's backers are hoping for traffic figures of 11 800 vehicles per day.

The coasts of Scandinavia are a road-builder's nightmare – deeply indented and jagged, a giant latticework of land and water. To overcome this problem, thousands of bridges have been constructed, no fewer than 17 300 in Norway alone. Many of these are built in the face of daunting technical difficulties. The Atlantic road from Molde to Kristiansund includes a stretch of eight bridges in just over 5 miles (8 km), linking island to island over a frequently stormy sea. Farther south, the road from Bergen to Stavanger takes a dizzying route along Åkrafiord that makes use of 24 bridges and 12 tunnels in a distance of 15 miles (24 km).

Works of engineering art

The boldness of some of these structures suits the landscape perfectly, their long curves and soaring piers setting off the dramatic natural contours and giving stunning views of the surrounding scenery. Perhaps the finest of all is the Ölandsbron, 3.75 miles (6 km) long, connecting the island of Öland to Kalmar, in southern Sweden. Opened in 1972, this is the second longest bridge in Europe. It carries some 55 000 visitors a year to the beaches and picturesque villages of the island.

Another classic bridge crosses the magnificent Svinesund fiord near Halden at

The Øresund bridge Opened in 2000, this historic land-link between Denmark and Sweden is 10 miles (16 km) long.

the southern end of the Swedish-Norwegian border. Completed in 1946, its span is 508 ft (155 m) and its roadway passes 196 ft (60 m) above the water, allowing ships of any size to pass below.

Many of these bridges are fine examples of the architecture of their time. The Storstrøm bridge in Denmark, which joins the south of Sjaelland to the island of Falster, is typical of the Functionalist movement of the 1930s, and for 40 years was the longest bridge in Europe. A few miles to the east, the Farø bridge is a more recent, but equally impressive, structure. Built in 1985, its 2.4 mile (3.3 km) span is a marvel of late-20th century elegance.

A Danish giant

Not so long ago, the two halves of Denmark were separated by the narrows of Store Baelt, 11 miles (18 km) wide. On the west side lay Jutland and Fyn; on the

Mountain link One of thousands of bridges in Norway's spectacular landscape.

east Sjaelland, Falster and Lolland. For 200 years, a ferry service had operated across the narrows. By the 1980s, the ferries were carrying 10 000 passengers and 6000 tons of merchandise every day – the busiest shipping lane in the country. Bad weather sometimes stopped the ferries sailing, however, and in harsh winters interruptions were frequent.

In 1986 the Danish government decided to build a bridge across the Store Baelt. The project, the most ambitious in the nation's history, took 12 years to complete. Queen Margrethe II opened the bridge on June 14, 1998. It now takes just ten minutes to cross the Store Baelt, either by car or train.

The bridge is made up of three separate parts. An undersea road and rail tunnel 4 miles (6.6 km) long connects Fyn with the small island of Sprogø. From there the railway continues to Sjaelland underground, while the road is carried by an enormous suspension bridge, its pylons towering 833 ft (254 m) above the water – the tallest structures in Denmark.

The Store Baelt bridge has dramatically reduced crossing times, and it is open in all weathers, 365 days a year. Only the most exceptional high winds have stopped the traffic flowing.

Denmark to Sweden in half an hour

The success of the Store Baelt project encouraged the Danish government to pursue another long-cherished dream – to throw a bridge across the straits of Øresund and link Denmark to Sweden.

The bridge was officially inaugurated on August 14, 1999. In a simple symbolic ceremony, Prince Frederik of Denmark met his second cousin, Princess Victoria of Sweden, at the midway point of the straits. Each had travelled the same distance from their native shore: a gesture of friendship that was designed to stand for ever more open relations, not only between Denmark and Sweden, but between Scandinavia and Europe as a whole.

Opened to traffic in July 2000, the Øresund bridge is 10 miles (16 km) long. It connects Copenhagen to Lernacken, a toll station south of Malmö. An artificial island 2.5 miles (4 km) long divides the bridge into two halves. It carries both road and rail traffic – partly by tunnel, partly by means of a huge double-decker bridge.

Inland waterways Canals and rivers, with their systems of locks and swing bridges, are part of a long tradition of water transport.

Sjaelland in Denmark and Skåne in Sweden, with a total of 3.5 million inhabitants, are now effectively joined. This densely populated region is an economic powerhouse that accounts for 25 per cent of the combined GNP of the two countries. By bringing them together, the Øresund bridge has created what is likely to become a key centre of cultural, political and business life in Europe.

High wires The suspension bridge over the estuary of the River Daugava at Riga, the Latvian capital.

Small is beautiful A footbridge in a park in Palanga, Lithuania.

By land and water

Apart from a few remote coastal settlements, the Scandinavian ports are all now accessible by road. This is the result of more than a century of work by architects and civil engineers, who have overcome the most daunting obstacles, from stormy seas to glaciers, to throw a network of roads, bridges and tunnels across this challenging landscape. Up to the end of the 19th century, people and goods were largely transported by water. This meant that fishing communities could exist in places inaccessible by land – for example, at the foot of steep cliffs in the west of Norway – staying in touch with the outside world entirely by boat. Something of that old lifestyle can still be seen on a Norwegian coastal voyage.

The Baltic capitals: targets for conquest

For centuries, Tallinn, Riga and Vilnius have passed from one foreign overlord to another. Today, at last, they are independent. But as history shows, these cities have almost been too attractive for their own good.

Old Tallinn *One of the most fascinating medieval city centres in Europe.*

The Estonian capital, Tallinn, sits opposite Helsinki on the Gulf of Finland. It is exactly halfway between St Petersburg and Stockholm, a site of enormous strategic importance and historically coveted for both military and commercial reasons.

Tallinn, medieval masterpiece

The origins of Tallinn go back to the 1st millennium BC, when it was little more than a fortified village. Historical records tell us that by the 12th century it had become a town. In 1219 a Danish army moved in and built a fort on Toompea hill. Trade flourished, and in 1285 Tallinn became a member of the Hanseatic League, a commercial network that dominated business and political life in the Baltic and North Sea region from the 13th to the 15th century. In 1346, the city was sold to the Teutonic Knights, but when their order was dissolved in 1561, possession passed to Sweden. Tsar Peter the Great seized the city in 1710, and it remained under Russian rule until 1918. A brief period of independence followed, but was cut short by the Soviet invasion of 1940.

The heart of Tallinn, within its ring of fortifications, is one of the finest medieval city centres in Europe. The Church of St Olaf, whose origins go back at least 700 years, stands on Pikk Street alongside a series of quaint houses. The Great Guildhall, built in 1417, is an impressive symbol of Hanseatic wealth. Nearby is the Saiakang, a tiny passage leading to the square where the 14th-century Rathus (Town Hall) stands handsomely beneath its soaring Baroque belfry. On a hill overlooking the town, the late 19th-century Orthodox Cathedral of Alexander Nevsky reminds the citizens of Tallinn of the centuries of Russian dominion.

Riga today *A city of almost 1 million inhabitants, Latvia's capital city is home to one-third of the country's population.*

Riga, a turbulent history

Straddling the banks of the River Dvina, Riga was founded in 1201 by Albert of Buxhövden, Bishop of Livonia. From the early years Riga retains its Gothic Cathedral of St Mary and a number of houses, all in the same gabled style. Also dating from the medieval period is the headquarters of the Brotherhood of the Black Heads, where foreign merchants would gather to do business. Like Tallinn, Riga was a member of the Hanseatic League, then passed to the Teutonic Knights until their order was dissolved in 1561. In 1581 the city became part of Poland, although it was conquered by Gustavus Adolphus of Sweden in 1621. A new phase of building began, including the Swedish Gate and reconstruction of the 15th-century castle.

Peter the Great laid siege to Riga in 1710, taking the city after more than two-thirds of its inhabitants had been killed. Thanks to its position and active business community, Riga was the third most prosperous city in Russia by 1914. After 1918 came two decades of independence, but the Russians returned in the Second World War followed by the Germans from 1941 to 1944. Executions and deportations left a depopulated city, which the Russians soon filled up with their own emigrants. By 1970 only 41 per cent of the population was Latvian. On the eve of independence, this figure had fallen to 30 per cent.

Ancient and modern *The huge television mast on the far bank of the Daugava dominates the skyline of Riga, with its churches, old merchants' houses, pedestrianised streets and wealth of Art Nouveau buildings.*

A heritage of Art Nouveau

In the early 20th century, Riga was immensely wealthy and many buildings in the Art Nouveau style were commissioned. Much of this architecture remains, characterised by florid wrought-ironwork, coloured glass and architectural ornament inspired by plant forms. Mikhail Osipovitch Eisenstein was a leading exponent of this style. A house he designed in Alberta Street is typical: its entrance hall has turquoise pillars decorated with serpentine patterns of leaves. Another enthusiast was Wilhelm Bockslaff, who designed the stock exchange building – now the Academy of Art. The Art Nouveau movement inspired the Riga School, a romantic national style of painting and decoration that also drew from folk art and the traditions of rural life.

Tourist destination
The Lithuanian capital, Vilnius, founded in the 14th century, was once Eastern Europe's leading centre of Jewish culture. Today, a new wave of prosperity and popularity brings tourists to see its churches, its fascinating old streets and lively markets (right).

Vilnius, home of the Jagiellon

On a hill at the confluence of the rivers Neris and Vilnia stand the ruins of the Castle of Gediminas, named after the Grand Duke of Lithuania who founded the Jagiellon dynasty. He dreamed of an iron wolf howling on this spot, and in 1323 chose Vilnius as his capital. After destruction by the Teutonic Knights in 1377, Vilnius was rebuilt and became self-governing in 1387. The city soon prospered, its culture blossoming under Sigismund II Augustus, King of Poland and Grand Duke of Lithuania from 1548 to 1572, who built the Church of St Anne, a masterpiece of Gothic architecture. In the same period a printing press and university were established, with a library that was one of the largest in Renaissance Europe. Its collection of 180 000 manuscripts survives to this day.

Like other Baltic cities, Vilnius was a tempting prize for foreign conquerors: the Russians in 1655-60, the Swedes in 1702 and 1706, the French in 1812, the Germans in both world wars. In 1795, under the Third Partition of Poland, Vilnius passed into Russian hands. Many of its Catholic churches, built by Jesuits, were taken over by the Russian Orthodox clergy. Since independence, however, the Catholic Church has been reclaiming its property.

Annexed by Poland in 1920, then occupied by Russian troops in 1939, Vilnius for much of the 20th century suffered the same fate as Riga: massive ethnic cleansing as its native population was deported and Russians and other nationalities moved in. Of its present population of 500 000 only 50 per cent are Lithuanian.

The urban heritage

The Scandinavians are proud of their past, and go to great lengths to keep it alive in their beautifully preserved historic towns and cities.

Few medieval towns can rival Ribe in Denmark. Set among water meadows on the west coast of Jutland, its 14th-century cathedral bell-tower is visible from miles away. Cobbled lanes meander between half-timbered houses with red-tiled roofs and carved wooden doorways. Owned and protected by the Danish National Trust – who provide a singing, storytelling night watchman in the summer months – Ribe also has an open-air Viking museum that hums with activity, especially in summer, when the main square is so lively you could easily be in a Mediterranean town.

Defying time

On the waterfront at Bergen, on Norway's west coast, a row of ancient wooden houses bears witness to the grandeur of the city's past: 58 buildings, all in the harbour area of Bryggen, which have escaped the countless fires that have ravaged the rest of the city. Their historic importance is such that they have been designated a World Heritage Site by UNESCO. Today they attract visitors from all over the world.

Norwegians have a special fondness for Bergen. Partly it is the extraordinary setting, at the meeting-point of seven mountains and seven fiords: above all, though, it is the city's history. Throughout the Middle Ages, and up to the middle of the 19th century, Bergen was the country's principal city. It remains one of Scandinavia's liveliest seaports and a thriving cultural centre, with a famed International Festival. In 2000, it was a European City of Culture.

In the 14th century, merchants of the Hanseatic League set up their warehouses in the Bryggen district, with a monopoly of Norway's international trade granted by royal charter. The main item of trade was dried fish from the north of the country, which Scottish, German, Dutch and English merchants exported to the rest of Europe. Bergen became one of the League's four biggest overseas trading stations. When the city withdrew from the League in 1559, its merchants were forced to choose between leaving and changing nationality, but the German style of architecture, the prosperity and the cosmopolitan culture remained.

The old copper-mining town of Røros lies 250 miles (400 km) north of Oslo, in the county of Sør-Trøndelag. Founded in the 17th century when copper deposits were discovered nearby, it has retained its original character and is now, like Bryggen, a World Heritage Site. The first mineshaft was dug here in 1644, near the falls on the River Hitterlava, which flows across the site. A wooden shed was built over the minehead. This was soon followed by other buildings, all laid out on a neoclassical grid of the kind that was

Viking colony Århus, in Denmark, is a busy, lively town, with a beautifully preserved historic centre.

Work to be done

Despite the wealth and commercial importance of their ports and cities from the Middle Ages to the 17th century, the Baltic countries have found it hard to preserve their architectural heritage. The restoration of old buildings is not yet seen as a priority by the newly independent Baltic republics, even if they do place great value on their past and make every effort to keep their traditions alive. According to an 11th-century manuscript, Tartu, Estonia's second largest city, is also its most ancient. History has been cruel to it, however: over the centuries its strategic position has made it a target for every passing army and it has been burned to the ground no less than 55 times. Despite this violent past, a handful of ancient buildings have escaped destruction, and these can be seen in the old quarters of the city that lie outside the predominantly neoclassical centre.

In Lithuania the port of Kaunas, with its cobbled streets and charming houses with red-tiled roofs, has been well preserved by the civic authorities. In the main square of Kaunas stands the old town hall, nicknamed the 'White Swan' for its unusual and elegant white tower. Museums, stalls, restaurants, bars and traditional shops line the square, encouraging visitors to linger and enjoy a taste of the region's colourful past.

Island capital Visby, on the island of Gotland, is one of the finest medieval towns in Sweden.

Living museum Designated by UNESCO as a World Heritage Site, Bryggen (the harbour area of Bergen) is a magnificent townscape of timber-framed houses and cobbled streets.

River port *The handsome old Finnish trading town of Porvoo, with its warehouses lining the banks of the river, gives the visitor a lingering sense of another world, another way of life.*

fashionable at the time of Christian VI, known as the 'Miner King'. The last copper was extracted at Røros in 1986. By then the preservation of the town was well in hand. Seven buildings were classed as historic monuments in 1923, and several others were restored with great attention to detail. Among the most remarkable is the Baroque church, which can hold a congregation of 1500. It was built in 1784, at the height of the community's prosperity, 'to the glory of God and the beauty of the town'. Nearby is the manor house that once belonged to the hunter Hans Olen Aasen, who first discovered copper in the mountains to the east of Røros.

Mixing old and new

Gothenburg (Göteborg) on the west coast of Sweden is a perfect marriage of past and present. The old town nestles snugly between the Göta river and canal, a fascinating network of picturesque streets, squares and canals that still reflects the ideas and tastes of its original Dutch planners in the 1620s.

An enormous variety of architectural styles is displayed in Gothenburg, especially in the fine houses built by Dutch, English and German merchants who settled here in the 18th and 19th centuries, often with oriental touches inspired by the Swedish East India Company and its trade with the Far East. The town's main street is the Kungsportavenyen, a wide, handsome boulevard lined with trees, restaurants, pubs and cafès; it is known by the locals as 'the Champs-Elysées of the North' – an easy, stylish, sociable place.

Timeless tranquillity

A visit to Finland would not be complete without a trip to Rauma. This, the largest and best-preserved timber-built city in the north, was the first Finnish site to be given World Heritage status by UNESCO. Most of the 600 houses and 160 shops in the old town date from the 18th and 19th centuries. They are now used mainly by jewellers, lacemakers and craftsmen of various kinds, whose workshops provide a living link with the past.

Another place where time seems to have come to a halt is Kokkola, a village that grew wealthy in the 17th century through the extraction and sale of bitumen. It later became a busy port for cargo ships and ferries sailing to Sweden. Today the quiet, lovely streets of Kokkola are a pleasure to walk in, providing a place of refuge from a hyperactive world.

CHAPTER 4
LIVING IN NORTHERN EUROPE

The Scandinavians' way of life is regarded with respect and admiration: they have the fairest, most open, tolerant and least discriminatory society in the world. Their social achievements are remarkable: they have the ability to produce wealth without social division, to pursue education, knowledge and happiness while maintaining harmonious relationships both with the rest of the human community and with nature. Some Scandinavian countries still have royal families, whose privileges have been preserved for centuries without bloodshed or violence, and who continue to be popular at the heart of thoroughly mature democracies. Other countries in the region have chosen to become republics: it seems to make little difference. Despite strict laws, the Scandinavians are great lovers of freedom, and have done more than any other people on Earth to guarantee that precious commodity for the largest possible number.

Students at the University of Turku in Finland taking part in the celebrations to mark the start of spring.

Modern royal families

In the modern world, the idea of hereditary rule by a single family seems out of place. In Scandinavia, with its long and respected tradition of democracy, the idea seems doubly strange. Yet three of the four Scandinavian states are monarchies – and happy ones, too.

Denmark has been ruled by the same dynasty since the 10th century, making it the oldest monarchy in the world. Sweden runs it a close second, with a monarchy that goes back to the year 1000. Norway's royal family is much more recent but, as if to make up for its junior status, it is hugely popular with the people.

An evolving tradition

The role of the kings and queens of Denmark has changed considerably over the centuries. Originally they were tribal chieftains, chosen as leaders for their wisdom and strength in war. Gradually,

King of Sweden *Charles XVI Gustav, the present king of Sweden, is descended from one of Napoleon's marshals, Jean-Baptiste Bernadotte, who came to the throne by invitation in 1818. Behind the pomp and ceremonial of royalty, King Charles and his queen, Silvia, live thoroughly modern lives.*

Constitution Day The people of Bergen turn out in all weathers for the country's biggest public holiday on May 17. Norway became an independent state only in 1905, after a long struggle, first against Denmark then against Sweden.

a dynasty evolved, a kind of gene pool of talent, from which monarchs were selected. In the late Middle Ages the nobility bore an equally important share of power, only to lose it in the period of absolute monarchy when royal authority was at its height. In 1660, Frederick III imposed absolute rule, but with the French Revolution of 1789 sending shivers throughout monarchist Europe, ideas began to change. After some brief rebellions in Schleswig and Holstein, the Danish 'revolution' took a typically peaceful and reasonable form: a reform movement some 10 000 strong demanded a liberal constitution and a democratically elected government. King Frederick VII accepted, and on June 5, 1849, the Danish parliament met for the first time since Viking days. The king was now outside the political process.

Since then the constitution has been revised several times, and the monarchy plays an entirely symbolic role, limited to approving the laws voted by parliament – which can dethrone a sovereign who refuses. The royal family must belong to the Protestant Church, and is expected to refrain from voting in elections or playing a part in national debates.

During the Second World War, King Christian X maintained a correct but icy relationship with the occupying Germans – an attitude that earned him great respect from his people. His son, Frederick IX, who came to the throne in 1947, set about modernising the image of the monarchy. When Queen Ingrid bore him three daughters, they decided to send the girls to normal state schools. At the time the constitution allowed only male heirs to succeed to the throne, but in 1953 this rule was changed and in 1972 the eldest daughter became Queen Margrethe II. Today Denmark's royal family remains simple, accessible and widely respected.

Privacy and the Press

The royal families of Scandinavia have perfected the art of fitting into everyday life. As royalty, they are public figures – like politicians or film stars – and they get their share of media exposure, although the press are careful not to intrude too far into their private lives. Recently, a newspaper published photographs of the crown prince of Denmark frolicking naked in a swimming pool with a pretty young female singer. There was a huge public outcry – not at the prince's antics, which were accepted as perfectly normal for a young bachelor, but at the vulgarity of the newspaper.

adopted the principle of cognatic succession, whereby the crown passes to the eldest child, whether male or female.

King Charles and his family are as popular as their fellow Scandinavian monarchs, although there has been some difficulty over intrusions by the press into their private lives. In 1998, the Palace let it be known that Victoria, the heir apparent, was suffering from an eating disorder, probably anorexia. The newspapers had a field day, whipping up public interest in the case to an excessive degree. Since then Princess Victoria has gone to study at Harvard University in the USA and managed to regain a measure of privacy.

Norway's young monarchy

From the 14th to the early 20th century Norway was a subject state without its own king. It was governed first by Denmark, then by Sweden, until 1905. In that year the Norwegian parliament, the Storting, decided to seek independence, offering the crown to Prince Carl of Denmark. Carl accepted, adopted the name Haakon VII, and promised to respect the Norwegian constitution – said to be the most liberal in the world. This had been drawn up in 1814, at a time when Norway was ridding itself of Danish rule, only to fall under the power of Sweden shortly after. Under the present constitution, the king has no powers but enjoys huge popularity.

When Hitler invaded Norway in 1940, King Haakon VII, Crown Prince Olav and the entire administration left the capital just a few hours before the German army arrived, refusing absolutely to collaborate with the occupying forces. After the surrender of June 1940 they were forced to leave the country, taking refuge in London, where the king established a government in exile and set up the Norwegian resistance. Queen Märtha, with the rest of the children, moved to Sweden, and then to the safety of the United States. Crown Prince Olav returned to his country on May 13, 1945, and was joined by the rest of the family three weeks later.

The monarchy's popularity continues under the present king, Harald V, the first Norwegian sovereign to be born in the country since 1370. In 1968, as crown prince, he came close to triggering a dynastic crisis when he married a commoner, Sonja Haraldsen, but the public took his side and the crisis passed.

Changing the guard This daily event at the royal palace in Copenhagen is as popular with Danes as with tourists.

The common touch

The present king of Sweden, Charles XVI Gustav, came to the throne in 1973, the 47th in a line that goes back 1000 years. He belongs to the House of Bernadotte, which has ruled Sweden since 1818. This was the year when, in the absence of a royal heir, the French army marshal Jean-Baptiste Bernadotte was offered the Swedish throne. The country already had a powerful parliament, the Riksdag (founded in the 15th century), and a constitution dating from 1809. Relations between the monarchy and the Riksdag were tense for the whole of the 19th century. The result was a complete loss of royal prerogatives in 1919: the sovereign was not even allowed to approve new laws.

Today's king, like his counterparts in Denmark and Norway, was brought up as a normal citizen of his country. He married Silvia Sommerlath, a girl he met at the 1972 Munich Olympics, where she was working as a guide. The royal couple have three children: Victoria, Charles Philip and Madeleine. In 1980, the Swedes

Queen of Denmark Margrethe II and her French husband, Count Henri de Montpezat, whose official title is Prince Henrik, at the wedding of their daughter, Princess Alexandra.

The aftermath of communism

The collapse of the Soviet Union plunged the whole of Eastern Europe into chaos. The Baltic States recovered faster than many other countries of the communist bloc – but can they sustain the necessary momentum of change?

Ski fighters   *Winter training for the Estonian army. These troops could soon be serving with NATO.*

Estonia, Latvia and Lithuania were never very enthusiastic about the socialist system forced on them by their Soviet 'Big Brother'. As soon as the cracks began to appear in the communist monolith, the Baltic States were among the first to claim their freedom. On August 23, 1989, massive human chains were formed, with an estimated 500 000 people from the three nations protesting against the Molotov-Ribbentrop pact, an agreement signed 50 years previously by the foreign ministers of Stalin and Hitler, with secret clauses granting control of parts of Eastern Europe to the Russians.

The protest movement quickly found support in the West. Denmark was the first to recognise Estonia, Latvia and Lithuania as sovereign states: the Danish action caused an immediate crisis in diplomatic relations with Moscow. Other nations waited until September 1991, when communism finally collapsed in Russia, to grant official recognition to the independent Baltic States.

Momentous decision   *Voting in the Latvian referendum on independence, held in 1991.*

Toppled idols   *A statue of Joseph Stalin, symbol of the hated Soviet empire, lies waiting to be carried off to the scrapyard in Lithuania.*

A tough regime

War on inflation was declared by the Estonian government in the 1990s, in order to ease the country into the free market economy. The Estonian Central Bank was forbidden to increase the money supply, no new government debts were taken on, and no treasury bonds issued. State spending was cut, to 10 per cent below average European levels. Income tax was reduced to a single rate of 26 per cent, with a high income threshold so that most people did not have to pay. To balance this, wages were frozen. The result was a reduction in the annual rate of inflation to 13 per cent (from 89 per cent in 1993), and unemployment stabilising at 10 per cent, and then 5 per cent in the late nineties.

Knocking on Europe's door

Under the communist regime, political power in the Baltic States was held almost exclusively by Russians, so when the opportunity for independence came, the local people were quick to seize it – dismantling the old order was a positive pleasure to them. They had two important advantages: an industrial sector that was a great deal more efficient and successful than others in the old communist bloc, and a geographical position that made trade with Western Europe relatively easy to set up. Since 1995, several Western companies have been tempted by the presence of a skilled workforce and low wage levels to set up factories and joint ventures in the Baltic countries. If these prove successful, the likelihood is that wages and living standards will gradually rise to meet Western levels: at present, for example, an Estonian pilot and a Danish pilot flying the same routes for the same airline are paid vastly different salaries – the Dane gets 400 per cent more.

Indications are that the process of integrating fully in the global free market economy, which Estonia, Latvia and Lithuania have begun so successfully, will continue without a hitch. They have already achieved a remarkable level of economic stability and plans for becoming full alliance members of NATO by May 2004 and members of the EU on May 1st 2004 are well underway.

Minorities old and new

The peoples of Scandinavia are some of the most ethnically homogeneous in Europe, with the question of minority remaining a marginal issue. In the Baltic States, though, ethnic tensions are high.

At the start of the 1970s, with the Scandinavian economies booming, workers from Southern Europe and the Middle East came and settled – not in vast numbers, but enough to bring a distinctive new feel to life in the big cities. There have been a few outbreaks of racism, but generally the new immigrants are accepted and appreciated for bringing new cultures and ways of life.

Tolerance and integration

Tolerance is the norm in Scandinavia. In Finland there are two official languages: Finnish and Swedish. Finnish is spoken in two of the country's national theatres, Swedish in the third. Swedes make up 5 per cent of the population in Finland, and they are totally integrated.

In the same way, the Sami (or Lapps), who live by herding reindeer in the subarctic tundras of northern Norway, Sweden and Finland, have adapted fully to the modern world while preserving their ancient language and culture.

Mediterranean presence *A wave of immigrants from Southern Europe and the Middle East came to Scandinavia in the boom years of the 1970s.*

New faces *Scandinavia's traditions of tolerance and political maturity help ethnic minorities become successfully integrated.*

Ethnic tension

The Baltic States, on the other hand, are living on a knife-edge of ethnic tension. This was created by the Soviet policy of 'Russification' (deporting locals and importing Russian settlers). In Lithuania, 20 per cent of the population was replaced in this way; in Estonia 40 per cent; in Latvia 50 per cent. The last two figures have been reduced during the 1990s to 35 per cent and 44 per cent respectively by granting citizenship only to those from families who were Estonian or Latvian before the Soviet occupation. This has, of course, meant the eviction of large numbers of Soviet-era settlers. In 2000 following international criticism, laws were passed to end discrimination against the Russian minorities.

The situation today is far from happy. The Baltic peoples are still haunted by the fear of losing their language, cultural identity and homeland, and relations with Moscow remain fairly tense.

Russian wedding *An Orthodox church in Latvia, where about one-third of the population is Russian.*

The Danish model of integration

Throughout its long history, Denmark has had to struggle to defend its southern frontier from its powerful neighbour, Germany. Until 1864, Danish territory included the whole of the Jutland peninsula, reaching almost as far as Hamburg. But the population of the Duchy of Holstein, in southern Jutland, was largely German, while Schleswig to the north was half German and half Danish. The situation became explosive in 1848, when the German-speaking populations of the two duchies claimed that they belonged to Germany, which had recently been unified into a single state. Denmark suppressed the revolt after three years of fighting, but in 1864 Prussia invaded southern Jutland. Denmark lost a fifth of its territory and a third of its people. After the end of the First World War, a powerful Danish nationalist movement tried to regain the lost territories, but only the population of Northern Schleswig voted to revert to Denmark under a plebiscite in 1919: Southern Schleswig and Holstein voted to remain as part of Germany. The new frontier left a Danish minority in Germany and a German one in Denmark. These communities coexist peacefully, with newspapers in their own languages.

The future of the welfare state

The people of Scandinavia enjoy one of the highest standards of living in the world. Ever since the 1930s they have been committed to the principle of the welfare state, despite the high financial cost involved.

The 19th-century Danish writer Nikolai Grundtvig defined the welfare state as a society where 'a few have too much and fewer still have too little'. His thinking helped shape the ideas of the social democratic parties that dominated Scandinavian politics throughout the 20th century. Even the opposition parties, in their brief periods of power, have stuck to the same social philosophy.

A *fair distribution of wealth*

The system is based on a progressive scale of taxation, which is more or less double the rate in other Western countries – between 50 and 68 per cent. This gives the state a huge cash income, which it is able to spend on providing an exceptionally high level of social

Cell phone *Phone calls are part of a humane prison service.*

care: free education and medical services, family allowances, unemployment benefit, old-age pensions and retirement homes. This means that all members of society have the same opportunities in life and the same benefits when they need help. The welfare state is not seen as a system of handouts to the less well-off: to Scandinavians, it is a question of basic human rights.

A *turning point*

The oil price crisis of 1973-4 and rising levels of unemployment in the 1980s gave the welfare system and its supporters some nasty shocks. People began to ask questions about the efficiency of public services, which had grown hugely through the boom years and had vast numbers of employees. In Denmark, for instance, one-third of the total workforce was employed by the government. With a monopoly on public services, were they giving the country value for money? In Norway, the discovery of North Sea oil allowed social programmes to continue at former levels, but elsewhere the welfare system came under attack. With taxation income falling and social security payments rising as a result of unemployment, the number of state employees in Denmark, Sweden and Finland had to be cut drastically. To make up for reduced public services, private schools, hospitals and retirement homes began to appear. Tolls were charged on new highways and bridges (now financed by a mix of public and private investment), on the principle that the user pays. Gradually, the welfare state has been adapting to a competitive, cost-conscious world.

Help for the aged *Home visits by social and health workers are standard in Scandinavia.*

Counter measures *Falling birthrates, a concern across the whole of Europe, have led to schemes to help couples share the work of raising children. Fathers as well as mothers get time off.*

Party of the discontented

In 1973, a new political party, the Fremskridtspartiet, took its first seats in the Danish parliament. Its policies included abolition of all taxes and the dismantling of the public sector. National defence would be taken out of the hands of the armed forces and replaced by a telephone answering machine with the message (in Russian) 'We surrender'. For a while, the party was the second biggest in Denmark. Its satirical approach is typical of the Danish sense of humour, but it also expresses a genuine sense of unease about levels of public spending. The Fremskridtspartiet has forced the government to make cuts both in staff numbers and in the amounts of cash available for social programmes.

Raising tomorrow's generation

Education is a top priority for Scandinavians. These are countries which have to rely on technical superiority and innovation to stay in the first league of industrial nations – and that means having a highly educated workforce.

After class A cornerstone of Scandinavian beliefs is that young people must have time to play.

Every child in Scandinavia has the right to free schooling up to university age. The state schools are generously funded, with well-trained teachers and excellent facilities. Pupils who go to university are expected to study full-time, and are given grants to enable them to do this without the distraction of part-time jobs.

There are free nursery-school places for all – essential in a society where both parents tend to be in full-time work. At the age of seven, children enter the first year of the school system, where they benefit from the highest educational budgets anywhere in Europe. They take exams at the end of years 9 and 10, and are then streamed either into vocational schools (leading to various trades and professions) or into academic schools (leading to university). To get into university, students have to get good marks in the school-leaving exams.

Folk high schools: Grundtvig's dream

In 1844 Denmark's first folk high school for adults opened at Rødding, in southern Jutland. Although the purpose was educational, the choice of site was not accidental: the area was a hotbed of nationalist agitation at the time, as Denmark and Germany tussled

Join the club!

There may be some truth in the saying that as soon as three Scandinavians meet, they form a club with a president, vice-president and treasurer. Every neighbourhood has its youth club, where young people can take up a range of activities, from sport to music to stamp-collecting. Forming groups, clubs and associations is right at the heart of Scandinavian life. Youth clubs are run on a voluntary basis by parents and are highly effective in discouraging juvenile delinquency.

The right note Danish primary school children take part in a musical discovery class.

over ownership of the duchies of Schleswig and Holstein. The school was an immediate success and similar institutions sprang up elsewhere – first in Denmark, then in other parts of Scandinavia.

Folk high schools were inspired by the thinking of Nikolai Grundtvig (1783-1872), a clergyman, poet, historian and educationalist, who wanted the poor people of the countryside to be able to improve themselves and broaden their mental horizons. The schools were residential and courses lasted five to six months. They offered lessons in the language, literature and culture of Denmark, foreign languages, history, arithmetic, politics and economics. Music and singing also played an important part: Grundtvig himself composed more than 1500 songs, hymns, psalms and canticles, which are still part of the popular repertoire.

The folk high schools were initially funded by the government, which saw them as a means of building up a national consciousness. As their numbers grew it was unable to fund them fully, but continued to make a contribution to their costs. The schools are still going strong today, offering a chance for working people to take educational time out from their normal lives, or to break out of a pattern of unemployment, hopelessness and social exclusion.

Living together in harmony

The Scandinavians are probably the most relaxed people in the world. Open-minded, tolerant and unshockable, they accept any behaviour so long as it causes no harm to others.

Marriage certificate *Homosexual marriages have been legally recognised in Denmark since 1990. For most people there is no social stigma in such unions.*

Not so long ago, Denmark and Sweden had a reputation for free morals and sexual liberty. This was due in large part to their tolerance: in 1967, the Danes took the unprecedented step of legalising pornography – the first nation in the world to do so, and, even more remarkable at the time, the legislation was passed by a Conservative Christian government. Since then, newsstands and shops have openly sold pornographic publications. Foreigners are often astonished, but the Danes themselves, whether young or old, regard it as quite normal.

Equality for all

When it comes to equality between the sexes, the Scandinavians have led the field for a long time. They have been a model for feminists worldwide since at least the 1970s, when the American Lindsy Van Gelder wrote in *Newsweek*, 'I would be happy if women in

My way *The right to be different, gay, transsexual or transvestite is widely accepted in Scandinavia, long famous for its tolerant and open attitudes.*

America raised themselves to the level of women in Denmark.' Since the 1960s most women have had full-time jobs, whether they are single, married or mothers, and there is no type of work or level of responsibility from which women are excluded. At present, 80 per cent of married women between the ages of 20 and 50 are in salaried employment, compared with 50 per cent in 1965. Although some kinds of work (nursing, for example) are still reserved for women, all the traditionally male jobs have now been opened up to both sexes: firefighting, police work, even the queen's personal bodyguard – the ultimate bastion of masculinity.

In couples where both partners work, household jobs are shared. Surveys show that men do almost as much cooking, cleaning and washing as women. When a baby is born, the father is present at the birth and is expected to take equal responsibility for the care and upbringing of the child. He can claim paid paternity leave from work, and when the parents return to their jobs the child is looked after in a public crèche.

Decline of marriage

Today, around 20 per cent of all Danish couples live together without any formal union. Similar figures apply to the rest of Scandinavia and the Baltic States. Like other Europeans, the Danes are committed believers in the nuclear family, although they have long been relaxed about sex before marriage. Marriage itself remains a sacred institution, but there is a growing tendency for couples to marry after the birth of their first child. The divorce rate, which has gone up significantly in recent decades, is about 25 per cent.

Almost 40 per cent of Danish children are born to unmarried mothers. This does not necessarily mean that the parents are single: about 40 per cent of unmarried couples have a child and 15 per cent have two or more. These new patterns owe much to the changing status of women in Danish society. Free contraception and abortions have led to greater sexual freedom and a general change in lifestyle. Women follow the same courses of study and have the same career opportunities as men. There remains some discrimination in salaries, but women are now financially independent of men, which means marriage is not necessary for security, and divorce no longer means social and financial ruin.

Equal opportunities *Swedish universities encourage women as much as men to go for the best jobs.*

Making it official

In recent years Denmark and Norway have recognised homosexual marriages. Same-sex partners, whether male or female, now have exactly the same legal rights as heterosexual couples, including the automatic right of inheritance. One of the most high-profile of these marriages took place in 1999, when the Danish Minister of Health, Torbent Lund, a divorced father of two, married his male partner in Copenhagen's City Hall. The couple were then invited to Queen Margrethe's annual ball. Nor has Lund been the only example: a number of sports celebrities, actors and musicians have had similar weddings.

Young, idealistic and free *The 'free town' of Christiania in the heart of Copenhagen started life as an anarchist commune. Today its alternative shops (above) and funky communal gatherings (right) attract tourists from around the world.*

Composite families, made up of a couple with children from more than one relationship, are now relatively common in Denmark, particularly in the more advanced and cosmopolitan south. In the north, where life is harsher, and is more ruled by tradition and the Church – and where there are fewer jobs – marriage remains sacrosanct, and, for women in particular, a material and social necessity.

Christiania, a 'free community' within the capital

In 1971 a group of five anarchist students occupied a set of disused naval huts in Copenhagen and announced that they were founding a new, free community, called Christiania, barely 2 miles (3.2 km) from the Danish parliament. Their aim was to build a society based on communal living and personal liberty, including the liberty not to pay tax or rent. The authorities tried hard to evict them on several occasions, but more than 30 years later the community is still there, and doing very well.

The government had good legal reasons for eviction: the land belonged to the state; the people who lived there paid nothing for public services; and the area was notorious for drug trafficking. Yet, as the years went by, public opinion came round to the idea

that the commune might be a positive thing. The houses, once built of scrap, have now become noticeably more stylish, and the streets of Christiania boast the city's best restaurants and cabarets. The creative note is unmistakable, and it has led to some popular and successful schemes, such as the famous Christiania bicycles with their spacious carrying-boxes.

Although freedom is very much the watchword, the commune has developed its own rules and now cooperates with the national and city authorities. Every year, hundreds of thousands of tourists come to peer into this alternative world. But you will not find many Swedes and Norwegians among them: to them, Christiania is a den of vice, violence and drugs. Although it is certainly true that marijuana is easy to buy on the aptly named Pusher Street, the locals keep up a constant battle against the dealers in hard drugs and against crime generally.

Warm hearts in a cold climate

At a first meeting, Scandinavians can often seem as cold and distant as the landscape in which they were born. But the moment trust is established, their warmth, generosity and hospitality know no limits.

The right pace *One of the best ways to explore Iceland's interior is on horseback.*

The first thing a traveller to Scandinavia tends to notice is the silence. This may not seem so remarkable in remote villages, but it does strike the visitor to the region's cities, where no hubbub of conversation disturbs the drone of traffic. When Scandinavians talk, they prefer to do it in the privacy of their homes; in public places they keep words to the minimum and speak in subdued tones. It is generally regarded as the height of rudeness to address a stranger on a bus or train.

In the countryside and small provincial towns – even in some big cities – foreigners tend to be treated with caution. Once they are known and accepted, however, a friendly relationship soon develops.

Oslo sun *Young people relaxing on the lawns in front of parliament. After the rigours of Norway's winter, summer days are intensely enjoyed.*

Traditional boats *Wooden rowing boats were once the universal form of transport for people and goods. Today, they are used for sport, pleasure and ceremonial, a symbol of proud traditions. This one is festooned with branches for St John's Day in the central Swedish region of Dalarna.*

Welcome among friends

The moment you become friends, and particularly if you are invited into a Scandinavian home, the coolness disappears and another side of the Nordic character comes out. Old and new friends alike are welcomed with open arms. There are, however, a few simple rules to be obeyed: dinner guests are expected to arrive on time, and before touching their wine or schnapps, guests must wait for the host to raise his glass, look everyone in the eye and wish them welcome to his home. The business of toasting (*skål*) is in fact quite a ritual: everyone must look their fellow guests in the eye before taking the first sip, and again immediately afterwards.

Lure of the Mediterranean

Much as the Scandinavians love their own landscapes, they are irresistibly attracted by the sunshine of the Mediterranean. Every summer the holiday resorts of Italy, Greece, Spain and the South of France draw thousands of fair-skinned northerners, following in the steps of their Viking ancestors to the lands of vine and olive.

Rules of hospitality are one thing, national rivalries another. Each of the Scandinavian nations nurses prejudices about the others. The Danes think of the Swedes as rather stuffy and hidebound by custom, while they see themselves as refreshingly irreverent and rebellious. Both Danes and Swedes regard Norwegians as stubborn and old-fashioned, while the Finns are seen as boorish and over-fond of their drink. Such stereotypes are seldom very accurate, but if taken (and meant) in good part, they can be amusing – until they are used as a pretext for aggression. It is mystifying to an outsider to hear the Scandinavians describe each other in these terms. They are, after all, so similar, with deeply shared tastes, attitudes and values: love of nature and landscape; a passionate belief in democracy; pride in their political and civic traditions; earnestness about life, tempered by gently self-deprecating humour.

Brought up in a spirit of independence and self-reliance, the Scandinavians are scrupulous in their respect for the freedom of others, which they will often defend with great vigour. Their record in defending human rights across the globe is second to none. It is no surprise that the Swedish chemist, Alfred Nobel, bequeathed part of his fortune to institute the Nobel peace prize when he witnessed the wartime uses of his inventions, dynamite and nitroglycerine.

Ferries to everywhere

Endless ferry services crisscross the waterways and seas of Scandinavia, with their fiords, gulfs, lakes and rivers. Vessels range from the big modern car ferries that ply the Baltic and Norwegian seas to small craft linking islands.

Great lakes *On Lake Inari, in Finnish Lappland, a small seaplane prepares to take off.*

South of Copenhagen, where the great new Øresund bridge crosses The Sound to Sweden, there is still a ferry service, as there has been for the past 200 years. The ferries sail under the bridge, which opened in July 2000, with a motorway and railway line covering the 27 miles (45 km) to Lernacken, south of Malmö. The commercial and business traffic has all moved to the bridge, but some people still take the ferry, which is like an old friend – in particular to housewives who like to go shopping in Sweden when prices are right, the ferry trip still makes a pleasant day out.

Roads of water and ice

All around the coasts of Scandinavia, the lives of small communities depend on water transport. Denmark is made up of 406 islands, with 67 different ferry services (not including international freight lines) running regularly between them. In the Åland Islands off Finland, even the post is brought by boat, along with food, wine, newspapers and merchandise of every kind. If the sea is too rough, no boats sail and no goods arrive. This makes living and working on the islands an unpredictable business – so much so that many of the locals have left to seek jobs elsewhere. With the

advent of the Internet and the opportunities this gives of working from home, there are high hopes that this trend can be reversed.

In winter the waters of the Gulf of Bothnia, between Finland and Sweden, freeze over. People used regularly to cross with wheeled vehicles, but now the shipping lanes between main ports are kept open by icebreakers.

Stern first *A huge modern car ferry manoeuvres into Copenhagen harbour. Maritime services remain a key part of Scandinavia's system of communications and transport.*

The Coastal Express

Winter and summer, every day of the year, a ferry sets out from Bergen for Kirkenes in the far north, while another one sets off from Kirkenes for the journey south. The round trip of 3216 miles (5146 km) takes 11 days. The service, known in Norwegian as Hurtigruten, was inaugurated in 1893. It carries post, cargo and passengers to a total of 35 ports along the coast, half of them within the Arctic Circle. The Hurtigruten has also proved attractive to a growing number of tourists, who experience an unforgettable scenic journey, threading through fiords and among islands, while eating, drinking and going ashore to visit a small fishing community, church or local museum. As the ship travels north, it calls in at the Lofoten Islands, allowing its passengers to discover the hidden beauty of their austere and rugged mountain chain.

The Göta Canal, an idyllic voyage

You can still take a boat up the Göta Canal between Stockholm and Gothenburg. It takes four days to do the 250 mile (400 km) journey, either by hotel boat or on a hired cruiser. The canal crosses two of Sweden's largest lakes and includes 65 locks along the way. Opened in 1832 to transport iron and timber out of central Sweden, it took 60 000 soldiers over 22 years to complete the canal. It offers one of the most picturesque journeys in Sweden, passing through lovely countryside and historic towns such as Vadstena, built around the monastery of St Brigitte, and Söderköping with its cobbled streets and fine wooden houses.

Education for life

Scandinavian universities are some of the best and most highly regarded in the world. They reflect a deep commitment to education and knowledge that goes back many centuries.

Teaching and learning   *A class in Copenhagen, where there is a long tradition of interactive teaching. Through a range of activities, including research and discussion, students become involved in the learning process.*

Copenhagen University, founded in 1479, has long been a centre of scientific innovation and discovery. Throughout its history it has produced thinkers and researchers of great originality and distinction. In the second half of the 17th century, Tycho Brahe, one of the fathers of modern astronomy, carried out the first exhaustive survey of the Solar System and established the exact positions of 777 stars. In 1675, Ole Römer calculated the speed of light, and just over 100 years later, Christian Ørsted discovered electromagnetism. In 1903, Niels Finen was awarded the Nobel prize for medicine for his work on the effects of light and ultraviolet rays in the treatment of disease. In 1922, Niels Bohr won the Nobel prize for physics for his studies on the structure of the atom.

Graduation day   *Students celebrate the awarding of their degrees at Uppsala.*

Today, the university occupies several sites and buildings across the city. It has 7000 staff and 32 000 students from all over the world. There is a particularly strong student presence from Iceland and the Faeroe Islands, which do not have universities of their own.

Great tradition of science and technology

The Karolinska Institute is one of the world's most prestigious scientific bodies, and is responsible for awarding the Nobel prizes for medicine and physiology. In 1895, Alfred Nobel, the inventor of dynamite, chose the medical faculty of the University of Stockholm as the awarding body for the prize that bears his name. Since then, seven Swedish scientists have won the prize, five from that faculty.

Uppsala, the oldest university in Scandinavia, was founded in 1477. Today it has 36 000 students, and is Sweden's top academic institution. Several Nobel prize winners are among its alumni, including the economist and statesman Dag Hammarskjöld (1905-61), a highly respected and admired Secretary-General of the United Nations, who was awarded the Nobel peace prize in 1961 for his work in international relations.

In Finland, a new university was founded in Helsinki when the capital was transferred from Turku in 1640. Today it has a formidable reputation in the field of advanced technologies, with a particularly strong department of computer sciences.

Downtown academy   *Oslo University, Norway's oldest academic institution, is one of the city's main landmarks.*

Freezer science

Tromsø is Norway's smallest and newest university, and the most unusual. Located inside the Arctic Circle, with two months of permanent darkness each winter and two months of constant light in summer, it specialises in scientific and cultural studies associated with the polar environment. These include research into atmospheric phenomena such as the aurora borealis, biotechnology, multicultural societies, the Sami, social medicine, ecology and oceanography. Students come from more than 100 nations, often on exchange programmes. The cosmopolitan spirit of the campus reflects growing concern for the Arctic environment, which was largely taken for granted until the dangers of global warming began to be understood.

A Lutheran christening   Despite a decline in religious attendance, the great ceremonies of life continue to be celebrated in church.

The Lutheran tradition

The teachings of Martin Luther spread quickly around the Baltic in the 16th century. All the Nordic countries, including Latvia and Estonia, adopted the Reformed Church, while allowing individual freedom of worship.

Religion and politics in Finland

In Finland 86 per cent of the people belong to the Lutheran Church. The president of the republic, who is elected for a six-year term, is head of the Church and commander-in-chief of the armed forces.

Christianity came late to these northern latitudes, with the first conversions in the 9th and 10th centuries, and pagan beliefs and cults enduring for many years after that. In the early 16th century, the Reformation begun by Luther in Germany found willing supporters in Scandinavia. There had always been a certain mistrust of Rome – partly because of the ostentatious wealth of the Catholic Church, partly because it was so far away, so rooted in an utterly different culture and climate. Protestantism insisted that the sacred texts, prayers and hymns of the Church be translated from Latin into local languages, allowing simple, uneducated people to understand what was going on. Reformed Church architecture was plainer, less sumptuously decorated, and the ritual of church services was simplified to go with it.

While these reforms gave new life to Christianity, there was also a destructive side to the movement. Monasteries and convents were burnt down, their communities disbanded, and lands confiscated by the state. This at once deprived society of its charitable

hospitals, which had provided care for the poor, sick and infirm. Also, by placing emphasis on individual faith and a personal relationship with God, Protestantism failed to encourage acts of charity. This meant that weaker members of society were left to their fate until the arrival of the welfare state.

Church and state

With the exception of Sweden, where the Church was disestablished in 2000, the Evangelical Lutheran Church is the official state religion in all Scandinavian countries. This means that feast days in the Protestant Church calendar are also public holidays, and that all citizens are expected to pay a church tax. Each country's constitution declares the monarch to be the head of the Church, and he or she must, therefore, be a Lutheran. Over the centuries this has required a number of royal conversions: a recent example is Prince Henrik of Denmark, the French husband of the present queen, who had to renounce Catholicism.

At the same time, the constitution guarantees freedom of worship, so any citizen has the right to leave the established church and refuse to pay its tax. In practice, most Scandinavians happily pay up, yet few of them, particularly in the south, go to church on a regular basis. Farther north, religious observance is generally stricter: Iceland, the Faeroe Islands, northern Norway and Finland are fertile ground for a growing number of puritanical and even fundamentalist Christian sects. Meanwhile the Sami and Estonians still keep up many pagan cults dedicated to the forces of nature.

The Church in Lappland
Kautokeino, northern Finland: in this small provincial town, a wedding is held in the recently evangelised Sami community.

The art of living comfortably

Nowhere in the world do people care so much about the way their houses look and feel. Comfort, warmth and beauty are essential. Small wonder that Scandinavian furniture and interior design have been so successful right across the world.

The Norse word *hygge* – originally used to describe the sensation of being in a warm and welcoming environment, sheltered from the icy winds outside – remains uppermost in people's minds when they make a home in Scandinavia. Furniture, décor and household objects are all designed for this purpose.

In the 20th century, Scandinavian design was influenced by a movement known as Functionalism. This became the dominant trend in European design between the two world wars, defined by simple, clean lines, plain shapes and neutral colours, with minimum decoration. It was led by the Bauhaus school in Germany until Hitler closed it down in 1935. Arne Jacobsen and Poul Hennigsen created several original designs for chairs and lamps in this style in the 1930s, but it was only after the Second World War that Scandinavian designers achieved widespread recognition.

A home by the water

Second homes tend to be simple and rustic, built of wood and located deep in the countryside, preferably by a beach, river or lake. Used mainly in the summer, they are perfect for fishing, swimming, boating or any of the outdoor activities so avidly pursued by the nature-loving Scandinavians.

Style for all

A typical Scandinavian home is comfortable, modern, warm and as pretty as a shop window. Colours harmonise beautifully and everything is immaculately arranged. It is clear that a great deal of pride and effort goes into keeping the place looking good, but also that elegant design is a high priority. And even if most people are unlikely to own an original Poul Hennigsen chair, Kenneth Wegner sofa or Alvar Aalto vase, they can rely on firms like IKEA to provide them with handsome furniture at affordable prices.

The Swedish manufacturing giant IKEA has been around for more than 50 years, but its global expansion, with shops as widely scattered as Hong Kong, the USA, France and Britain, is more recent. Using talented young designers who work exclusively for the company, IKEA supplies self-assembly furniture to suit all budgets, with a particular focus on the younger end of the market. The formula is simple enough: clean lines, good quality materials (especially wood) and soft colours, all enhanced by subtle lighting. Behind the company's philosophy lies the Scandinavians' love of the home and their mastery of the art of living comfortably.

Changing fashions

In the 1960s, a new style of home appeared on the market: a ready-made, industrialised product that people could buy from a catalogue, then just walk into and start living. Prices were competitive, and the novelty of the idea soon caught on. Swedes, Finns, Norwegians and Danes started buying these houses in large numbers, and new residential districts filled with rows of identical houses all painted the same colours began to spring up on the edges of the major towns. These became known as *parcelhuskvarter*. Now they are no longer fashionable and have a dated look. Part of the problem was that they split people off into box-like individual family units, going against the Scandinavian ideal of community living. Recent urban housing has attempted to be more open to the community, while still offering that precious quality of a really comfortable private home.

City living Snug suburban homes in Oslo, built mainly of wood and carefully designed to offer a sense of privacy while preserving the feeling of life in a community, which remains an important ideal.

Home comforts A typical living room, with plenty of space, good modern furniture and a relaxed, uncluttered feel.

Traditional foods

Fish, sour cream, potatoes and black rye bread are the basic ingredients of Scandinavian cooking: simple, healthy and delicious. A more subtle and sophisticated cuisine can be found in Sweden, while Denmark rivals France for its lavish use of butter and cream.

Staff of life *A tempting bread display at Riga's central food market, one of the biggest in the world.*

Open-air grilling *A fish barbecue in Finland – with serious equipment. Scandinavians are keen outdoor cooks.*

Whether it is served cold, smoked, fried, baked, stewed, grilled or even raw, fish is the key ingredient. Salmon, sole, trout, halibut and cod are most common, while delicacies include eel smoked over juniper twigs and herrings marinated with dill, sugar and vinegar. At Christmas, the traditional meal begins with *lutfisk*, a dish of dried cod soaked for several days in water, slaked lime and soda. To children and foreigners it is an unappealing sight, translucent and jelly-like, and the taste is as dull as its appearance – but the mustard sauce that comes with it is a delight. Another acquired taste is *surströmming*, or fermented herring. This has such an overpowering smell that it is usually served only in fine weather, outdoors!

'Take whatever you have...'

So begins a recipe for soup in an 18th-century Scandinavian cookbook. In those days, the range of agricultural products available was limited, although the forests were full of wild berries, mushrooms and game – elk, deer, pheasants and reindeer. Today, the availability of imported foods has totally changed Scandinavian cuisine.

The gastronomic traditions of a nation are determined by what is most readily available. The diet in the Baltic countries is based on salt pork, barley broth, smoked or salted fish, and excellent rye bread. Lithuanian dishes tend to use a lot of salt, black pepper and nutmeg, with honey cakes a speciality on feast days. A delicious 'Thursday soup' is made with yellow peas, bacon and thyme. Fish is seasoned in exciting ways: pike with horseradish, shrimps with dill. For St John's Day, the Latvians make a cheese spiced with caraway seeds – as do the Lithuanians, but with a much stronger flavour. Large numbers of savoury dishes are garnished with mushrooms and berries – fruits of the extensive heaths, moors and forests. For the adventurous palate there are countless delights and gastronomic surprises, such as black pudding and sausages with cranberry jam, rosehip or bilberry soup served as a dessert, or even for breakfast, and smoked reindeer tongues.

Gravadlax

This traditional delicacy, with a taste like mild smoked salmon, is easy to make. Fillet a salmon, leaving the sides whole and the skin on. Make a cure of two tablespoons each of honey, salt, crushed black peppercorns and brandy, and rub into the salmon with plenty of dill. Lay one side on the other, with more dill above and below. Cover with foil and weights and refrigerate for 48 hours, turning every 12 hours. Serve with brown bread and butter, and a dill and sweet mustard mayonnaise.

Winter treats

All over Europe the feast of St Martin, on November 11, was the day for slaughtering animals to salt and preserve their meat for winter. It was a feast in every sense: in Scandinavia, goose was traditionally served, starting with a rich soup made with the blood of the bird, apple and prune juice, cognac, madeira, ginger and cloves.

At Christmas, pork is the traditional festive dish: roast pork ribs with sauerkraut and cumin in Norway; ham pie and puréed turnips in Finland; braised ham with apples and red cabbage in Sweden. (Denmark is the exception, where they eat roast goose stuffed with prunes and apples.) Christmas sweets include spicy fruit loaves, petits fours with ginger and cloves, and the Finnish *joulutorttu*, a puff-pastry cake filled with prune jam. To drink there is *glögg*, a warming winter punch of hot red wine, vermouth, cardamom, cinnamon, cloves, orange peel, raisins and chopped almonds.

Eating out

Going out for a meal is not as common in Scandinavia as it is in the Mediterranean – partly because of the climate. Yet there is no shortage of pubs, cafés and restaurants in the towns, and they cater for every taste as well as every pocket.

Anyone who knows anything about food in Scandinavia is familiar with *smörgåsbord*, a dazzling array of seafood and accompanying dishes, served with white or rye bread and washed down with beer or aquavit (a 45° proof spirit, variously flavoured). Endlessly imitated, this king of buffets is generally thought to be a Swedish invention, although there are also strong claims by the Norwegians (who call it *smorbrod*), the Danes (*smörrebröd*) and the Finns (*voileipäpöyta*).

In restaurants, dishes are laid out on a large table and customers help themselves. Hearty eaters will usually fill their plates several times: the trick is not to eat too much, but as skilfully as possible to subtly combine flavours and textures. The first course is always herring – poached, marinated, smoked or spiced – with sour cream, mustard or curry sauce. Then comes a selection of other fish, often served with a *fågelbo* salad made with sprats, onion, lettuce, beetroot, capers and egg. This is followed by vegetables, pâté, salads and cold meats. The fourth course is often a selection of hot dishes; and finally there is fruit salad, or an assortment of pastries and cheeses.

Cafés and pubs

There are still plenty of attractive traditional taverns to be found in Scandinavia, particularly in the countryside, but today's city dwellers have acquired a taste for European-style cafés and pubs, with the décor coming straight from Italy, France, England and Ireland. These places are busiest at weekends, when young people go out to enjoy themselves, drink large amounts of beer, and chatter happily far into the night. Good basic food is informally served, and the atmosphere is sociable and friendly rather than rowdy, with the same relaxed style that you find in most restaurants, bars and even the smartest of nightclubs.

A wealth of choice

Of course, Scandinavian food goes far beyond *smörgåsbord*. There is a vast range of dishes to be found in every style. Denmark, a member of the EU since 1973, and the most cosmopolitan of the Scandinavian nations, has long been fascinated by exotic cuisines. There is scarcely a town of any size in Denmark without a Thai or Mexican restaurant.

Not that the Danes have abandoned their traditional style of cooking, which is based on their rich agricultural produce and makes great use of dairy products, poultry, pork, cabbage and potatoes. Classic dishes include loin of pork stuffed with apples and prunes, *frikadeller* (veal and pork meatballs), goose with red cabbage and apples, chicken with parsley, black pudding, and stuffed ox heart with cream. Their own version of the cold buffet (*smörrebröd*) includes liver pâté, sliced pork, salads, herrings, and scrambled eggs with bacon and cheese, all served on fresh dark bread and butter. It is such a national institution that one of the greatest

Gleaming copper vats
The world famous Carlsberg brewery in Copenhagen has its own brewing museum. Throughout Scandinavia, beer is the usual accompaniment to food, often alternated with shots of ice-cold aquavit.

Try this *Smoked fish is one of the oldest and most delicious of traditional Scandinavian foods.*

Arctic nightlife The university town of Tromsø, in northern Norway, offers plenty of lively bars, cafés and clubs, often with live music. Although the beer flows freely, the atmosphere is relaxed and friendly.

Table talk In Iceland, hospitality and the pleasures of the table are an important part of life. At the annual sheep-herding in Landmannalaugar (right), everyone eats and drinks together after a hard day's work.

The food in Norway, Iceland and the Faeroe Islands is also very fine. Their *smörgåsbord* is every bit as lavish as the Swedish or Danish versions, with their own special varieties of fish freshly caught from the icy waters of the Atlantic or Arctic Oceans. A popular place to sample these delights is the Lofoten Fiskrestaurant in Oslo, overlooking the harbour at Aker Brygge.

Breakfasts in Norway are a memorable experience, especially when you stay at a guesthouse on a farm. As well as bread, butter, fruit jellies and jams, there are herrings, cheeses and air-dried hams of beef, pork, lamb or reindeer. You may also be offered *rommergrøt*, the Norwegian national dish, which is a porridge with butter, cinnamon, sugar, raisins, sour cream and blackberry or redcurrant juice. On July 29 each year, it is traditional to eat a dish of *rommergrøt* in honour of St Olaf, the country's patron saint.

Fish and lamb are the basis of much of the cooking in Iceland and the Faeroe Islands. The food is excellent, if occasionally a little surprising to foreign palates. Sheep's heads are still eaten, for instance, and one of the favourite traditional dishes is *skaerpkød*, a dried leg of lamb with an alarming smell but superb flavour. But step into a restaurant like The Gallery in Reykjavik, and there is no hint of rough peasant fare. Wild game, seafood and gravadlax are exquisitely prepared and served in elegant surroundings.

A Finnish speciality is salmon served with fresh dill and boiled potatoes, or made into a soup with the same ingredients. The

Swedish treats

Swedish coffee is the best in Northern Europe. A good place to try it is in a *konditori* (cake shop), where you will find it hard to resist the delicious pastries. Open sandwiches are also available, with generous toppings of pâté, cheese with green peppers, meatballs, prawns in mayonnaise, smoked salmon, caviar – even reindeer.

Summer in Tallinn Sunshine brings out the café tables – and plenty of people to sit at them – in the Estonian capital.

honours for a public figure is to have a special version of *smörrebröd* named after them. One of these is the 'Victor Borge', created at the famous Ida Davidsen restaurant in Copenhagen for the great Danish comedian and pianist. It consists of salmon, fresh lumpfish roe, lobster, Greenland prawns and lemon or dill mayonnaise. Although the classic accompaniment to such dishes is beer or aquavit, the Danes are becoming increasingly keen and knowledgeable wine-drinkers, too.

Danish pastries and sweets are deservedly renowned, and include such specialities as *rodgrod* – a chilled dessert of red fruits and white wine – pancakes with vanilla ice cream, and deliciously buttery apple and jam tarts.

Finnish *voileipäpöyta* is likely to include smoked reindeer or elk. There are also some great savoury tarts, such as *piirakka*, made with rye pastry and filled with fresh cheese, rice and fish. Typical drinks are *ryyppy* (a powerful grain alcohol) and *lakka*, made with Arctic cranberries. Famous restaurants in Helsinki where traditional fare is served include Amadeus, in a delightful old town house near the south harbour, specialising in game, reindeer and mushroom dishes, and the Savoy, designed by Alvar Aalto and overlooking the Esplanade Gardens, where the war hero and statesman Karl Gustaf Mannerheim often dined. Specialities at the Savoy include *vorschmack* (a rich lamb and salt herring stew with garlic and onions), *läski soosi* (pork in a rich dark sauce) and reindeer fillets.

Life beyond the Arctic Circle

The north of the Scandinavian peninsula extends far beyond the Arctic Circle. We tend to imagine the region as a bleak and hostile environment where life is a perpetual struggle – but there is a lot more to it than that.

The climate beyond 66° 32′ north is much less extreme than most people imagine. This is because the coast lies in the path of the Gulf Stream, a warm water current that flows across the Atlantic from the Gulf of Mexico, making winters less harsh. Even in the coldest months of the year, the temperature rarely falls below −18°C (−0.4°F).

Sheltered by fiords

Yet few people choose to settle here: in Lappland, the northernmost province of Finland, the population density is five inhabitants per sq mile (two per km²) – eight times less than the national average. In the far north of Norway, all the villages are huddled around fiords on the west coast where, thanks to the maritime climate and the Gulf Stream, most ports remain ice-free throughout the year. A little to the east the climate is too vicious, and the mountains are uninhabited. Where the populations cluster, communities and individuals rely on one another in times of trouble – a sort of mutual insurance if conditions turn severe.

Generally, however, the Swedes, Finns and Norwegians who live in these northern regions are accustomed to the cold. Rather than fear it, they take up the challenge and enjoy it. Winter sports are a passion, with cross-country and downhill skiing popular among all ages. Cross-country skiing was once the most practical way to move around in winter. Today it is seen more as a sport or leisure activity, offering an invigorating form of exercise that combines the pleasures of walking with the excitement of skiing. But for daily getting about, locals now prefer mechanised transport: the age of the snowmobile has arrived.

On dark days *Students at the University of Tromsø study under special lights which counteract the sunless northern winter.*

Hazard to shipping *Once pack ice starts to form, shipping routes can close, but in the Gulf of Bothnia, icebreakers keep the waters navigable.*

For people in remote places the snowmobile is an essential link to the rest of the world. For the Sami, it has replaced the reindeer as a means of transport, and herdsmen now ride them – or even travel by helicopter – as they follow the herds of reindeer that are still their principal source of income. In the growing holiday and leisure industry, treks and expeditions use convoys of sledges towed by snowmobiles to carry food, fuel, baggage and equipment.

In this harsh environment you would hardly expect to find many farmers, but one form of 'farming' works very well here: fur farming. This highly successful – if controversial – activity is concentrated largely around the Finnish coast between Vaasa and Kokkola, south of the Arctic Circle. The most valuable species farmed are mink, muskrat, Siberian squirrel and Arctic fox. The fur trade remains an important sector of the economy in Sweden and Finland, and every year the Finns hold an auction for fur dealers from around the world.

Snowmobiles – for and against

Snowmobiles can reach speeds of up to 80 mph (130 km/h), but they rarely do more than 20-25 mph (32-40 km/h) on long journeys, as fuel supplies may be hundreds of miles apart in the Arctic tundra, making economising on fuel essential. Although snowmobiles are immensely popular, they are far from perfect machines: they are noisy and pollute the air, and can wreak havoc on plantlife where the snow cover is thin. It is illegal to use them where they are likely to cause damage to the environment.

Sapmi: a territory without frontiers

The majority of Sami live north of the Arctic Circle – the only European people to do so. They have now adopted a modern way of life, yet they remain deeply aware of their own separate identity, which is expressed in their remarkable arts and crafts, their flag and their dialects.

Lobbying for rights

The Sami are deeply attached to their traditions. Young Sami writers, well-educated and cosmopolitan, believe strongly in preserving their own culture. Seventy per cent of Sami still speak one of seven dialects. Children can go to Sami schools, or to state schools where they take courses in their own language. Sami interest groups work to retain exclusive pasturing rights for their animals – which are usually granted – and to gain a monopoly of fishing rights in the Sapmi territory.

There has been a craftsman's market in the Swedish village of Jokkmokk since the 17th century. It is held every February in this Arctic outpost, providing a vivid splash of colour and activity in the snow. The goods on sale are magnificent: drinking flasks made of white elk horn, knives with finely carved bone handles, baskets of woven birch bark, reindeer harness, embroidery, knitted woollen hats, jackets, trousers, and mittens in leather or fur.

The Sami dress up splendidly for the occasion, wearing their traditional costumes trimmed in red, green and yellow passementerie, with their capacious 'all weather' red pompom hats. It was these motley garments that earned them the name 'Lapp' – a word that means 'patched up'. They prefer to be called Sami, which is their own name for themselves.

Handmade The annual craft market at Jokkmokk in northern Sweden, which has been attracting visitors since the 17th century to buy Sami handiwork.

The land of the Sami

The Sami's name for their territory, which extends from the Kola peninsula in Russia to the Atlantic coast of Norway, and crosses the borders of four countries, is Sapmi. There are around 62 000 Sami in Scandinavia: 5000 in Finland, 17 000 in Sweden and 40 000 in Norway. They often coexist with other peoples, who worry as little about frontiers as they do. Northern Sweden, for example, includes whole regions where Finnish is the main language spoken. The vast, sparsely populated landscapes show few signs of human presence. Forests, lakes and streams, high mountain plateaus and wild, rocky coasts fringed with islands – such is Sapmi, land of the midnight sun and the magical northern lights.

Old colours, new ways Traditional ways are still followed by some Sami (inset), but the young have moved on to new, international fashions and mechanised transport. At Kautokeino, in the Finnmark region of Norway, technology and reindeer herding go hand in hand. The old nomadic lifestyle belongs to the past.

Tradition and change

The Sami no longer live in tents or *kåta*, slender birch frames draped with cloth or woollen blankets. Large numbers of them work in forestry or mining, live in comfortable houses, and are fully integrated in the modern Scandinavian lifestyle. The shamans who once called up spirits, healed the sick and foretold the future with the aid of a magic drum, have disappeared. Their rituals and practices were ruthlessly suppressed by the Protestant Church, and their instruments burned, in the 18th century. A few artefacts have survived in museums. But the *jojks* or improvised chants sung by the shamans are popular among the young today, who continue to compose and perform them at festivals each year.

CHAPTER 5

SPORT AND THE GREAT OUTDOORS

Skiing is an ancient tradition in Scandinavia: rock carvings thousands of years old show people on strips of wood that can only be skis. As soon as children can walk, they are taught to ski and skate. But winter sports are only half the story: when spring comes, a new set of outdoor pleasures and activities awaits, from sailing to rock-climbing. Scandinavians love the natural life and defend their environment fiercely. This is one of the main attractions for visitors – the beauty of the wild landscapes and natural habitats is unrivalled in Europe. In the Baltic States, Nature has not been so carefully protected, but the situation is improving as people are educated to appreciate the importance of a healthy environment. Of the competitive sports, football is universally popular and played at every level. Tennis is keenly played, too, and Sweden has produced some outstanding champions, notably Björn Borg, Stefan Edberg and Mats Wilander.

Iceland's hot springs, bubbling up from the volcanic earth, make outdoor swimming a luxurious experience.

Football and tennis

They love any ball game: volleyball, hockey, basketball, badminton, tennis ... But the one they love most, in Scandinavia and the Baltic States alike, is football.

The smaller countries of Northern Europe have struggled to make their mark in football, despite some great individual players and managers and some fine performances in international tournaments. But economic realities are against them: even the biggest clubs in Scandinavia and the Baltic States find it hard to retain their best players in the face of temptation from the likes of Juventus and Manchester United. To stop this leakage of talent, they are looking for ways of tempting their young stars to stay.

Tennis, a Swedish speciality

Football may be the Swedes' favourite spectator sport, but tennis seems to bring out something special in them. A series of champions – Mats Wilander, Stefan Edberg, Magnus Larsson, Thomas Endqvist and Magnus Norman – have kept Swedish tennis at the centre of the world stage. It all began with the 18-year-old Björn Borg winning the men's singles title at Wimbledon in 1976, then again a further four years in succession. He won 62 international tournaments between 1974 and 1981. With his long blond hair and lithe physique, an unorthodox two-handed backhand and a serve of astonishing power and accuracy, he was an idol for an entire generation.

Tennis champion Pictured here at Flushing Meadow in 1985, Mats Wilander was one of a line of Swedish players admired wherever they appeared for their skill and good sportsmanship.

The Scandinavian school

In the 1958 World Cup Final, played in Stockholm, Sweden faced Brazil. Thanks to a young genius on the Brazilian side – 18-year-old Pele – the Swedes were beaten 5-3. Sweden were also in the front rank in the 1994 World Cup, held in the USA, where they finished third overall. Sweden was back in the news in the winter of 2000-1, when a crisis in the England team led the FA to choose Sven Göran Eriksson as the first-ever England manager from overseas.

Norwegians have recently become a force to reckon with as well, with their cool, precise, scientific style of play – said to be inspired by British football, although the German influence is probably just as strong. There are currently some 50 Norwegian players appearing for British clubs.

Iceland, Finland, the Faeroe Islands, Latvia, Estonia and Lithuania are not in the same league, despite some creditable performances. The wheel of fortune may turn for them, though, as it did for Denmark in the *annus mirabilis* of 1992. . .

The Danish miracle

June 26, 1992, is a date that no Danish football supporter will ever forget. On that day they became champions of Europe – the first Scandinavian country to win a major international competition. It really was an extraordinary victory: Denmark had not even qualified for the contest, but war had just broken out in the Balkans and the Yugoslavian team were unable to play. With a team that included Brian Laudrup and Peter Schmeichel (twice voted best goalkeeper in the world), they reached the final and beat Germany 2-0 in a thrilling game. In the days that followed the whole country went into a riot of celebration, unseen since the liberation of 1945.

Danish lightning
Michael Laudrup zigzags between opponents in the 1998 World Cup. Since the 1980s, Danish footballers have been famed for their passion and commitment. They were rewarded in 1992 by becoming European champions.

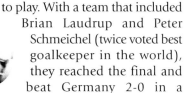

They were found in peat bogs in northern Finland and Sweden, and have been dated to between four and five thousand years old. Short and wide, they look more like snowshoes than today's skis. Meanwhile, in Norway, a rock carving has been discovered near the Arctic Circle, clearly showing two skiers; it dates from about 2000 BC. In the 9th and 10th centuries, the Vikings used skis, as did the Sami later. In more recent times, skiing became the usual means of moving around the countryside in winter all over Scandinavia and in many parts of Eastern Europe.

Home of skiing

The northern regions of Norway, Sweden and Finland are covered in snow for much of the year. In fact they say that people from up there are born with skis on …

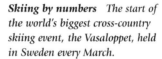

Skiing by numbers   The start of the world's biggest cross-country skiing event, the Vasaloppet, held in Sweden every March.

Ice hockey   Young Norwegians play one of their favourite games. With plenty of frozen lakes around, no rink is needed.

To the rest of the world, skiing means sport, winter holidays, leisure – but in Scandinavia it has always been an everyday, practical activity: Scandinavians strap on their skis to go and see friends or post a letter just as easily as others would hop on a bicycle or get into the car. Incredible as it may seem, there is even evidence that people used skis in prehistoric times.

When it comes to skiing as a sport, the Scandinavians are among the world's best. Many of the skiing competitions that regularly feature at the Winter Olympics were invented in Scandinavia: Nordic skiing (cross-country and ski-jumping) were events in the first Winter Olympics, held in 1924; alpine skiing (downhill racing and slalom) were added in 1948. Today there are several more events in the Nordic section, including cross-country over several distances, 70 m and 90 m jumps, cross-country relays, and Nordic combined – a mixture of cross-country racing and ski-jumping, both team and individual.

Until 1970, there was only one way of doing cross-country skiing – the 'classic' sliding step, with skis parallel. Then an American skier, Bill Koch, worked out a skater's V-shaped step, which proved much more effective. It required longer sticks and shorter skis, with high boots to support the ankles, but today all freestyle cross-country racers use Koch's step.

The Vasaloppet

Every March, in the county of Dalarna, north-east of Stockholm, the world's biggest cross-country skiing event is held: the Vasaloppet or Vasa Race. It was invented by a journalist, Pers Anders, to commemorate the ski-borne escape in 1521 of the future Swedish King Gustavus I Vasa from imprisonment in Denmark. The first Vasaloppet was held on March 29, 1922. A hundred and thirty-six contestants, watched by about the same number of spectators, raced 53 miles (85.5 km) between the towns of Sälen and Mora. In the week leading up to this event, there are a variety of other competitions for men, women, juniors and seniors, with a total of 13 000 enthusiasts of all ages joining in. The 2000 Vasaloppet attracted a record 40 500 participants. Today, coming first in the competition is regarded as one of the highest achievements – almost equal to a gold medal in the Winter Olympics or the World Cup.

Hundreds of skiing competitions take place throughout the winter, all over Scandinavia. Some, like the Holmenkollen Marathon, held at the famous Holmenkollen ski-jump on the slopes above Oslo, are huge events. Others are small, country village affairs. But whatever the event, it all adds up to a lively and very popular tradition.

Wild sports   Skiers at Inari in Finland go in for a spectacular form of racing – pulled along by galloping reindeer.

111

Water and steam

Outsiders think of Scandinavia and the Baltic States as having freezing winters and cool summers. Yet, especially in the south of the region, summer days can be deliciously warm. In Iceland, too, the sun often shines, making its thermal areas even more inviting.

As soon as the hot weather arrives, people crowd onto the sandy beaches that line the coasts of Denmark, Sweden and the Baltic States. They swim, sail, windsurf, play beach games, or just laze happily in the sun.

Danish sands

Within a 4 mile (7 km) radius of the Rådhuspladsen in the centre of Copenhagen, you will find dozens of beaches to choose from, starting with the most famous, Bellevue, north of the city. Known as 'the flycatcher', because it swarms with bathers the moment the sun rises on a summer morning, this beach on the Øresund Strait even attracts visitors from Germany. Go down to Falster, the southernmost of the country's many islands, and you will see the population swell in summer from 400 to over 40 000, as holidaymakers

Seaside spa   Pärnu in Estonia is a seaside town that also has thermal baths. Like many Baltic resorts, it is starting to attract foreign tourists, who can be sure of a warm welcome.

pour in to enjoy its 20 miles (32 km) of golden sand on the shores of the Baltic. Wherever you go in Denmark, you are never more than 25 miles (40 km) from the sea. There are dozens of seaside resorts, many of the best being in Jutland. They remain popular, despite cheap air fares to the Mediterranean – even the Danes seem surprised by the way they attract so many foreign visitors, as summer temperatures average a cool 16°C (61°F), and sunshine is by no means guaranteed. There may be weeks of fine weather, but there is an equal chance of rain.

The success of Scandinavian summer resorts is something the Baltic States would like to emulate. They certainly have the beaches for it, and since independence they have been working hard to bring in more foreign tourists to enjoy them.

Finnish saunas

Whether it is snowing, hailing or blowing a gale outside, the Finnish sauna ritual carries on regardless. Known as *bastu*, this national institution provides a good winter pastime. Clouds of steam sizzle off red-hot stones, as naked bathers lounge on wooden decking, whipping themselves with bundles of birch twigs or little wooden paddles until their skin goes red and starts to prickle. Then it is time to plunge into a pool of ice-cold water or, even better, roll about in the snow. These sudden thermal shocks are believed to stimulate the circulation – although they are not recommended for people with weak hearts.

Icelandic baths

Swimming off the beaches of Iceland, in the icy waters of the North Atlantic, is not an attractive proposition. But inland, in the volcanic lakes, it is another story – especially in winter, when the temperature drops below freezing. The water in the lakes is hot and, like the steam that comes off it, is said to be excellent for the health. With frosty air around your head and warm water enveloping your body, a dip in a thermal lake is an unforgettable sensation!

The natural life   This Norwegian beach, close to Oslo, has the additional attraction of unspoilt forest.

Choose your sauna

There are three different kinds of Finnish sauna. The *torrbastu* is a dry sauna, where the temperature can sometimes reach as much as 100°C (212°F). The *våtbastu* has more humidity in the air, but it is still very hot – up to 75°C (167°F). Then there is the cooler, but totally steamy, *ångbastu* at 60°C (140°F), which is similar to a Turkish bath.

Earth energy
From geothermal power stations in Iceland (left) to wind farms in Denmark (right), every means available is used to produce clean electricity.

The 'green lungs of Europe'

One positive aspect of the Soviet regime in the Baltic States was the complete lack of interest in forestry. This was a continuation of tsarist policy, and it has left some of the most magnificent forests in Europe almost untouched. Some have hardly been affected by human activity for 800 years, preserving flora and fauna that have long disappeared from the rest of the continent. In 1993, the United Nations declared these forests the 'green lungs of Europe', with an agreement on ecologically sensitive and sustainable management, and nature reserves to protect the rarest species of plants and animals from extinction.

Partnering Nature

The beauty and variety of the landscape in Scandinavia is partly natural, partly man-made. In recent years the most important human influence has been in protecting the environment.

In Norway and Sweden, there is a concept in common law known as *allemansrätt* (everyman's right), which gives free access to the countryside. Anyone can climb over a gate and walk across a piece of land, whether public or private, provided they keep a reasonable distance from people's homes and cultivated ground. Waterways, fiords and lakes are similarly open, with unrestricted navigation and mooring rights for boats. In pastures and forests you can pick flowers, mushrooms and berries – although there are some protected species – and pitch a tent wherever you like.

In most Scandinavian homes, you will find bins for different kinds of rubbish: paper, tins, plastic, glass, biodegradable items. A large proportion is recycled. In the shops, organic foods are becoming increasingly popular, despite higher prices: organic dairy products now account for 20 per cent of the Danish domestic market.

Clean sources of power
When it comes to protecting the environment, the Scandinavians have one enormous advantage: their main industries are almost completely non-polluting. Thanks to enormous supplies of hydroelectric energy from rivers and waterfalls, Norway and Sweden can power their steel and paper-making industries without pumping clouds of greenhouse gases into the atmosphere.

Factories tend to be located at the mouths of fiords to provide easy access to the sea, or in river gorges to take advantage of the fast-flowing currents. Unfortunately, these local measures can do nothing to stop the wind bringing atmospheric pollution from other countries. This falls as acid rain, with devastating effect. In Sweden, forests have been severely damaged and lakes in the west of the country have been poisoned. The government, working with associations of fishermen, has set up a lake de-silting programme, but this is a temporary measure that does not treat the cause of the problem and has to be repeated every few years.

Environmental protection
The Scandinavian countries generally, and Denmark in particular, have fought hard for environmental protection in Europe and across the world. Their expertise will be much needed in the Baltic States, where Soviet-era industrial policy has left a grim legacy. Even though the will may be there to modernise the old heavily polluting factories, the money and the means are still lacking.

Achieving a balance *Man's respect for the environment is visible here in Kerimälsi, Finland, where part of the forest has been cleared, but plenty has been left.*

Ramblers' paradise   *Urno-Kekkonen National Park in Finland.*

Expeditions and adventures

Early morning, and the sun is just starting to pierce the bands of mist that lie across the mountain slopes. The sunlit peaks seem close enough to touch. In the distance, a row of tiny figures can be seen moving off from a mountain refuge . . .

Denmark's gentle agricultural landscapes, with country roads running flat as a board as far as the eye can see, are an open invitation to cyclists. Everyone in Denmark has a bicycle and uses it regularly. You will often see whole families on tour in the summer, cycling with bulging panniers from campsite to campsite. As befits this major leisure activity, there are hundreds of miles of purpose-built cycle paths in the Danish countryside, many of them far from normal roads and leading to otherwise inaccessible places.

On two wheels   *A favourite activity in Denmark, cycling is also popular in Norway and Sweden.*

Scandinavians love hiking: they do it so frequently and enthusiastically that it might almost be part of their genetic coding. As soon as they get the slightest opportunity to escape from their daily routine, they step out of their front doors, take a deep lungful of fresh air, and set off for the nearest open space with a rucksack on their back.

There are marked footpaths everywhere in Scandinavia, many of them covering huge distances. The most famous of these, the Kungsleden, winds 300 miles (500 km) across Sweden, from Abisko to Hemaavan, through a series of spectacular landscapes. Along these paths there are plenty of refuges to welcome walkers at the end of each day. Things are rather different up north, however. Hikers in the great national parks and mountain fastnesses of northern Sweden and Norway have to fend for themselves, carrying with them a tent, sleeping bag, portable stove and provisions. What they get in exchange is unique: the privilege of wandering through the largest wilderness in Europe.

Journeys by water

Sweden, with more than 90 000 lakes and countless rivers and canals, is an excellent place for canoeists. Canoeing centres hire out equipment for a few days or several weeks, and there are hundreds of enthusiasts who use these facilities on a regular basis. The county of Värmland, in the west, is particularly rewarding for exploration, with its intricate network of narrow lakes and waterways stretching from Lake Vänern to the Norwegian border.

Also highly recommended are the waterlands of Ströms Vatterdal, near Strömsund in the more northerly province of Jämtland. This is ideal country for hiking and swimming, as Strömsund is the start of the Wilderness Way, a road that snakes off into splendid mountain scenery along the Norwegian border, passing silent blue lakes as it goes, before turning north-east across the desolate Stekkenjokk plateau and into Swedish Lappland.

A Swedish boating trip is never complete without fishing. Trout, perch, salmon, pike and many other species can be found in abundance. All you need to do is hang out a line, admire the beauty of the scene, and dinner will swim up and offer itself to your hook. In the evening, you can grill the fish over the embers of a wood fire and let the calm of nature fill your soul with contentment . . .

Life on the water   *Whether they prefer canoeing, white-water rafting or just fishing, the water is a major summer attraction for nature-loving Scandinavians.*

Tourist attraction   *Walking in Iceland, with its fascinating landscape of glaciers, volcanoes, lava deserts, beaches and waterfalls, attracts a growing number of visitors each year.*

Venturing into the wilderness

Volcanoes and glaciers, midnight sun, northern lights, vast empty expanses where time seems to stand still … To come to these northern tracts of wilderness from a world of cities, concrete and traffic jams is truly to feel the call of the wild.

Born out of fire and sculpted by ice and water, Iceland is still in the process of being formed. Smoking volcanoes and charcoal-black lava fields lie adjacent to white glaciers; geysers spit jets of boiling water and steam from the earth. These elemental landscapes of the interior, which seem like a throwback to the early, violent days of the Earth's creation, attract more and more visitors each year. But these are challenging, extreme places, and exploring takes careful preparation. There are no restaurants, inns or hotels, so hikers have to carry their own food and shelter on their backs.

Not all of Iceland is quite so untamed, however: in some parts there are networks of hiking trails with refuges along the way, where walkers can find simple cooking equipment and a bed for the night.

Norwegian Lappland is another great wilderness, now divided into three national

Open road *Liberty is a camper van.*

Whale watchers *Off the coast of Iceland, where once whales were hunted, tourists now come to see them in their natural habitat.*

parks. In 1996 the area was declared a World Heritage Site by UNESCO in recognition of its outstanding natural and cultural importance. It is home to the Sami people, who have lived in this hostile, awe-inspiring terrain since prehistoric times, herding reindeer and barely changing their way of life as the centuries have passed. Although the Sami now have mechanised transport and live in houses rather than birch huts and tents, visitors have reason to be thankful to them for keeping their land free from the scars of civilisation for so long.

Lands of the midnight sun

North of the Arctic Circle, around the time of the summer solstice, a strange and wonderful thing happens: the sun never sets. This affects plants and animals as much as human beings, and seems to bathe the whole of Scandinavia in an atmosphere of exhilaration. People sleep very little and party a lot. Plants and trees absorb all the light they can get over the short summer, accelerating their natural processes accordingly, going from bud to fruit in a few weeks, rather than months.

Once darkness returns, as it does with a vengeance in winter, the skies are lit by the magic of the northern lights. People who have stood in the Arctic wilderness and seen these, even if only once, never forget the experience. Most make a secret resolve to return and witness the mystery at least one more time in their lives.

An accidental nature reserve

The Soviet regime that ruled the Baltic States after the Second World War was not renowned for its environmental sensitivity. Heavy industrial pollution was its usual legacy, but at Cape Kolka, on the coast of Latvia, a nature reserve was created by default when the entire area was sealed off for military use. Schools and other public institutions were closed, and children were sent off to be educated in other areas. In fact, little military activity occurred there, and when Latvia became independent in 1991, Cape Kolka was found to have been neglected for 45 years. An area of exceptional natural beauty, it was immediately declared a nature reserve.

CHAPTER 6

HISTORY AND TRADITIONS

At the end of the last Ice Age, early hunter-gatherers followed the reindeer north into the Scandinavian peninsula. As they settled, they began to record scenes from their lives in rock engravings, the earliest form of art. In the 9th century, the Vikings became masters of shipbuilding and their skills in working wood were passed on to generations of sculptors and carpenters – the wooden churches of Scandinavia are great architectural treasures. In the Middle Ages and Renaissance, towns grew rich from trade: castles, cathedrals and palaces were built, and craftsmanship in iron, wood, pottery, glass and stone flourished. That heritage lives on today, preserved in the historic town centres and museums. But a culture is more than buildings and crafts: there are also words, ideas, stories and beliefs – a living folk tradition that continues to inspire the Nordic peoples with a sense of mystery, even in a technological age.

Snowy forests lend a fairy-tale atmosphere to the town of Sigulda in Latvia.

The carved stones speak

They date from the early period of human settlement in Scandinavia, and continued to be produced well into the Viking era – thousands of pictures and words engraved in rock, recording the events of vanished lives.

An Alta engraving

At the far end of a fiord in northern Norway, a network of ancient paths leads to the oldest rock engravings in Scandinavia. At Hjemmeluft, just outside the city of Alta, are 3000 images cut into the rocks along the coast, from the Neolithic period (the earliest date to around 4000 BC) to 500 BC. They have been designated a World Heritage Site by UNESCO. The engravings were made with stone chisels and hammers, then highlighted in red paint. They show human figures, boats and several types of animals: elks, bears, reindeer, seals and sea birds are all clearly distinguishable.

Animals and gods

More recent, but just as intriguing, are the Tanum engravings on the west coast of Sweden, dating from the early Bronze Age, 1500 to 500 BC. The site includes more than 400 different groups of engravings – the largest collection in the world – and is also a UNESCO World Heritage Site. The images have puzzled archaeologists for years: they are sketchy human forms in a series of complicated scenes that make little sense to a modern eye. They may represent myths or religious rituals, as there are a number of outsize human figures who could be gods or giants. Or are they perhaps chieftains or kings, part of an historical narrative?

Remembering the dead

In the 3rd century AD the first forms of writing appeared in Scandinavia. These were runic inscriptions, using an alphabet that is thought to be derived from Etruscan script (the pre-Roman, extinct language of modern-day Tuscany and Umbria). Some inscriptions are magical or ritual, others celebrate historical people and exploits. At Jelling in Denmark, in AD 940, Gorm the Ancient, founder of the royal dynasty, raised a stone in memory of his wife Thyra. Another stone, beautifully carved, was commissioned by his son, Harald Bluetooth, to commemorate his parents. The

Carved in stone *Viking life is depicted on this stone relief from Bunge.*

stone bears the first-ever inscription referring to Denmark as a unified country.

The Swedish region of Uppland, north of Stockholm, has about 1200 runic stones, all raised in memory of the dead. Inscriptions range from brief to long and intricate. The only illustrated runic stones in Sweden are to be found on the island of Gotland, where they were set up along roads or in cemeteries from the 3rd to the 9th century. The Bunge stone is the most celebrated of these: it tells a long story, in several acts, including a scene of sacrifice.

History re-enacted *At Stikkestad, Norway, a festival is held every year to commemorate the death in battle of Olaf, the country's patron saint.*

Iron Age village

In the Roskilde region of Denmark, 25 miles (40 km) west of Copenhagen, is the Lejre Forsøgscenter (Archaeological Research Centre), a 60 acre (25 ha) park with a reconstructed Iron Age village of six small houses. Every summer, a group of Danish farmers comes to live and work in the style of their ancestors 2000 years ago. Archaeologists and the public observe them as they build, mend, forge iron, make pots, herd animals and farm the land. Visitors can even join in, helping to cook, work the dairy, grind corn and paddle a dugout canoe.

Carpenters and craftsmen

*Even before the Vikings, who were superb craftsmen in wood, there was
a strong tradition of skilled carpentry. This has continued to develop over
the centuries and can still be seen all over modern Scandinavia.*

*Delicately carved Hopperstad
church at Vik in Norway, dating
from the 12th century, has fine
woodcarvings.*

In 1904, archaeologists excavating the Oseberg
mound in Oslo Fiord uncovered a magnificent
buried wooden ship. The ship's prow was carved with
twining serpents; her clinker-laid planking, all beautifully cut and planed, was caulked with horsehair;
her lines were so sleek that she seemed almost fragile.
She turned out to be the grave of a queen, dating
from shortly before the Viking age. No sails were
found, although Bronze Age rock engravings show
that sails had been in use for hundreds of years, and
a well-known 8th-century stone carving from the
Swedish island of Gotland depicts a square-rigged
sailing ship of just this kind.

On board the longships

The longships used by Viking warriors were similar to
the Oseberg vessel in their shallow draught, although
they stood higher out of the water, with tall masts
and large square sails that gave them a speed of
13-15 knots on the open sea. Stem and stern were
identically shaped, so the ships could go in either
direction, adding greatly to their manoeuvrability.

The Vikings used different vessels for trading. These
were the *knarr*, broad-beamed and squat, built of oak,
with a shorter mast and small sail. Examples of both
trading and fighting ships were discovered sunk in
the fiord at Roskilde in Denmark in 1957. Carefully
raised and restored, these superb specimens are now
on display at Roskilde's Viking Ship Museum.

Carved wooden churches

The first wooden churches, or *stavkirker*, were built in Norway
towards the end of the 10th century. Like the longships, they were
often decorated with carvings of dragons, symbols of Viking
strength and ferocity. These early wooden churches are fascinating
structures: instead of a single-span roof, they usually have several
smaller ones, with numerous gables. This makes them look as if
they were influenced by oriental architecture, but in fact the design
is due to the lack of trees tall enough to provide long beams.

The façades of these churches are often exquisitely carved with
scenes from Norse mythology. Hylestad, dating from about 1200,
shows the legend of Sigurd Fafnesbanne, the dragon-killer. Carvings
at Austad depict the sinister tale of
Atlakvida, in which King Atla watches
as the heart of his enemy Hogne is cut
out, with Hogne smiling all the while. . .

In the 14th century, Norway had more
than 1000 wooden churches. Most of
these have long since vanished,
destroyed either by fire or by zealous
pietists who thought the sculptures too
pagan. Those that did survive were
restored in the 19th century, and there
are now about 30 of these exquisite
buildings left.

Natural look

This is not a modern eco-house, but a
traditional Viking design. The Vikings
used to cover their houses with turf, which
is a good insulator against the cold. In
Iceland and Denmark, where wood is hard
to find, turf was the principal building
material. In Greenland, the Vikings built
their houses of stone, but insulated the
north-facing walls and the roof with turf.
A few examples of this type of house can
still be found in odd places today.

Castles and palaces

Built in the Middle Ages to defend borders and strategic positions, castles were converted into luxurious royal palaces during the Renaissance, with showy architect-designed interiors capable of housing a large administration and a culturally active court. Today, these grand residences and such fortresses as retained their military character are important symbols of national identity.

Pikk Herman Tower, on a panoramic hill above Tallinn, is a national monument to the Estonians. It was much visited in the years of independence between the world wars, when people would come to hear the national anthem, *Mi isämaa*, played each morning as the flag was raised. Today, after years of closure, it is open again, a symbol of Estonia's pride and new-found freedom.

Fortresses and strongholds

On the vast Lake Saimaa in Finland, the fortress of Olavinlinna stands guard on a small island near Savonlinna. Built in 1475 to protect the frontier with Russia, it saw countless battles before losing its strategic importance when the border moved to the west. Today this majestic site witnesses drama of a different kind, as a summer opera festival is held in the castle courtyard, bringing visitors from around the world.

Even more celebrated, however, is a castle far to the south, in Denmark. It stands on a promontory overlooking the Øresund, the strait that separates Denmark from Sweden. This is Kronborg Castle at Helsingør – known throughout the world as Elsinore, the setting of Shakespeare's tragedy *Hamlet*. On winter days, when the foghorn sounds across the straits, this turreted Gothic castle seems an apt setting for the sad and bloody story. From here Erik

Renaissance style
The 17th-century palace of Rundall in Latvia, a typically spacious and harmonious design.

Lakeside setting   Gripsholm castle, on Lake Mälaren, near Stockholm, is now home to the Swedish national portrait collection.

Brothers and rivals

While Swedish King Erik XIV was conducting the Seven Years War against Denmark, his brother and successor Duke Johan maintained a glamorous court with his wife Catherine Jagiellon at Turku Castle in south-west Finland. Johan and Erik were bitter rivals: Erik was convinced his brother was planning to kill him, and at Kalmar Castle built a secret passage to the roof from a hidden door in his bedroom. Erik imprisoned Johan and his wife for a while at Gripsholm Castle on Lake Mälaren. Erik's paranoia may have been justified – historians believe that Johan poisoned him with arsenic in 1569 – but to the royal family he was a madman. His portrait in the Golden Room at Kalmar Castle is smaller than that of other kings and hung high on the wall, as it was believed that his mental illness could be caught by looking into his eyes.

of Pomerania controlled all shipping through the Øresund, levying a tax on vessels trading between the Baltic and the outside world. The castle, which is open to the public, was modified in the 16th and 18th centuries, and has a magnificent interior that includes one of the longest and most splendid ballrooms in Europe.

The Danish Riviera

In North Seeland, the same region as Helsingør, 32 generations of monarchs have built a glorious variety of castles. Frederik II, a passionate lover of the hunt, bought the manor of Hillerødsholm in 1560. His son Christian IV transformed the place 40 years later,

building a sumptuous palace of brick and sandstone, and renaming it Frederiksborg. It was partly destroyed by fire in 1859, but restored with funds collected by King Frederik VII, including a major contribution from the Carlsberg Foundation. Today it houses the National Historical Museum and the National Portrait Gallery.

A few miles away, the elegant Baroque chateau of Fredensborg is the royal family's spring and autumn residence. Also known as the Castle of Peace, it was given this name by Frederik IV after a treaty with Sweden was signed here in 1722.

Haakonshalle

Constructed in Bergen in the mid-13th century, and endlessly tinkered with ever since, the royal seat of Haakonshalle is the oldest castle in Norway. King Haakon IV Haakonsson (1217-63), who built it, was a keen patron of the arts and able administrator whose reign was the start of a century-long 'golden age' in medieval Norway. Haakon was particularly fond of French chivalric literature and had several romances translated into Norse, including the famous story of Tristan and Isolde. Subsequent kings have continued Haakon's tradition of creating a brilliant artistic circle at court.

Kalmar and the Vasa

The Vasa dynasty of Swedish kings had a habit of building castles in exceptional surroundings – on strategic pinnacles guarding the coast, or hidden deep among the islands of an archipelago. Kalmar Castle, in Småland, is a particularly fine example, with its imposing corner towers, drawbridge, moat and battlements. Originally a medieval fortress protecting the country's southern frontier, Kalmar was rebuilt by Gustav Vasa in the early 16th century in a severe style. His two eldest sons, the future kings Erik XIV and Johan III, remodelled the interior of the castle into a jewel of the High Renaissance, with fantastically painted royal bedrooms and a magnificent Golden Room with inlaid wood panelling and sculpted ceiling.

Sweden's Versailles

On the island of Lovön, an hour by ferry from the centre of Stockholm, stands Drottningholm Palace, the permanent residence of the Swedish royal family.

Rooftops of Tallinn Toopmea, the upper, fortified town of the Estonian capital, offers fine views of the historic centre of the city.

Medieval stronghold Impregnably perched on crags, castles like Turaida in Latvia provide a stark reminder of the wars that once ravaged the country.

Designed by Nicodemus Tessin the Elder in 1662, it was completed by his son 20 years later. The florid rococo interiors were added in the 18th century after the palace was presented to Princess Louise Ulrika of Prussia at her wedding with Crown Prince Adolph Frederick. She had a theatre built in the grounds, which became a centre of artistic life in Sweden. The theatre's 18th-century machinery is still in working order, and visitors are given demonstrations of trapdoors, wind, lightning, thunder and other special effects.

Royal apartments A sumptuous bedroom at Frederiksborg (above), the Danish royal palace near Copenhagen. This majestic building (left) is now one of Denmark's major museums.

A world of fairy tales and legends

Long winters, scattered villages, a sense of Nature's majesty and power – these are some of the factors that inspire the incredible folk imagination of the Scandinavians, with their tales of wicked trolls and laughing ghosts.

Traffic hazard *Images of trolls are used to warn drivers of the consequences of illegal parking.*

In Norway, hundreds of place names begin with the word 'troll': Trollheim, Trolldalen, Trolltindane – which is a snow-covered mountain with a road called the Trollvegen, or trolls' way, leading up to it. Old, ugly and acquisitive, the trolls are said to live in mountains and forests, under huge stones: they cannot bear the touch of sunlight. Some have splendid underground halls glittering with silver and gold. Attracted by the beauty of humans, they pounce on solitary walkers or disguise themselves to seduce innocent young princesses. In most stories, young men beat them in combat or by deception, thus winning the hand of the fair maiden and half the kingdom. In Sweden and Norway, trolls are big and stupid, but in Denmark they are short and cunning to match the low-lying landscape, and they make their homes in boats or windmills.

Friendly chat *Stories of trolls and elves are a part of every young Scandinavian's upbringing.*

The society of elves

In Swedish elves are *vättar*, in Norwegian *huldrer*, in Danish *elver-folk*. In the north of Sweden they are said to keep great herds of white cows that produce extraordinary quantities of milk. They live in families or clans in a kind of parallel society to our own, and spend most of their time doing wicked deeds. Stealing children is not unknown. They can on occasion be kind, however, and anyone who returns an object lost by an elf is always richly rewarded. They have feelings, too, and there are even tales of elves who fall in love.

Another species of elves are the small grey kind who live under houses, or in stables where they take care of the horses. Sometimes they can be seen, tiny figures just a few inches tall, hurrying through the garden of a lonely house. Then there are the nature spirits, solitary beings who dwell in springs, lakes and forests. In the Baltic States, it is believed that spirits take on the form of bears or wolves, and their mocking laughter can drive bewildered travellers into deadly swamps. Young girls must take care not to be enchanted by Näcken, a water sprite in the shape of a handsome young man who entices them into whirlpools. It is said that some musicians learn their most beautiful melodies from him, and when they play a certain passage from Näcken's polka, the dancers are so carried away that they are swallowed up in deep water.

Tales of the Baltic forests

The Baltic countries are rich in legends. The *Kalevigpoeg*, the national epic of the Estonians, tells of the giant Kaleva and mythical heroes who fight trolls. In a famous Lithuanian folk tale, a girl called Egle is bathing in a stream when a snake steals her clothes, promising to return them if she will marry him. Egle agrees and becomes queen of the serpents. Many years later she gets permission to visit her family, taking her daughter and two sons with her. Egle's brothers force the daughter to reveal a spell that attracts the snake from its home so that they can kill it. In the end Egle is turned into a pine tree, her sons into an oak and an ash, and her daughter into an aspen.

Festivals of light

In the long Nordic winters, when the cold and dark go on for months, festivals of light have a special meaning. A candle in a window is a sign of warmth and hospitality. And when summer comes, bonfires are lit in celebration.

Early in the morning of December 13 each year, children whisper and laugh excitedly as they make the final preparations for St Lucy's Day. As soon as St Lucy is ready in her long white dress, with her crown of bilberry leaves and candles, her stable-boy Staffan reaches up and lights the wicks. Then the children go upstairs and wake their parents with a tray of coffee and cakes.

The feast of St Lucy is celebrated all over Sweden, in homes, offices and schools. Young girls sing St Lucy's hymn, and in the evening they gaze out of their windows to see the saint ride by in a horse-drawn gig, wrapped in white furs. St Lucy was a 3rd-century Christian martyr from Syracuse in Sicily, executed by order of the Roman Emperor Diocletian. Legend says that she plucked out her own eyes rather than submit to an evil seducer, and was then put to death by Roman soldiers. The patron saint of opticians and protectress of eyesight (the name Lucia is derived from the Latin word *lux*, light), St Lucy is commemorated in both Southern and Northern Europe. In Sweden, after a special breakfast on St Lucy's Day, a traditional period of fasting before Christmas begins.

Symbol Dressed in white and crowned with candles, St Lucy symbolises the return of light at the darkest point of the winter.

Each Sunday in December, families light a new candle in their Advent candelabra. They hang decorations, often made of straw, in windows and on doors. On Christmas Eve, four candles are lit to celebrate the birth of Jesus. Father Christmas is a relative newcomer to the festivities. He appeared in Scandinavia at the end of the 19th century, when fathers dressed up in red robes and a white beard, and handed presents to their children, sometimes with an accompanying poem.

Fires in the night

On the eve of May 1, the Swedes get together in the open air and sing songs around bonfires to welcome the arrival of spring. Known as Walpurgisnacht (St Walburga's night) and celebrated in various forms throughout Europe, this ancient seasonal rite is meant to chase off wild beasts and evil spirits at a time when the forces of nature are stirring into new life. (Walpurgisnacht is also a night of revelry for witches, when they meet to dance with the devil on the Brocken, the highest peak of the Harz Mountains.)

The summer solstice, or midsummer's day, is also marked by the lighting of fires. In Denmark they light them on the beaches and children throw dolls representing witches into the flames. In Sweden the solstice is celebrated with dancing and maypoles decked with flowers, a pagan symbol of fertility that has endured into the Christian era. Throughout the country, the afternoon is dedicated to children, with games and dancing round the pole to traditional folk tunes played by accordion bands.

Light in the darkness Christmas lights and festivities have a special meaning in Scandinavia's long dark winters.

Midsummer's day A time of dancing and joy, especially for children, the summer solstice is party time all over Sweden.

Treasures and museums

*Some of the finest museums in the world can be found in Scandinavia.
As well as the art collections of kings and business magnates, there are
superb museums of traditional crafts and maritime exploration.*

The National Art Museum in Stockholm, Sweden's largest collection of fine and applied art, houses hundreds of major works acquired by the royal family over nearly 500 years, from the Renaissance to the start of the 20th century. There are medieval masterpieces from all over Europe, Russian icons, paintings by Cranach, Bellini, Rembrandt, El Greco, Rubens, Gainsborough, Canaletto and Renoir. Some of these treasures were looted by Swedish armies during 17th-century wars, but many were bought by collectors such as the diplomat and statesman Count Carl Gustav Tessin (1695-1770), son of the royal architect Nicodemus Tessin the Younger, who was educated in France and Italy and was a knowledgeable and shrewd connoisseur of art.

Art and commerce

Not all the major art collections in Scandinavia were put together by royalty and court officials, however. Right in the heart of Copenhagen, the Ny Carlsberg Glyptotek was presented to the city in 1888 by Carl Jacobsen, son of the founder of the Carlsberg brewery. Jacobsen used his enormous wealth to create a magnificent collection of ancient and classical art – the largest in Northern Europe – and to indulge his well-informed taste for contemporary French sculpture. He visited Paris once a year to see artists' work and place new orders.

Watching me watching you
The Modern Art Museum of Stockholm, one of many in Scandinavia dedicated to 20th-century artists' work.

Halge Jacobsen, Carl's son, inherited his father's excellent taste and continued to buy works of art on a grand scale. As a result the Ny Carlsberg Glyptotek has 24 sculptures by Rodin and an outstanding collection of Impressionist paintings, including 32 works by Gaugin, and others by Van Gogh, Manet, Cézanne, Bonnard and Monet.

The citizens of Gothenburg

Gothenburg Art Museum was founded in 1861 by a group of citizens who gave their private art collections and financial backing. One of them, Pontus Fürstenberg (1827-1902), paid for galleries with works by Carl Larsson and other national romantic painters who specialised in scenes of 19th-century life. Most of the collection is Swedish, but it is balanced by works from other Scandinavian countries and paintings by Rembrandt, Rubens, Guardi, Canaletto, and the French Impressionists.

Oslo's sculpture garden

Gustav Vigeland (1869-1943) was Norway's most prolific sculptor. Apprenticed as a woodcarver, he was influenced by Rodin in his youth, but later developed his own more realistic style. His major work was Fountain Square, a sculpture garden in Oslo's Frogner Park. Around it he placed some 200 structures, including a bridge, a fountain, a mosaic maze and a forest of life-size granite statues. Beyond the bridge rises a monolith, 57 ft (17.37 m) high, carved from a single block of granite weighing 270 tons. There are 121 figures here, making the total cast of characters in the park more than 600. The theme is human life in all its forms, from childhood to old age.

Light and space

Scandinavia's museums of 20th-century art are all stunning examples of modern architecture. Glass is used everywhere to bathe the exhibition spaces in light and link them with the landscape outside. A particularly beautiful example is the museum of Louisiana, overlooking the Øresund north of Copenhagen, which is filled with works by 20th-century masters from Joseph Beuys to Jackson Pollock. Another is on the island of Bornholm, where a newly built gallery of modern art, which houses paintings by Edvard Weie, Karl Isakson and Olaf Rude, slopes gently down to the seashore, following the contours of the land. Stockholm's Museum of Modern Art is also in a contemporary building, designed by Jose Rafael Moneo. Its vast, uncluttered spaces provide the perfect setting for a full range of 20th century art forms.

Of ships and the sea

The maritime museums of Norway are all you would expect from a great sea-going nation. In Oslo, the Fram Museum is dedicated to a ship used by two famous Arctic explorers. The *Fram* was specially built for Fridtjof Nansen (1861-1930), who wanted a ship that would be lifted rather than crushed by the polar ice. Setting out in 1893, Nansen reached the farthest point north yet visited by a human (86°N), making important discoveries about Arctic Ocean currents on the way. Eighteen years later, the same ship was used by Roald Amundsen on his historic trip to the South Pole. Nearby is the Kon Tiki Museum, containing the balsa wood raft that Thor Heyerdahl sailed across the Pacific in 1947 to prove that Polynesian islanders came originally from South America. Also in the museum is the *Ra*, a copy of an Ancient Egyptian reed boat, in which Heyerdahl crossed the Atlantic in 1969, demonstrating that the pre-Columbian Americans could have had contact with the Egyptians.

The Kon Tiki *Thor Heyerdahl's raft, on which he crossed the Pacific in 1947, is now exhibited at its own museum in Oslo.*

Øresund view   A piece by English sculptor Henry Moore at Louisiana, a magnificent modern art museum overlooking the Øresund, near Copenhagen.

The resurrection of the *Vasa*

One of Stockholm's attractions is the *Vasa*, a warship built by Gustavus II Adolphus in 1625, shortly before the outbreak of the Thirty Years' War. Armed with 64 cannons, she set sail on her maiden voyage in 1628, watched by a huge and enthusiastic crowd. Then, as her cannon-ports were opened to fire a salute, she keeled over and sank to the bottom of the harbour. For three and a half centuries the *Vasa* lay in the mud, before being rediscovered by a diver and raised to the surface in 1961, complete with her contents. Now restored, she can be seen again in her glory, with her bows and stern covered in gold leaf, and over 700 pieces of sculpture and relief-carving. The officers' cabin is still visible, where 12 men slept in spartan conditions.

How it was
Traditional crafts and ways of life are lovingly preserved, as in this museum of fishing in Iceland (left).

Creative spaces
Museum design is some of the most daring in the world. Right: A room in the National Museum, Copenhagen.

Country life

Open-air museums have become popular in recent years, with new ones being opened regularly on the outskirts of major cities and in rural areas. The first was Skansen, opened in 1891 and today Scandinavia's foremost tourist attraction. Arthur Hazelius, its creator, wanted to give visitors an idea of life in the different regions of Sweden. He assembled traditional farm buildings, houses, windmills and workshops, and brought them alive with displays by craftsmen.

The medieval centre at Nykøbing Falster in southern Denmark is run on similar lines. In a 14th-century harbour village visitors can see a blacksmith, a weaver or a coppersmith at work, while women draw water from wells and tend vegetable gardens. The same idea has spread to the Baltic. The Ethnographic Museum of Latvia, on Lake Jugla, east of Riga, has around 100 farmhouses, windmills and churches dating from the 18th and 19th centuries, with staff dressed in traditional costumes.

Faeroes holiday

The Faeroese celebrate the arrival of summer in grand style. During the longest days of the year, from late May to the end of July, they hold a series of feasts and festivals in every corner of the islands.

All dressed up
Traditional costumes are often worn during the summer festivals.

Summer is regatta time in the Faeroe Islands. The first competition of the season is the *nordoyastevna* at Klaksvig. After weeks of preparation, the town is hung with flags, there are fanfares and parades through the streets, welcoming speeches, church services, meetings, and then the boat races. After Klaksvig come the festivals of Skálafiord, Syderø, Fuglefiord, Vågø and Vestmanhavn. The starting gun for the first race is the signal that summer has begun.

Crews of 6, 8, 12 or 14 row traditional wooden boats, similar in design to Cornish gigs, each with a helmsman to shout encouragement and steer the most advantageous course. Young and old, male and female, all take part in a variety of competitions and categories. Usually there will be at least 250 rowers in each race.

The competitions are a traditional way of training the young in an essential activity. Until quite recently, rowing boats were the only form of transport to and from the remote villages (*bygd*) scattered around the islands. Every village sends a crew, and victory is fiercely contested, bringing high status to the winners. Training begins in January, with daily practices and workouts. For six months before the final competition at Olavsøku on July 29, rowers concentrate on getting themselves into peak physical condition. Most avoid alcohol for the training period, but once the final is over, they do their best to make up for lost drinking time.

Hardship and faith

Life has always been tough in the Faeroe Islands, whether for farmers struggling to make a living on difficult land, or for fishermen exposed to the dangers of storms and high seas. But harsh lives often make good Christians, and the Faeroese find a strength in their faith that more comfortable societies might envy. In the quiet, intense simplicity of their religion they seem close to the spirit of their ancestors, who first heard the Christian gospel a thousand years ago. This is not a joyless, censorious Christianity, however. The summer festivals are good-humoured, carefree and happy, expressing the instinctive pleasure the locals feel in seeing the sun shine, people out on the streets and quaysides, and the rowing boats cutting through the bright waters.

'Ein litlan?'

When the summer festivals are in full swing, there is so much going on in the way of sporting events, meetings, shows and concerts that no one can see it all. But the most important and pleasurable activity of all is one that is never mentioned in the programme – letting yourself be carried along with the crowd, all in their finest clothes, many in national costume, as they flow down the main street. Some move against the tide of people, hoping that they will bump into friends and acquaintances as they go past. No alcohol is served in bars during the festival, but friends will often take a hip-flask from an inner pocket and offer a gulp of schnapps, known in local parlance as *ein litlan*.

St Olaf's day *The national holiday in the Faeroes is marked by a special regatta at Tórshavn, with crews of all ages battling hard to win their races and the applause of an enthusiastic crowd.*

Popular pastime A singing festival in Lithuania, with the crowd-pulling power that you find at football matches in other countries.

Folk traditions return

The Lithuanians have started a powerful revival of interest in folk traditions that is now spreading to its neighbours. Despite their officially Christian faith, they have never completely abandoned their old pagan deities: all over the country you can find old temples, sanctuaries, ritual sites and sacred forests. There are ceremonies to mark the stages of life – *Krikstynos* (baptism), *Vestuves* (marriage), *Laidoruves* (death and burial) – as well as turning-points of the year: *Kucios-Kaledos* (winter solstice and new year), *Velykos* (spring equinox), *Rasa-Kupoline* (summer solstice) and *Velines* (autumn).

Lithuanian festivals

Among the Baltic States, Lithuania has been the most successful in keeping its popular traditions alive. Somewhere in the country there is a picturesque local festival – pagan or Christian – almost every month.

Street music
Bands like this are one of the delights of Vilnius.

The eve of Ash Wednesday, known as Mardi Gras or 'Fat Tuesday' in Catholic countries, is the last day before Lent. It is also the climax of Carnival, a day of wild exuberance and revelling – nowhere more so than in Lithuania.

The world turned upside down

Villages in the region of Zemaitija are renowned for their spectacular processions. Led by Kanapinis, the master of revels, a series of grotesque figures parade in carnival costume. There are several stock characters: Lasaninis, the Jewish Peddler, who hawks his wares in a stammering voice; the Prying Gypsy on the lookout for loot; and More, the Old Serving Woman, who rides through the streets on a farmer's cart with a flail in one hand and a broom in the other, a symbol of the struggle between winter and spring, unable to make up her mind whether to finish threshing last year's harvest or start this year's spring cleaning. On this wild day, when women dress as men and men as women, everyone throws themselves with abandon into the spirit of Carnival.

Much has changed in Lithuania in the past 50 years. Many old customs have died out, but you can still find country marriages celebrated in traditional style. As the happy couple come home from the church or town hall, they find the tables for the wedding feast

already occupied by 'Gypsies', who are sitting alongside a grotesque couple of cross-dressed newlyweds, a female groom and a male bride. A bargaining session takes place, and finally the Gypsies (who are neighbours in disguise) give up their seats to the real wedding guests in exchange for a bottle of schnapps. When the food arrives, everyone takes a mouthful and begins a traditional wedding song: 'Bitter, bitter is the food, but how sweet it will taste when the groom has kissed the bride!' Then the guests shower the couple with advice for the wedding night and the years of married life ahead.

One of the most dramatic moments of the feast is the 'execution' of the matchmaker. Shortly before the end of the meal, the bride's brothers and sisters accuse the luckless go-between of making the bride's family pay too big a dowry. The matchmaker is tried and duly condemned. He will be burnt alive in water, frozen to death in an oven, roasted in ice – or sent into the barn with all the village girls. Before facing this terrible fate, the matchmaker asks to say goodbye to his friends. He daubs his face with soot, then tries to kiss all the ladies of the house, until the bride or her mother have mercy and grant him a pardon by laying a napkin on his shoulder. The matchmaker is saved and a dummy is hanged in his place.

Fancy dress A group of mummers keep folk traditions alive in Latvia.

CHAPTER 7

ART AND CULTURE

The arts have a special place in Scandinavian life. In every field, artists have created works that are true to the lives, beliefs and realities of their home communities, yet are also universal. Classical composers like Edvard Grieg, Carl Nielsen and Jean Sibelius; writers like Henrik Ibsen, August Strindberg, Selma Lagerlöf and Karen Blixen; the Skagen School of painters, Edvard Munch, Inger Sitter, Asger Jorn; film directors Ingmar Bergman, Carl Theodor Dreyer, Bille August; architects and designers like Alvar Aalto, Eliel Saarinen, Kjell Lund and Nils Slatto. Despite such dominant figures, the arts do not exist only for a sophisticated élite: music encompasses everything from amateur choirs to huge international singing festivals, while paintings and quality design are part of the décor of ordinary people's houses. Culture, like education and health, is seen as everyone's right – an essential element of a strong democracy.

Jazz clubs, like this one in Norway, can be found in all the cities of Scandinavia.

The musical soul of Scandinavia

Like other late 19th and early 20th-century composers, Edvard Grieg and Carl Nielsen drew inspiration from folk music, a tradition that is still very much alive. The old songs can still be heard at festivals – but then so can almost any other kind of music you choose.

For hundreds of years, folk music in Scandinavia had a special place in the life of rural communities. Itinerant musicians used to turn up in villages and towns, bringing dancing and good cheer to weddings and festivals, and brightening the long winter nights. They played traditional songs and dance tunes, usually on a violin and accordion, without drums or percussion. Rhythms were clapped or stamped by the listeners. These musicians also acted as a kind of country newspaper, passing on news that they had picked up on their travels.

Oral tradition

In Iceland and the Faeroe Islands you can still hear performances of the *kvad* – medieval epics sung unaccompanied by a *skipara* or captain, while a ring of dancers beat the rhythm and sing choral refrains. Although their subject matter belongs to history, the *kvad* remain popular even today.

In Sweden, songs called *visor* are all the rage, as they have been for centuries. With short, humorous or lyrical texts based on contemporary life, this type of song was turned into an art form by Carl Michael Bellman in the 18th century. Composing his own tunes or adapting popular melodies of the day, he wrote wonderful ditties of Stockholm life, full of wit, romance, gaiety and gentle mockery. Bellman was a great poet whose ability to express the pleasures of life, while suggesting the shadows that lie beyond, is unrivalled.

A passion for song

The huge, living repertoire of folk songs in the Baltic States has kept people in touch with their cultural traditions despite years of Russian rule. Most people belong to community choirs and know hundreds of popular and traditional songs by heart. One that is common to all the Baltic nations is *Gaudeamus* (the Latin name means 'Let us rejoice'). The singing of this medieval song is a key moment in village festivals, especially at the summer solstice.

Icelandic star Björk was a leading figure in the pop world in the 1990s. Film director Lars Von Trier revealed her acting talent in Dancer in the Dark, *for which she won Best Actress Award at the Cannes Film Festival in 2000.*

Traditional instruments

Flute, violin, guitar and accordion – the standard instruments of Central European folk bands – are also found in the Baltic States. They have special instruments of their own, too, such as the *torupil*, or bagpipes, played in Estonia and Protestant parts of Lithuania, and the Latvian *kokles*, or zither, which is played all over the Baltic, including Finland, under a variety of names. Perhaps the most magical is the cimbalom, a dulcimer with a silvery echoing sound, played with light wooden hammers in Latvia and the Catholic areas of Lithuania.

Sami singing
Traditional songs form an important part of the ancient Sami culture. Here a group of singers performs at the opening of the Sami parliament in Trondheim, Norway.

Sometimes the oral tradition is helped along by written music. In Latvia and Lithuania, many *daina*, a type of melancholy folk song, were transcribed between the 15th and 17th centuries. Several of the songs were much older, of course, but their written forms ensured their preservation for posterity.

Music and patriotism

Folk songs were immensely important to two of the greatest Scandinavian classical composers: Edvard Grieg (1843-1907) from Norway and Jean Sibelius (1865-1957) from Finland. Both were

Piano virtuoso *Edvard Grieg, Norway's greatest composer, drew much of his inspiration from folk songs. He suffered from ill health for most of his life, but toured widely, performing his famous* Piano Concerto, *a popular classic, in London in 1888. Other famous works include incidental music for Ibsen's* Peer Gynt *and his* Norwegian Peasant Dances.

Jazz in the soul *The Finns organise some of the biggest and best music festivals in the world (Oulu, Jazz Espoo, Tampere Biennale, Kainuu Jazz, Kuopio, Naantali, Savonlinna). These are known and appreciated by music lovers everywhere. Pori Jazz (left), held every July, always boasts a glittering array of top names.*

working at a time when their countries were fighting for independence and attempting to create, through education and the arts, a national identity. Both composers looked for the source of that identity in the old myths and sagas. In their music, which was deeply influenced by German romanticism, they brilliantly conveyed the beauty of their native landscapes, as well as the passion and drama of their troubled histories. Grieg's most famous works are the *Norwegian Peasant Dances* and the *Peer Gynt Suites*, which he

composed for theatrical performances of Ibsen's play. Sibelius, who is regarded as the founder of Finnish music, composed seven symphonies filled with powerful patriotic emotion, a magnificent violin concerto, and several symphonic poems. One of these, *Finlandia*, has become an unofficial national anthem. In Sibelius's honour the name Finlandia was given to a great concert hall in Helsinki designed by Alvar Aalto.

The Romantic influence was also felt by the Danish composer Carl Nielsen (1865-1931), whose music is filled with echoes of folk songs and his own feeling for the landscape of his native region, Fyn. A violinist and conductor as well as a composer, Nielsen taught for many years at the Royal Copenhagen Conservatory, developing a forceful and highly personal musical idiom. This can be heard in one of his best-known works, *Spring in Fyn*.

Opera, jazz and rock

People are often surprised by the variety and quality of music festivals in Scandinavia. Most of these take place in summer, when travel is easier and the evenings are long. Finland hosts a number of outstanding classical music festivals, among them Naantali in June and Savonlinna in July, an opera festival in a medieval castle in the heart of the Lake District.

Denmark has made a speciality of jazz, with July a particularly 'hot' month in Copenhagen. Its rock fans, meanwhile, get their big opportunity at Roskilde, 'the Nordic Woodstock', a festival that has been going since 1970, attracting audiences as well as stars from around the world.

Abba, a global success story

In 1974, four young Swedish singers won the Eurovision Song Contest with the catchy disco sound of 'Waterloo'. The writers of the song, Benny Andersson and Björn Ulvaeus, were already successful as

the creators of two of Sweden's most popular groups in the 1960s, The Hep Stars and The Hootenanny Singers. They joined forces with their fiancées, Agnetha Fältskog and Anna-Frid Lyngstad, and shot to international fame as Abba. Their songs were not to everone's taste, and their costumes did little for the reputation of Swedish design, but there was no denying their appeal. By the end of the 1970s, the group was Sweden's third biggest export earner after Volvo and Saab. Abba split up in 1982, but their records, tapes and CDs have continued to sell in their millions. They have turned down many offers to get together again.

The storytellers

The Norse sagas, which were written down in the early Middle Ages, already show the characteristic concerns of Scandinavian literature – love of life, the search for justice, belief in a tragic destiny, and the hope of final redemption.

From the 12th century *History of the Danish Kings and Heroes* by Saxo Grammaticus to today's international bestsellers, story-telling has always been a strong point of Scandinavian literature. In the work of contemporary novelists – Göran Tunström or Kerstin Ekman from Sweden, Peter Høeg from Denmark, Jan Kjaerstad from Norway – the link to the past is clear.

Beyond the barriers of language

A brief look at the history of Scandinavian literature reveals its variety and influence on other cultures. The sagas deal with three different themes: life among the early settlers in Iceland, the history of Norway's kings, and legends of great heroes. Their influence has been enormous, not only on later Scandinavian writing, but on other forms of art, too – leading to the creation of such works as Wagner's *Ring des Nibelungen*. The 18th century saw a golden age in writing, with figures such as dramatist, essayist and historian Ludvig Holberg (1684-1754), philosopher and scientist Emmanuel Swedenborg (1688-1772), and songwriter and poet Carl Michael Bellman (1740-95), whose *Fredman's Epistles* paint such a delight-fully bittersweet portrait of Stockholm life.

The 19th century produced a number of writers of world stature, such as Hans Christian Andersen (1808-75), whose *Fairy Tales* have been translated into over 100 languages. Norwegian playwright Henrik Ibsen (1828-1906) was the most influential dramatist of the century, bringing serious political and social issues onto the stage for the first time in 100 years. August Strindberg (1849-1912) is important for his psy-

Tortured genius *Swedish dramatist August Strindberg, author of* The Dream Play *and other highly influential works.*

On stage Miss Julie, *one of Strindberg's most powerful plays, in performance in Paris, with Niels Arestrup and Isabelle Adjani.*

chological dramas, while philosopher Søren Kierkegaard (1813-55) was one of the most original 19th-century thinkers, with his defence of the individual's freedom of choice.

Among these giants stand others: Selma Lagerlöf (1858-1940), who wrote novels of rural life and a children's book, *The Marvellous Adventures of Nils*; critic Georg Brandes (1842-1927); novelist, poet and champion of social progress Johannes Jensen (1873-1950); feminist novelist Sigrid Undset (1882-1949); Karen Blixen (1885-1962), author of *Out of Africa*; Knut Hamsun (1859-1952), of whom the American writer Isaac Bashevis Singer said, 'the whole modern school of fiction in the 20th century stems from him'.

Scandinavian winners of the Nobel prize for literature include Hamsun, Lagerlöf, Jensen and Undset; Danish novelists Henrik Pontoppidan (1857-1943) and Karl Gjellerup (1857-1919), Swedish novelist and playwright Pär Lagerkvist (1891-1947), and Icelandic novelist Halldor Laxness (1902-98).

Ultimate storyteller *A statue of Hans Christian Andersen in his home city of Copenhagen.*

Classics reinvented *Ibsen's* Peer Gynt *in performance at Lake Gol in Norway.*

From runes to sagas

The runic inscriptions, which date from the 3rd century AD, are the earliest form of Scandinavian writing. They record some intriguing spells, riddles and poems, but show nothing like the complexity of thought and narrative skill that is evident in the later sagas. These were the product of an oral storytelling tradition that had reached a level of high art by the time the sagas came to be written in the 12th and 13th centuries.

The Skagen group

Around 1870, a group of artists began to form in the fishing village of Skagen, at the northern tip of Jutland. Inspired by the long vistas of dunes and the constantly changing light, painters Michael and Anna Ancher were joined by Holger Drachmann, P.S. Kroyer and others. Like the French Impressionists, they concentrated on capturing the play of light over the physical world. More than 1500 of their works can be seen at the Skagen Museum and the Brøndums Hotel, where the group often gathered for dinner.

Mother and daughter *A typically powerful picture by Norwegian painter Edvard Munch.*

Northern light *The light in Danish artist Vilhelm Hammershoi's work is reminiscent of Flemish painting.*

Great 20th-century painters

Because of its geographical isolation, Scandinavia remained on the margins of European art for hundreds of years. But in the 19th century, as travel became easier and art became more international, that all changed.

From the Middle Ages to the 17th century, foreign artists were employed to decorate the churches and palaces of Scandinavia. It was only in the 18th century that national academies of art were set up. In Sweden, the first truly national style developed during the Gustavian Enlightenment, led by the sculptor Johan Tobias Sergei (1740-1814). In Finland, painting only began to emerge in the 1830s, with the growth of nationalist sentiment. At the end of the 19th century, Akseli Gallèn-Kallela (1865-1931) became the first Finnish artist to achieve major renown.

Edvard Munch and Expressionism

Born into an educated Oslo family, Edvard Munch (1863-1944) grew up in the shadow of tuberculosis: first his mother, then his elder sister Sophie died of the disease. Although he achieved great success as a painter, sorrow and anguish were the enduring themes of his work. In 1885, on a scholarship to Paris, Munch discovered the work of Seurat, Gauguin and Van Gogh, adapting their techniques with colour and line to express his own bleak vision of the soul. In his most famous work, *The Scream*, violent colours and twisting forms create a terrifying image of a screaming figure on a bridge beneath a wild sky. Although his later work is calmer, Munch is chiefly remembered for his ability to reveal the psychology of pain through art.

Documentary realism The Blacksmith *by Carl Larsson, Sweden's great 19th-century painter of everyday life.*

From abstraction to landscape

Perhaps because Munch was so influential, abstraction was slow to catch on in Norway and its exponents – painters like Knut Rumohr, Ludvig Eikaas, Jacob Weidermann and Inger Sitter – were unrecognised until after the Second World War. Elsewhere in Scandinavia, foreign ideas were more quickly absorbed. Asger Jorn in Denmark, for example, worked in a style that combined elements of Abstract Expressionism with Surrealism, and in 1948 founded the CoBrA group together with Corneille from Belgium and Van Appel from Holland (the name is made up of the first letters of Copenhagen, Brussels and Amsterdam). Several Scandinavian painters diversified into different art forms after the war. Asger Jorn became interested in ceramics and writing, while another Dane, Per Kirkeby, branched out from oil painting to cinema, poetry and sculpture.

Recently there has been a return to landscape painting. Nature's most awe-inspiring and violent aspects have inspired a new generation of Icelandic painters, including Jón Thorleifsson, Gunnlaugur Scheving and Jón Engilberts. It is as if, after all the movements and fashions of the 20th century, artists have felt the need to renew their contact with the earth and the remarkable landscape in which they live.

The art of film

Denmark and Sweden have made an enormous contribution to world cinema – not just through the work of their two greatest directors, Dreyer and Bergman, but through a wider tradition of film-making that addresses the deepest issues of the age.

I n 1906 Ole Olsen, a travelling showman, created Nordisk Film. Olsen was unimpressed by the mediocre content and poor technical quality of the films that were on offer commercially, so he decided to make his own. Within ten years he was running the second largest production company in the world, with an annual output of 200 films. And as there was no soundtrack in those days, language was no barrier to exports.

Until the First World War, Denmark ran a close second to Germany as the world's leading maker of films. Actresses like Asta Nielsen were international stars. With the arrival of sound, however, and the growth of Hollywood in the USA, the market for Danish and Swedish films was suddenly and drastically reduced.

Healing food *First and best of the 'foodie' films,* Babette's Feast *(1987) starred Stéphane Audran in the title role and was directed by Gabriel Axel. It won an Oscar for Best Foreign Film.*

Dark secrets *Winner of the Jury Prize at Cannes in 1998,* Festen *by Danish director Thomas Vinterberg is the story of a family torn apart by incest.*

An early genius

The pioneering years of Danish cinema produced one director of genius: Carl Theodor Dreyer (1889-1968), who joined Nordisk Film at the age of 23 as a writer of subtitles. He made his first full-length feature, *The President*, in 1919. A perfectionist with a hot temper, he always had difficulty financing his projects, and had to go to France to raise money for his 1928 film *The Passion of Joan of Arc*. This masterpiece of silent cinema introduced two new techniques to the art of film-making: the dissolve and the close-up. By fixing the camera on his actors' faces, Dreyer captured every nuance of emotion, intensifying the drama, but also annoying the set-designers, whose work was often out of shot.

Joan of Arc established Dreyer's international reputation and he remains one of the giants of cinema history, but his unwillingness to compromise artistically made financial backers wary. His first talking film, *Vampyr* (1932), only came out thanks to the help of a wealthy patron. In later years, Dreyer found it increasingly hard

Dogma, essential cinema

I n 1995 four Danish film directors – Soren Kragh-Jacobsen, Kristian Levering, Lars Von Trier and Thomas Vinterberg – founded a collective called Dogma. Their aim was to limit budgets by having no artificial lighting, no camera trolleys or tripods, no specially recorded music and no costumes for the actors. Several films have been made in this style, and have won important prizes: *Idiots* won the Jury Prize at Cannes in 1996, and *Festen* in 1998. In 2000, Lars Von Trier won the *Palme d'Or* with *Dancer in the Dark*, starring the Icelandic singer Björk.

to work. He made *Dies Irae* in 1943, then *Ordet* (*The Word*) in 1955. After completing his last film, *Gertrud*, in 1964, he was reduced to working as the manager of a cinema in Copenhagen.

Ingmar Bergman

By the 1940s, as the early energy of Danish cinema was faltering, the Swedes were starting to produce some remarkable films of their own. The outstanding director in the postwar years was Ingmar Bergman. Working both in the theatre and cinema, a brilliant scriptwriter as well as director, Bergman's first international success was the comedy-drama *Smiles of a Summer Night* (1955). He went on to direct over 40 acclaimed films, including such classics as *The Seventh Seal* (1956), which won several awards at Cannes. Among his later films are *Wild Strawberries* (1957), *The Touch* (1971), *Cries and Whispers* (1972), *Autumn Sonata* (1978) and *Fanny and Alexander* (1983).

Very much an artist of the cinema, Bergman has worked repeatedly with a group of favourite actors: among them Max Von Sydow, Bibi Andersson and Liv Ullmann. Bergman's films vary from bittersweet comedy to the darkest tragedy, but he is one of the

Migrants' story
Bille August's Pelle the Conqueror, *starring Max Von Sydow, was a huge critical and box-office success, and won the* Palme d'Or *at Cannes in 1988. It tells the story of a father and son who move to Denmark from Sweden at the end of the 19th century.*

Director's cut *Born in 1918 in Uppsala, Ingmar Bergman was one of the key figures in world cinema for nearly 50 years. As well as a director of films, he was also a brilliant screenwriter and theatre director.*

most philosophical and intense of directors, exploring the great moral and spiritual questions of life, looking deeply and unsentimentally at love and marriage, personal identity, and the relationship between man and God.

A new generation

Bergman is no longer directing, but he has continued to write, and his screenplay for Bille August's *The Best Intentions* contributed to the film's *Palme d'Or* at Cannes in 1992. August is one of a new generation of directors who have made their distinctive mark on the international scene. His *Pelle the Conqueror* won the *Palme d'Or* in 1988, as well as an Oscar from Hollywood. Tempted over to the United States, he saw his next film, *Smilla's Feeling for Snow* (1997) flop painfully at the box office. But he regained his form with *Les Misérables* (1998), based on Victor Hugo's novel, which is a superb piece of cinematic storytelling.

Lasse Hallström is another outstanding Swedish director, whose gently humorous *My Life As A Dog* (1985) led to a chance to work in the USA and make *What's Eating Gilbert Grape?* (1993) with Johnny Depp and Leonardo Di Caprio. Another successful 'transplant' is Renny Harlin from Finland, who specialises in action films such as *Cliffhanger* (1993).

Despite the limited market for foreign-language features, Scandinavian art films continue to be made, with new directors like Lars Von Trier emerging from time to time via the prize and festival circuit. Meanwhile the governments of the Scandinavian countries, believing strongly in the importance of cinema, encourage film production through generous subsidies.

Stars from Sweden

In the Hollywood golden years, a little-known Swedish actress became a household name: Greta Garbo. With her delicate but sensuous beauty and magnetic screen presence, she thrilled audiences as Mata Hari, Anna Karenina and Ninotchka. But in many ways she did not play by Hollywood rules. Known as 'the sphinx of the screen', she never gave any interviews.

Another great Swedish star was Ingrid Bergman. She stole the hearts of American moviegoers with her freshness, intelligence and spontaneity, and was perfect playing the part of a loving wife, an important role model in the troubled 1940s. Among her many great films are *Casablanca* (1942), *For Whom The Bell Tolls* (1943), *Spellbound* (1945), *Notorious* (1946) and *Anastasia* (1956). In 1974 she won an Oscar for her part in *Murder on the Orient Express*.

Masters of modern design

From huge office buildings to the smallest everyday objects, Scandinavian design stands out for its excellent workmanship, brilliant use of space and light, and fresh ways of using traditional materials.

One of the finest examples of early 20th-century architecture is Helsinki's central railway station. It was designed by Eliel Saarinen (1873-1950), once a keen exponent of national romanticism, who adopted the new principle of functional architecture for this important public project. Later he emigrated to the United States, where, together with his son Eero, he had a powerful influence on American urban planning.

Working in a similar idiom, but far surpassing Saarinen in both fame and influence, was another Finnish architect, Alvar Aalto (1898-1976). Aalto first came to prominence in the 1930s for his highly original use of wood. He designed not just buildings but objects of all kinds, from jewellery to furniture, transforming everything he touched with his sober, graceful lines. His principal aim was to bring out the connections between man, nature and buildings. He first achieved this with Villa Mairea at Noormarkku in western Finland, one of the most remarkable modern houses in the world.

After the Second World War Aalto became interested in urban design and was given the task of rebuilding Rovaniemi, the capital of Finnish Lappland, which had been burnt down by the retreating Germans. He gave the city a visionary new plan, based on the shape of a reindeer's antlers. Individual buildings were integrated into the landscape – a famous example being the city's cultural centre, Lappia-talo, which echoes the rising and falling skyline of the nearby mountains.

Aalto's heirs

The Norwegian architects Kjell Lund and Nils Slatto followed in Aalto's footsteps, adapting traditional techniques in wooden construction to the constraints of modern industrial production. One of their most important projects was the Franciscan monastery of Enerhaugen in Oslo (1966), which consisted of a cube

Lines of the future   Helsinki railway station (1914), designed by Eliel Saarinen, one of the key buildings of the modern era. The giant lamp-bearing statues are by Emil Wikström.

Industrial chic *Verner Panton, born in Denmark in 1926, was one of the major designers of the late 20th century. His furniture, wall panels and lamps (left and right) used industrial manufacturing processes and synthetic materials to create a contemporary effect.*

Illuminating details

At the Exposition Universelle in Paris, in 1924, Poul Hennigsen presented his first 'PH' lamps made with metal plate, which won first prize in the lighting competition. The secret of the lamps, now valuable collectors' items, lies in the careful arrangement of the metal surfaces. These hide the bulbs while directing the light downwards, and are angled so that the beams of light are reflected only once. The edges of the metal are shaped to soften the contrast between illuminated objects and the walls of the room. As a final touch, Hennigsen coloured the inside surfaces red, which tones down the brightness of white light.

Danish building abroad

Some Danish architects are better known abroad than at home. Jørn Utzon, for instance, designed the Sydney Opera House (arguably the world's most famous modern building) and the new Parliament building in Kuwait. Born in 1918, and inspired by Alvar Aalto, Utzon was one of the first architects to integrate his buildings with the surrounding spaces. His work in Denmark includes the concert hall in Esbjerg, Bagsvaerd Cathedral, and the Kongo residential district in Helsingør. Another Dane, Otto Spreckelsen, partnered Erik Reitzel in the design of the Grande Arche de la Défense on the outskirts of Paris. This gigantic but supremely elegant structure contains 860 000 sq ft (80 000 m²) of offices, conference rooms and exhibition spaces, and has become one of the city's most admired landmarks.

surrounding a circular church. In 1975 they were commissioned to design the new headquarters of Bureau Veritas, the Scandinavian ship classification agency, in the town of Baerum. This was completed in 1985, a structuralist building in brick and concrete. The following year an even more prestigious project came to fruition with the acclaimed Norwegian Central Bank on Oslo's Bankplassen.

Putting on the style

In the 1920s, Poul Hennigsen was a key figure in Copenhagen. He designed several villas, a few additions to the Tivoli gardens, and the interiors of two theatres. He published poems and wrote articles about architecture and contemporary society – but he is remembered most of all for his novel theories of lighting in the home, and for his extraordinary lamps and chandeliers.

While Hennigsen taught people to think differently about space and light, Sigvard Bernadotte in Sweden was starting to gain a reputation as a designer of fine furniture. Bernadotte was an aristocrat, related to the royal family. He trained as an architect, but soon ventured into interior decoration, ceramics, textiles, furniture, and objects in aluminium, plastic and glass.

In the early part of his career, Bernadotte worked for Acton Bjørg's studio in Copenhagen. Later he started his own company in Stockholm, which became a nursery for young talent in contemporary design. Over the years he diversified further, becoming interested in industrial, mass-market products of the most varied kinds, from vacuum flasks to kitchen utensils. Yet he kept up the more exclusive side of his business too, creating a celebrated set of silver cutlery for Georg Jensen, the Copenhagen jeweller.

In the 1960s, the chocolate-maker Marabou asked Bernadotte to redesign the company logo in a more contemporary style; the manufacturer Rosti commissioned a salad bowl, which they still make and sell today; and the Stockholm Metro consulted this versatile designer on the exact shade of blue to use on their trains.

Easy chair
This simple yet graceful plywood chair, dating from 1931-2, was one of many furniture designs by the great Finnish architect Alvar Aalto.

Craftsmen and style

Design is not the exclusive domain of architects. Scandinavia has large numbers of artisan schools where design is an essential element of the training. Many of the graduates from these schools become artists in their own right. A well-known example is Hans J. Wegner, born in Denmark in 1914. He trained as a cabinet-maker in Copenhagen and started designing furniture for the architectural studio of Arne Jacobsen and Erik Moller in 1938. In 1942 he opened his own office in Gentofte, producing a design for a complete apartment in collaboration with Borge Mogensen. This was shown in Copenhagen in 1946 and quickly made his name. In a long and successful career, Wegner has designed sofas, chairs, bookshelves, cupboards, tables – all now regarded as modern classics.

137

MAPS, FACTS AND FIGURES

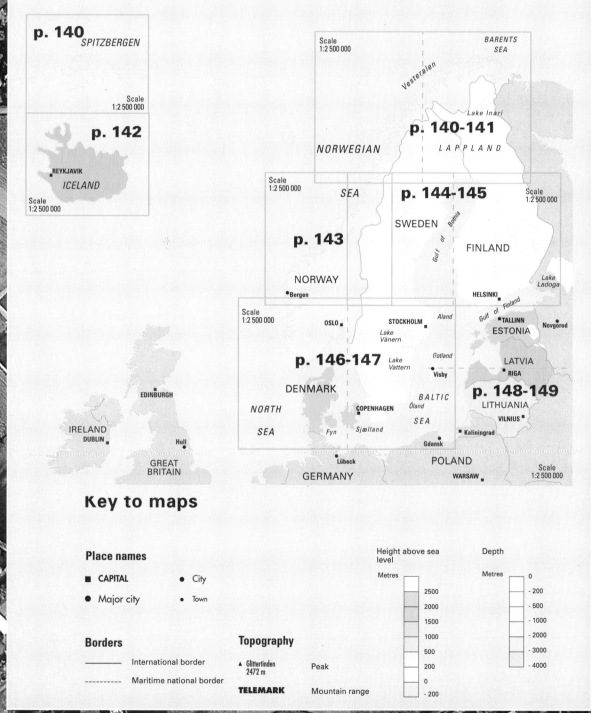

Key to maps

Place names

■ **CAPITAL**   ● City

● Major city   • Town

Borders

——————— International border

----------- Maritime national border

**Height above sea
level**

Metres

	2500
	2000
	1500
	1000
	500
	200
	0
	- 200

Depth

Metres

	0
	- 200
	- 500
	- 1000
	- 2000
	- 3000
	- 4000

Topography

▲ Glittertinden
2472 m   Peak

TELEMARK   Mountain range

Svalbard inset (Greenland Sea / Spitzbergen)

GREENLAND SEA

SJUØYANE
K. Platen
FOYNØYA
KVITØYA
LÅGØYA
K. Brunn
STORØYA
MOFFEN
80°
80°

NORDAUSTLANDET

DANSKØYA
Wijdefjorden
Haakon VII Land
Andree Land
Kapp Mohn
Erik Eriksenstretet
ABELØYA
79°
Eidsvollfjellet 1 454 m
K. Mitra
Kong Karls Land
79°
KONGSØYA
Tre Kroner 1 225 m
SPITZBERGEN
SVENSKØYA
Olgastretet
PRINS
Oscar II Land
Svanbergfj. 962 m
K. Bessels
BARENTSØYA
KARLS
Olav V Land
FORLAND
Forlandsundet
Isfjorden
Longyearbyen
K. Pechuel Løsche
Salpynten
Grumantbyen
78°
Barentsburg
K. Melchers
78°
Sveagruva
EDGEØYA
Van Mijenfjorden
Heer Land
Bellsund
Diskobukta
Wedel Jarlsberg Land
Storfjorden
Tjurfjorden
HALVMÅNEØYA
Tanefjellet 933 m
77°
77°
Hornsund
Sørkapp Land
HOPEN
30 miles
50 km
SØRKAPPØYA

Jan Mayen inset

JAN MAYEN
Nord Kapp
Jan Mayen Radio
Beerenberg 2 277 m
71°
Rudolf Toppen 769 m
Sør Kapp
15 miles
25 km

Main map (Northern Norway)

VANNA
Fugløysund
RINGVASSØY
Tromsø
Lyng
KVALØYA
Berg
Nordkjosbc
SENJA
Finnsnes
Andenes
ANDØYA
Ånderdalen
Bardufoss
Mälselva
Bardu
Alteva
VESTERÅLEN
Andfjorden
Harstad
Altevа
Vadvetjåkko
LANGØYA
Sortland
Riksgränsen
Bø
Ofotfjord
Narvik
Abisko
ABISKO
AUST-VÅGØYA
Ballangen
Stetsteuinstjellet 1 901 m
Tornet
Svolvær
HINNØYA
Bognes
Kebnekaise 2 111 m
Vagan
VEST-VÅGØYA
Bogness
STORA SJÖFALLETS
Moskenes
Nordfold
Lake Akkajaure
MOSKENESØYA
VÆRØY
Folda
Sarek 2 089 m
RØST
Sørfold
RÅGO
PADJELANTA
Stora Lulevate
Bodø
Fauske
SAREKS
Saltfjord
Suliteima 1 914 m
Kvikkjokk
Lomi
Lønsdal
Vuoggatjålme
Snøtinden 1 594 m
Sädvaluspen
Hornavan
Svartisen
PIELJEKAISE

L   M   N   O   P   Q   R

24°   26°   28°   30°   32°   34°   36°   70°

BARENTS SEA

North Cape   MAGERØYA   C. Nordkinn   Berlevåg

3

ROLVSØYA   Honningsvåg   Nordkynhalvøya   Tanafjorden   Hamningberg

Repvåg   Porsangerhalvøya   Lebesby   Tana   Varangerhalvøya   Vardø

Poluostrov Rybachiy

OSTROV KIL'DIN

SØRØYA   Hammerfest   Vadsø   Varangerfjorden   299 m   Port-Vladimir   Teriberka

KVALØYA   Skaidi   Kunes   Polmak   Bugøynes   Linakhamari   Tyuva Guba   69°

Pechenga   Polyarnyy   Severomorsk

SEILAND   Kirkenes   Zapolyarnyy   Roslyakovo

TJERNØYA   STABBURSDALEN   Lakselv   Rastegaissa 1 067 m   Utsjoki   Nikel 631 m   Murmansk   Kola

Cuekkarassa ▲ 1 139 m   Skoganvarre   Sevettijärvi   Kil'dinstroy

Alta   Finnmark   Øvre Pasvik   Shonguy

nangen   Burfjord   Karasjok   RUSSIA   Tuloma   Kola   4

Reisaelva   Karigasniemi   Inarijarvi   Virtaniemi   Talvik'ulla   Verkhnetulomskiy   Taybola

Nordreisa   Pealdoaivi 567 m   Verkhnetulomskoye Vodokhranilishche   Laplandiya

Reisa   NORWAY   Inari   Lotta   907 m   Olenegorsk   68°

Gora Elgoras 997 m   Monchegorsk   Gora Chasnachor 1 191 m

Haltiatunturi 1 328 m   Ivalo   Raja-Jooseppi   714 m   Javra   LAPLANDSKIJ   Ozero Imandra   Apatity

Kautokeino   ØVRE ANARJOKKA   Kilpisjärvi   Könkämaalven   LEMMENJOEN   Nattaset 567 m   URHO KEKKOSEN KANSALLISPUISTO   Afrikanda   5

VIDAL   Enontekiö   Porttipahdan tekojärvi   Lokan tekojärvi   Kovdor   Zasheyek   Nivskiy

Kelottijarvi   Kemijoki   Kandalaksha   67°

Lainioälven   Karesuando   PALLAS-OUNASTUNTURIN   Palojoensuu   Pallastunturin 807 m   Lokka   Sorsatunturi 629 m   Zelenoborskiy

Nedre Soppero   Lappland   Muonio   FINLAND   Luiro   Martti   Alakurtti   Ozero Kovdozero   6

Kiruna   Kittilä   Sodankylä   Kittinen   Pelkosenniemi   Kelloselkä   Kuolayarvi   Zarechensk   Tumcha   Arctic Circle   32°

Vittangi   Kolari   Pyhätunturi 540 m   Salla   Yakkonen

Svappavaara   Anttis   Lohiniva   PYHÄTUNTURIN KANSALLISPUISTO   Joutsijarvi   OULANGAN KANSALLISPUISTO   Ozero Tiksheozero

Fjällåsen   Pajala   Meltaus   Kemijärvi   Kemijärvi   66°

Koskullskulle   Malmberget   Tarendo   Vikajärvi   RIISITUNTURIN KANSALLISPUISTO   Sofyanga

Gällivare   Pello   Rovaniemi   Yli-Kitka   Kuusamo   Ozero Topozero

Porjus   MUDDUS   Kauliranta   Posio   471 m   Tikhtozero   7

SWEDEN   Luleälven   Overtorneå   Simojärvi

Jokkmokk   Polcirkeln   Overkalix   Tervola   Ranua   Iso-Syöte 431 m   Taivalkoski   Voynitsa

Kalixälven   Karungi   Kemijoki   Kiantajärvi   65°

Kåbdalis   Boden   Kukkola   Tornio   Kemi   Simojoki   Tannila   Pudasjärvi   Suomussalmi   Ladvozero

Töre   Kalix   Karlsborg   Kuivaniemi   Iijoki   Ämmänsaari

Luleälven   Räneå   Haparanda   Seskaro   Livojoki

20°   66°   22°   24°   26°   28°   30°

141

Iceland

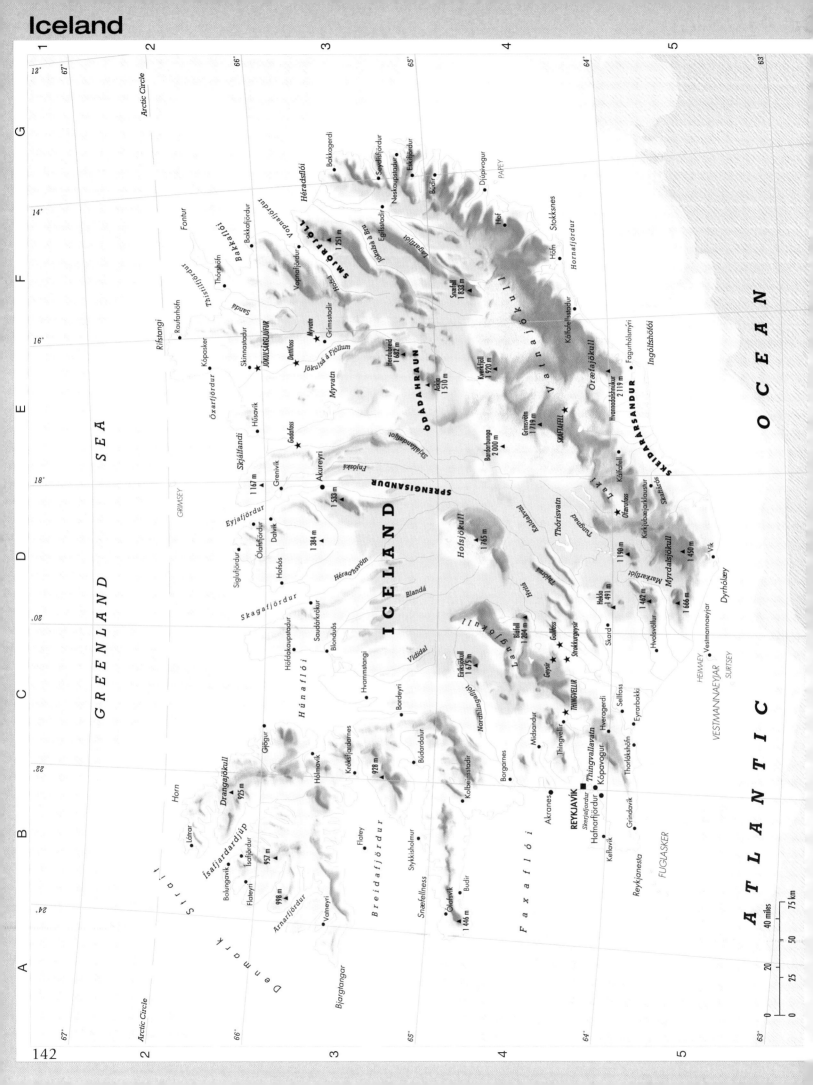

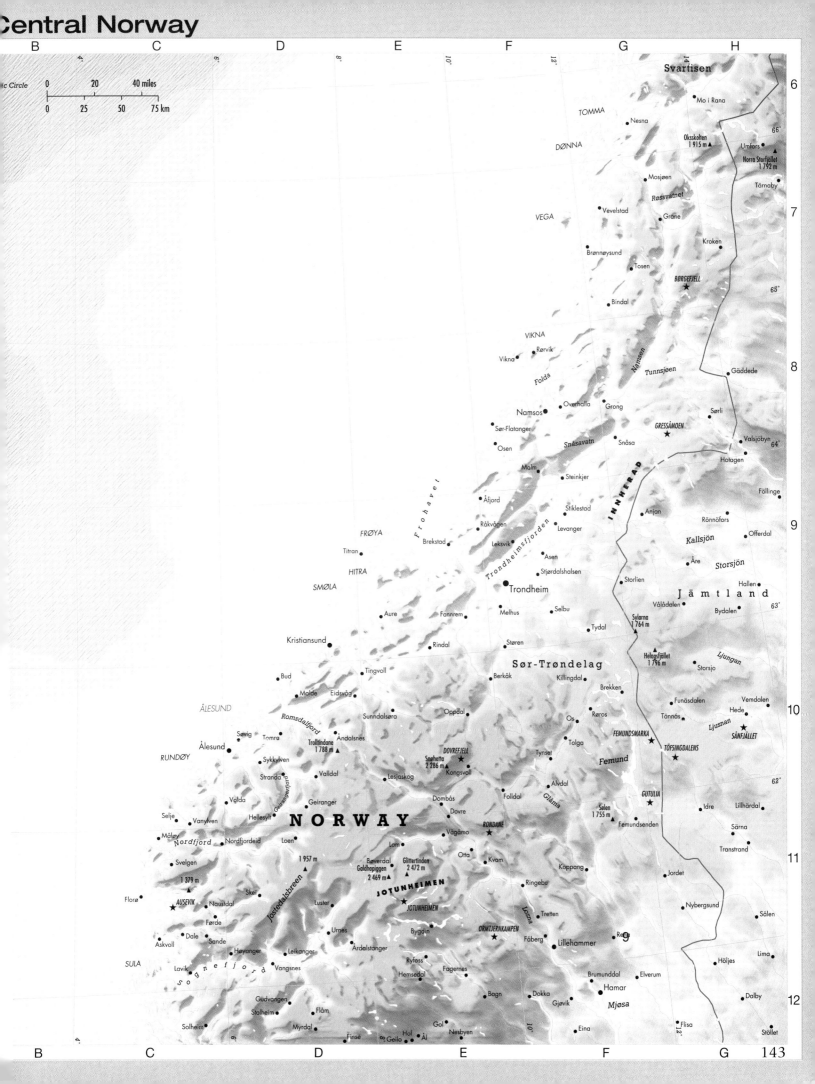

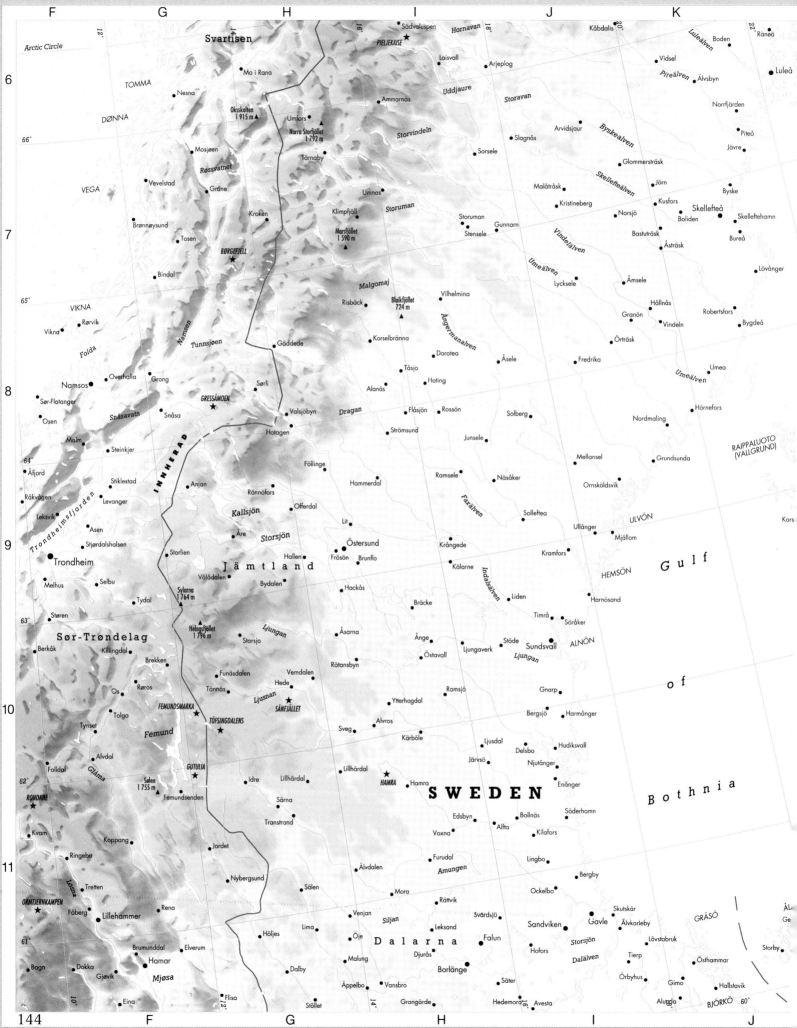

Arctic Circle

Svartisen

TOMMA

Mo i Rana

Nesna

DØNNA

Oksskolten
1 915 m ▲

Umfors

Norra Storfjället
1 792 m

66°

Mosjøen

Røssvatnet

Ammarnäs

Storvindeln

Uddjaure

Hornavan

Laisvall

Arjeplog

Storavan

PIELJEKAISE

Sädvaluspen

Kåbdalis

Luleälven

Boden

Räneå

Vidsel

Älvsbyn

Luleå

6

Piteälven

Norrfjärden

Piteå

Jävre

Arvidsjaur

Byskeälven

Tärnaby

VEGA

Vevelstad

Gräne

Kroken

Umnäs

Klimpfjäll

Storuman

Slagnäs

Sorsele

Storuman

Stensele

Gunnarn

Malåträsk

Kristineberg

Skellefteälven

Norsjö

Jörn

Kusfors

Boliden

Skellefteå

Byske

Skelleftehamn

Brønnøysund

Tosen

Marsfjället
1 590 m ▲

Bastuträsk

Åsträsk

Bureå

Lövånger

7

65°

VIKNA

Bindal

BØRGEFJELL

Malgomaj

Risbäck

Blaikfjället
724 m ▲

Vilhelmina

Ångermanälven

Korselbränna

Hållnäs

Granön

Vindeln

Robertsfors

Bygdeå

Örträsk

Vikna

Rørvik

Folda

Namsen

Tunnsjøen

Gäddede

Dorotea

Tåsjö

Hoting

Åsele

Fredrika

Umeå

Umeälven

Overhalla

Grong

Sørli

GRESSÅMOEN

Valsjöbyn

Dragan

Alanäs

Flåsjön

Rossön

Solberg

Nordmaling

Hörnefors

8

Namsos

Sør-Flatanger

Snåsavatn

Snåsa

Hotagen

Strömsund

Junsele

Mellansel

Grundsunda

RAIPPALUOTO
(VALLGRUND)

Osen

Malm

Steinkjer

Ramsele

Näsåker

Örnsköldsvik

64°

Åfjord

INNHERAD

Följinge

Hammerdal

Faxälven

Sollefteå

Ullånger

ULVÖN

Kors

Råkvågen

Stiklestad

Levanger

Anjan

Rönnöfors

Offerdal

Lit

Kallsjön

Krångede

Kramfors

Mjällom

9

Leksvik

Åsen

Storlien

Åre

Storsjön

Östersund

Frösön

Brunflo

Kälarne

Indalsälven

HEMSÖN

Gulf

Trondheimsfjorden

Stjørdalshalsen

Vålådalen

Bydalen

Hackås

Liden

Harnösand

Trondheim

Jämtland

Melhus

Selbu

Tydal

Sylarna
1 764 m ▲

Bräcke

Ånge

Timrå

Söråker

of

Støren

Helagsfjället
1 796 m ▲

Ljungan

Storsjo

Åsarna

Östavall

Ljungaverk

Stöde

Sundsvall

ALNÖN

63°

Sør-Trøndelag

Berkåk

Killingdal

Brekken

Funäsdalen

Hede

Vemdalen

Rätansbyn

Ramsjä

Gnarp

Bothnia

Os

Røros

SÄNFJÄLLET

Ytterhogdal

Bergsjö

Harmånger

10

Tynset

Tolga

FEMUNDSMARKA

Tännäs

Ljusnan

Sveg

Alvros

Ljusdal

Delsbo

Hudiksvall

Femund

TØFSINGDALENS

Kärböle

Njutånger

Alvdal

GUTULIA

Idre

Lillhärdal

HAMRA

Hamra

Enånger

62°

Folldal

Glåma

Sølen
1 755 m ▲

Femundsenden

Särna

SWEDEN

Edsbyn

Bollnäs

Söderhamn

RONDANE

Transtrand

Voxna

Alfta

Kilafors

Kvam

Koppang

Jordet

Lillhärdal

Furudal

Lingbo

Bergby

11

Ringebu

Nybergsund

Sälen

Älvdalen

Amungen

Ockelbo

Bergby

ORMTJERNKAMPEN

Tretten

Rena

Mora

Rättvik

Svärdsjö

Skutskär

Gävle

Älvkarleby

GRÄSÖ

Storby

Fåberg

Lillehammer

Höljes

Lima

Venjan

Siljan

Leksand

Sandviken

Storsjön

Lövstabruk

Tierp

Östhammar

61°

Bagn

Dokka

Hamar

Elverum

Dalby

Öje

Dalarna

Djurås

Falun

Hofors

Dalälven

Örbyhus

Gimo

Hallstavik

Eina

Gjøvik

Mjøsa

Flisa

Stöllet

Äppelbo

Malung

Vansbro

Grangärde

Hedemora

Borlänge

Säter

Avesta

Aluoja

BJÖRKÖ

60°

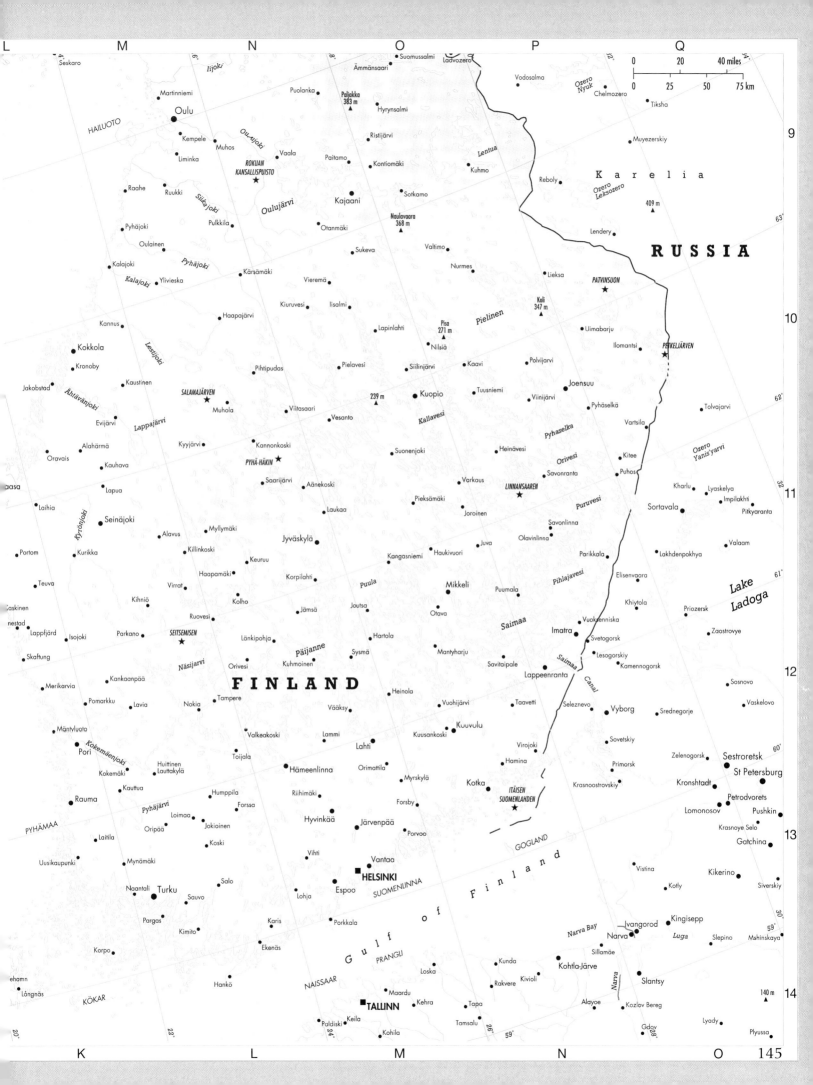

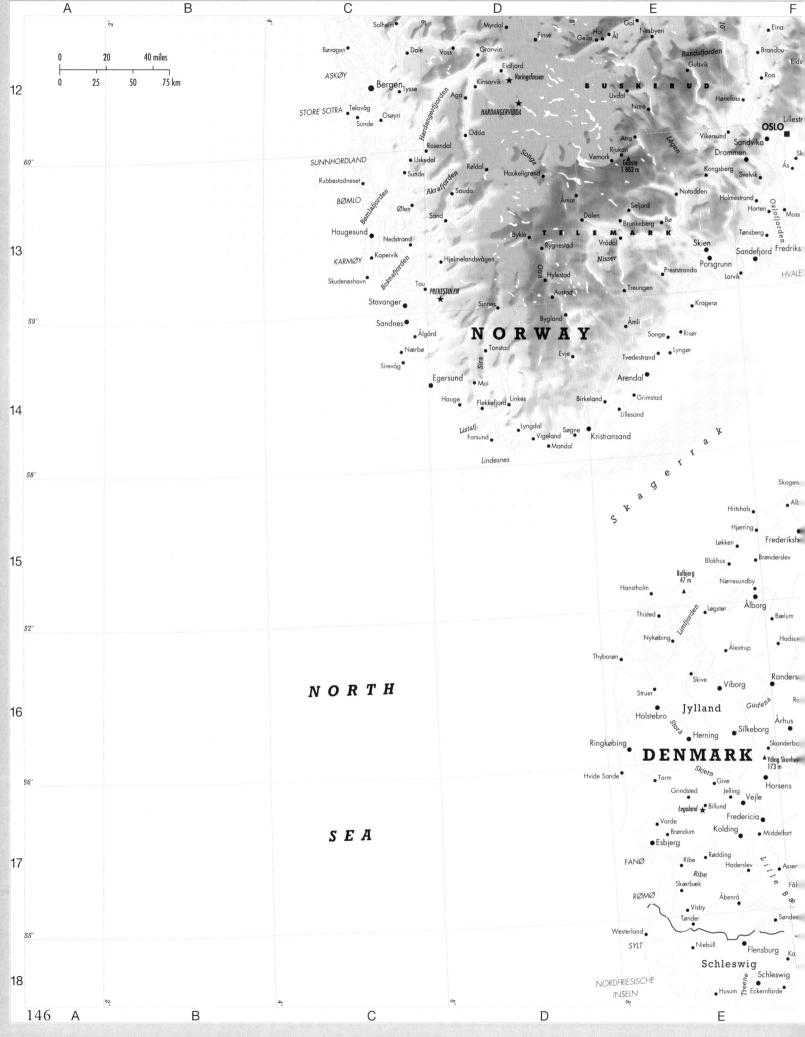

A   B   C   D   E   F

Scale

0   20   40 miles
0   25   50   75 km

12

Solheim
Bøvagen
Dale
Voss
Myrdal
Finse
Geilo
Hol
Ål
Gol
Nesbyen
Eina
Brandbu
Eids
Granvin
Randsfjorden
Gulsvik
Roa
ASKØY
Bergen
Tysse
Eidfjord
Voringsfossen
BUSKERUD
Hønefoss
STORE SOTRA
Telavåg
Aga
Kinsarvik
HARDANGERVIDDA
Uvdal
Nore
Lillestr
OSLO
Osøyri
Sunde
Odda
Vikersund
Sandvika
60°
Rosendal
Atrå
Rjukan
Lågen
Sandefjord
Drammen
SUNNHORDLAND
Uskedal
Røldal
Vemork
Gausta
1 883 m
Kongsberg
Svelvik
Ås
Sk
Rubbestadneset
Sunde
Haukeligrend
Åmot
Seljord
Notodden
Holmestrand
BØMLO
Akrafjorden
Sauda
Dalen
Bø
Horten
Moss
Ølen
Sand
Brunkeberg
Oslofjorden
Haugesund
Bykle
TELEMARK
Skien
Tønsberg
13
Nedstrand
Rygnestad
Vråbal
Sandefjord
Fredriks
KARMØY
Kopervik
Hjelmelandsvågen
Nisser
Porsgrunn
Skudeneshavn
Boknafjorden
Otra
Hylestad
Preststranda
Larvik
HVALE
Tau
Austad
Treungen
Kragerø
Stavanger
PREKESTOLEN
Sinnes
Åmli
Sandnes
Bygland
Songe
Risør
59°
Ålgård
Tonstad
Evje
Lyngør
Nærbø
Tvedestrand
Sirevåg
NORWAY
Arendal
Egersund
Moi
Grimstad
14
Hauge
Birkeland
Lillesand
Flekkefjord
Linkes
Listafj.
Lyngdal
Søgne
Kristiansand
Farsund
Vigeland
Lindesnes
Mandal
Skagen
58°
Skagerrak
Hirtshals
Alb
Hjørring
Frederiksh
Løkken
Brønderslev
Blokhus
15
Bulbjerg
47 m
Nørresundby
Hanstholm
Ålborg
Limfjorden
Løgstør
Bælum
57°
Thisted
Hadsu
Nykøbing
Ålestrup
Thyborøn
NORTH
Skive
Viborg
Randers
Struer
Jylland
Gud'ena
Re
16
Holstebro
Storå
Århus
Herning
Silkeborg
Ringkøbing
Skanderbo
DENMARK
Yding Skovhøj
173 m
Hvide Sande
Tarm
Give
Horsens
56°
Grindsted
Jelling
Vejle
Legoland
Billund
Varde
Fredericia
SEA
Brøndum
Kolding
Middelfart
Esbjerg
FANØ
Ribe
Rødding
Asser
17
Ribe
Haderslev
Lille
Fåb
Skærbæk
Åbenrå
RØMØ
Visby
Sønder
Tønder
55°
Westerland
SYLT
Niebüll
Flensburg
Ka
18
Schleswig
NORDFRIESISCHE
INSELN
Husum
Treene
Eckernförde

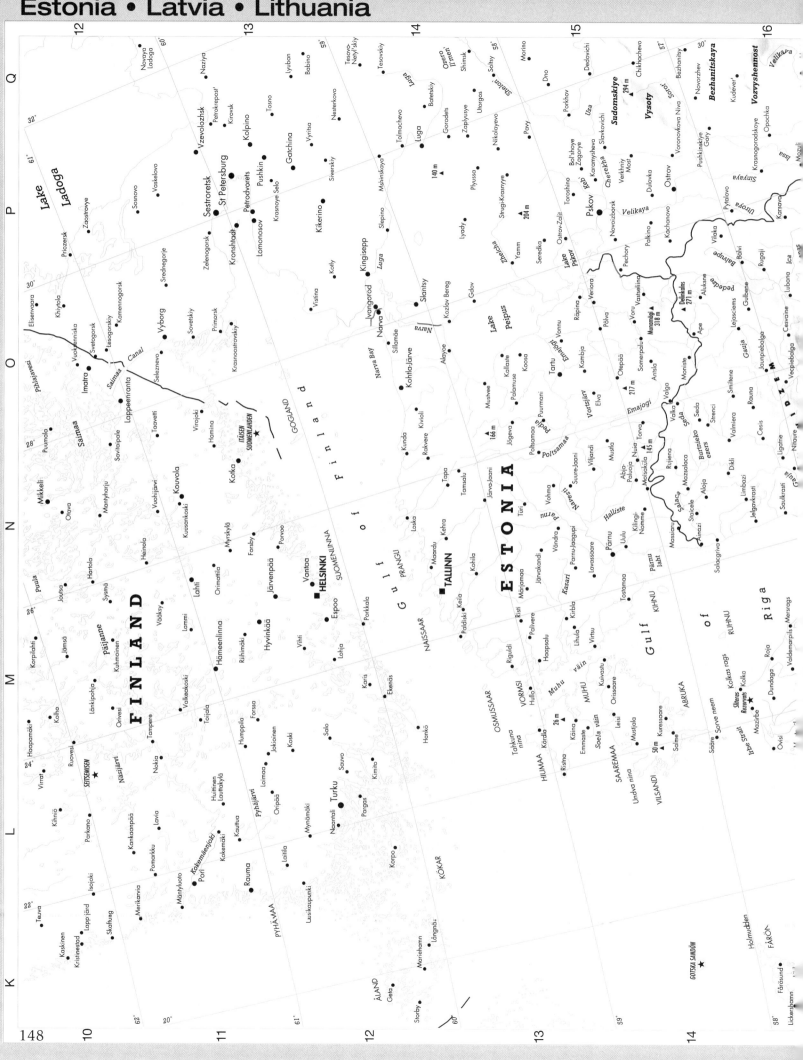

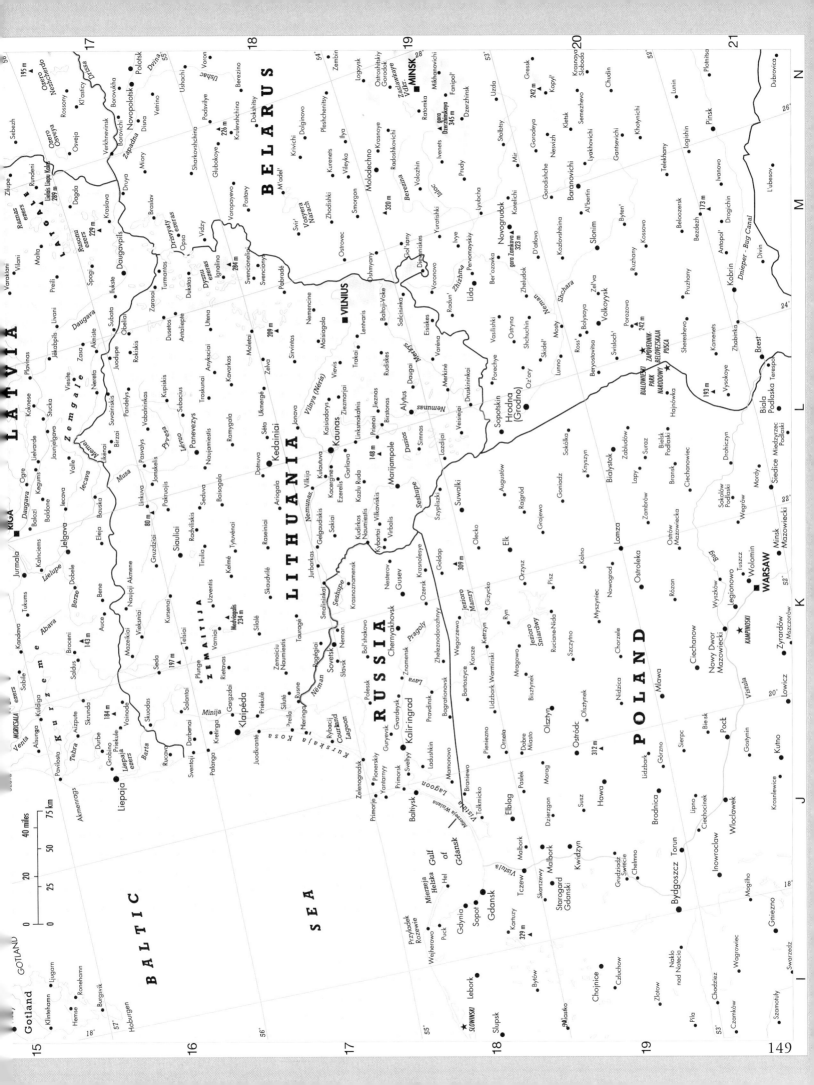

ICELAND

Official name: Republic of Iceland (Lydhveldidh Island)
Area: 39 768 sq miles (103 000 km²)
Capital: Reykjavik
Currency: Icelandic krona
Population: 281 000
Language: Icelandic
Government: Republic
Flag (date created): 1918
National holiday: 17 June
National anthem: O God of our country (Ó Gudh vors lands)

NORWAY

Official name: Kingdom of Norway (Kongeriket Norge)
Area: 125 050 sq miles (323 878 km²)
Capital: Oslo
Currency: Norwegian krone
Population: 4 513 000
Language: Norwegian (Bokmål and Nynorsk)
Government: Constitutional monarchy
Flag (date created): 1821
National holiday: 17 May
National anthem: Yes, we love this country
(Ja, vi elsker dette landet)

SWEDEN

Official name: Kingdom of Sweden (Konungariket Sverige)
Area: 173 732 sq miles (449 964 km²)
Capital: Stockholm
Currency: Swedish krona
Population: 8 833 000
Language: Swedish
Government: Constitutional monarchy
Flag (date created): 1906
National holiday: 6 June
National anthem: You ancient, free and mountainous north
(Du gamla, du fria, du fjällhöga nord)

DENMARK

Official name: Kingdom of Denmark (Kongeriget Danmark)
Area: 16 638 sq miles (43 093 km²)
Capital: Copenhagen
Currency: Danish krone
Population: 5 333 000
Language: Danish
Government: Constitutional monarchy
Flag (date created): 1219
National holiday: 5 June
National anthem: There is a lovely land
(Der er et yndigt land)

FINLAND

Official name: Republic of Finland (Suomen Tasavalta)
Area: 130 559 sq miles (338 148 km²)
Capital: Helsinki
Currency: Euro/
Population: 5 188 000
Language: Finnish
Government: Republic
Flag (date created): 1917
National holiday: 6 December
National anthem: Our land (Vårt land)

ICELAND

ESTONIA

Official name: Republic of Estonia (Eesti Vabariik)
Area: 17 400 sq miles (45 100 km²)
Capital: Tallinn
Currency: Kroon
Population: 1 377 000
Language: Estonian
Government: Republic
Flag (date created): 1991
National holiday: 24 February
National anthem: My country, my pride and joy
(Mu isamaa, mu õnn ja rõõm)

LATVIA

Official name: Republic of Latvia (Latvijas Republika)
Area: 24 900 sq miles (64 500 km²)
Capital: Riga
Currency: Lats
Population: 2 359 000
Language: Latvian
Government: Republic
Flag (date created): 1918
National holiday: 18 November
National anthem: God bless Latvia
(Dievs, sveti Latviju)

LITHUANIA

Official name: Republic of Lithuania (Lietuvos Respublika)
Area: 25 200 sq miles (65 200 km²)
Capital: Vilnius
Currency: Litas
Population: 3 488 000
Language: Lithuanian
Government: Republic
Flag (date created): 1918
National holiday: 16 February
National anthem: Lithuania, our fatherland (Lietuva,
tévyne müsu)

Baltic crossroads

Since the collapse of the Soviet Union in 1991, the Baltic region has changed radically. No longer split between two competing economic systems, it is returning to its historic role as a centre for trade between east and west, north and south. This was a role first glimpsed by the Vikings, then more fully conceived by the Hanseatic League in the Middle Ages. The region's economic potential has always been there – today it is becoming a reality.

SWEDEN

FINLAND

ESTONIA

NORWAY

LATVIA

LITHUANIA

DENMARK

Climate and landscape

The Nordic countries have perhaps the most challenging yet intriguing climate in the whole of Europe, characterised by long dark winters and brilliant summers of short nights. They also contain some of the continent's most unspoilt landscapes.

Contrasting regions

The geography of Scandinavia and the Baltic lands is a fascinating mixture of similarity and diversity. Norway and Denmark feel the full influence of the North Atlantic. Finland, Estonia, Latvia and Lithuania are in thrall to the Baltic Sea. Characteristic features of the entire region include indented coasts, vast forests and an immense number of island-dotted lakes – Sweden has 90 000, Norway160 000, Finland more than 180 000. As for diversity, the most obvious difference is the change from the flat plains of Denmark and the Baltic States, where the highest hills are 1000 ft (305 m) above sea level, to the mountains of northern Sweden and Norway, which reach more than 6500 ft (2000 m). There are important climatic differences, too, partly due to latitude, partly to the effects of the Gulf Stream, which brings warm air and mild weather to the western coasts. The farther north and east you go, the harsher the winters become.

Iceland is a separate geographical entity. Five hundred miles (800 km) from the nearest part of Europe, in the middle of the North Atlantic, this volcanic island is largely covered with glaciers, lava fields and black sand. The ocean brings some mildness to the west, south and east coasts.

Relief
altitude in metres

1500
500
200
0

LENGTH OF BOUNDARIES *(in miles/km)*		
	land	sea
Denmark	42/68	4545/7314
Estonia	393/633	2358/3794
Finland	1567/2521	2858/4600
Iceland	0/0	3100/4988
Latvia	670/1078	330/531
Lithuania	791/1273	67/108
Norway	1580/2542	3624/5832
Sweden	1275/2053	2000/3218

MEAN TEMPERATURES IN CAPITAL CITIES		
	January	July
Copenhagen	0°C/32.0°F	16.2°C/61.2°F
Helsinki	–5.5°C/22.1°F	16.5°C/61.7°F
Oslo	–4.3°C/24.3°F	17.3°C/63.1°F
Reykjavik	–4°C/24.8°F	11.2°C/52.2°F
Riga	–7°C/19.4°F	16.5°C/61.7°F
Stockholm	3.2°C/37.8°F	18°C/64.4°F
Tallinn	–7°C/19.4°F	16°C/60.8°F
Vilnius	–8°C/17.6°F	17.5°C/63.5°F

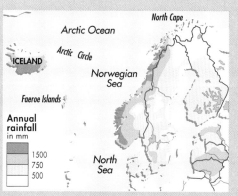

Annual rainfall in mm

1500
750
500

Hardwood forest
Mixed forest
Coniferous forest
Tundra
High altitude vegetation

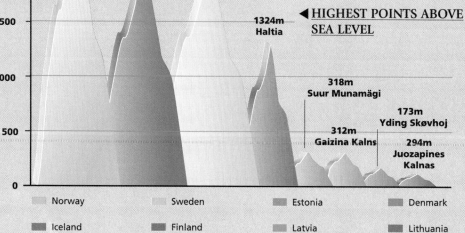

◀ **HIGHEST POINTS ABOVE SEA LEVEL**

2469m Galdhøpiggen
2119m Öraefajökull
2111m Kebnekaise
1324m Haltia
318m Suur Munamägi
312m Gaizina Kalns
173m Yding Skøvhoj
294m Juozapines Kalnas

Norway   Sweden   Estonia   Denmark
Iceland   Finland   Latvia   Lithuania

Rising lands

The last Ice Age ended about 10 000 years ago. Before that time the whole of Scandinavia lay under the weight of a vast ice sheet that was more than 1 mile (1.6 km) thick. As the ice melted, the land was freed from this crushing weight and it started rising, with the lowest-lying regions emerging from the sea. This process is far from over: in the most northern areas, where the movement is the greatest, the land is still rising at a rate of 3.3 ft (1 m) every 100 years. The Baltic Sea, which is the youngest sea in the world, is therefore likely to turn into a series of lakes over the course of time.

Population and society

The Scandinavian model of society is one that many others envy – not least their Baltic neighbours, who are only now emerging from a traumatic half-century of Soviet rule.

LIFE EXPECTANCY

	men	women
Denmark	74	79
Estonia	65	76
Finland	74	81
Iceland	77	81
Latvia	62	74
Lithuania	67	77
Norway	76	82
Sweden	77	82

UNEVEN DISTRIBUTION OF POPULATION

With the exception of Denmark, the Nordic countries tend to be sparsely populated. Most people live in the south, where the climate is more temperate than it is in the mountainous, densely forested north. Another factor affecting the distribution of population is the gradual emptying of the countryside, which began in the late 19th century with the rapid growth of industry, and has accelerated more recently with the development of the tertiary sector (service industries). Today, all the Nordic countries are predominantly urban. In Denmark, one-twelfth of the population lives in Copenhagen, the capital. Iceland is an extreme example: its total area is 39 768 sq miles (103 000 km²) and, of its 281 000 inhabitants, 40 per cent live in the capital, Reykjavik.

Population density

Denmark	318.51 per sq mile (123.75/km²)	Latvia	94.7 per sq mile (36.5/km²)
Estonia	79.13 per sq mile (30.53/km²)	Lithuania	138.4 per sq mile (53.49/km²)
Finland	39.7 per sq mile (15.3/km²)	Norway	36.0 per sq mile (13.9/km²)
Iceland	7.0 per sq mile (2.7/km²)	Sweden	50.8 per sq mile (19.6/km²)

The Sami: a special minority

Most countries are a hotchpotch of peoples and cultures, around whom state boundaries have been drawn in ways that make little sense. Scandinavia is unusual in that cultural, national and state identities make an almost perfect fit. Sweden's population is 94 per cent Swedish, Iceland's is 96 per cent Icelandic, Denmark's 97 per cent Danish, and so on. The only true ethnic minority are the Sami, whose homeland stretches across the national boundaries of Finland, Sweden and Norway, and who are physiologically different from the Nordic archetype: they tend to be short and dark-haired, with prominent cheekbones and oriental eyes.

The Sami population is around 60 000, and they live in an area that stretches from Trondheim to the easternmost point of the Kola peninsula. Their way of life has changed enormously in the space of a few generations, from a simple, nomadic existence to one where the latest comforts and technology are enjoyed. Most Sami are bilingual – a sure sign of openness to the outside world. Their unspoilt territory, with its mountains, vast snowfields, northern lights and midnight sun, is proving increasingly attractive to tourists.

Ageing populations

Although the Baltic States are 'young' countries, the region's population is growing older as a whole. This creates a problem, common to all developed societies, of renewing their human stock. One solution, immigration, is highly controversial. Until recently, Scandinavia had some of the most ethnically, culturally and linguistically homogeneous populations in the world. It is only in the past 20 years, with the arrival of economic and political refugees from abroad, that the situation has begun to change. This has led to a fear among some native Scandinavians of losing their cultural identity – and with that fear, a shift from welcoming immigrants to treating them with hostility.

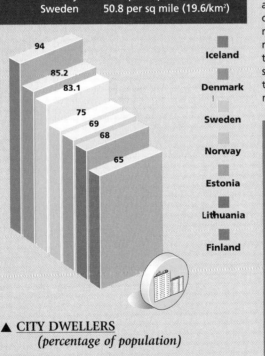

94	Iceland
85.2	Denmark
83.1	
75	Sweden
69	
68	Norway
65	Estonia
	Lithuania
	Finland

▲ CITY DWELLERS
(percentage of population)

RELIGION

When the 16th century Reform movement swept through the Roman Catholic Church, the Scandinavian countries were quick to convert. Protestantism remains the majority religion, with the Lutheran Church as the state religion in Denmark and Norway. The Swedish Lutheran Church was disestablished in 2000, and 85 per cent of the population now belong to the Church of Sweden. Of the Baltic States, Lithuania was least affected by the Reformation and is 80 per cent Catholic. Latvia is 23 per cent Lutheran and 20 per cent Catholic, and Estonia is predominantly Lutheran.

Lutherans in Northern Europe
(percentage of population)

Denmark	87.7 %	Iceland	95.8 %
Finland	86.2 %	Norway	87.8 %

AGE PYRAMID ▼

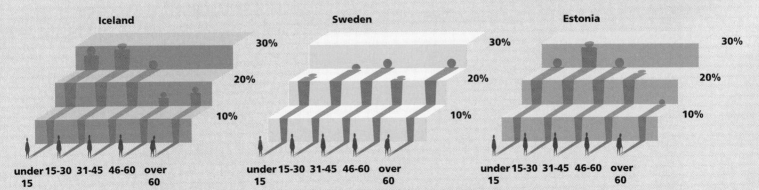

Iceland

Sweden

Estonia

under 15 · 15-30 · 31-45 · 46-60 · over 60

COMPOSITION OF THE POPULATION ▼ IN THE BALTIC STATES

Multicultural societies
The Baltic States have more diverse populations than their Scandinavian neighbours.

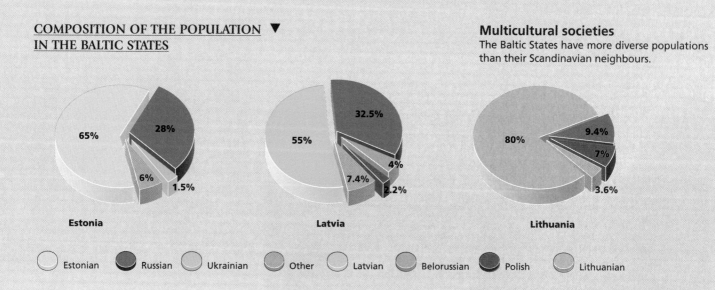

Estonia — 65%, 28%, 6%, 1.5%

Latvia — 55%, 32.5%, 4%, 7.4%, 2.2%

Lithuania — 80%, 9.4%, 7%, 3.6%

Estonian — Russian — Ukrainian — Other — Latvian — Belorussian — Polish — Lithuanian

Schools inspired by Rousseau

The ideas of the 18th-century French philosopher Jean-Jacques Rousseau have had a lasting influence on the Scandinavian educational system. Rousseau, one of the first Romantics, believed that human beings have a natural desire to be good and to learn. In Scandinavian schools, 'Give children time' is the governing principle: time to play, to dream, to grow. This philosophy is visibly reflected in the schools themselves, with their comfortable furniture, indoor plants, play-grounds, sports facilities, theatres, swimming pools, workshops and computer rooms.

Continuing education

Despite the fact that they are thinly populated, the Nordic countries are very active culturally. Music groups, choirs, concerts, festivals, art galleries and museums, cinema and theatre, are all immensely popular. If you look at the number of books published each year relative to the size of population, Iceland is the most literate country in the world: the figure there is 1 title per 188 inhabitants – three times as high as Great Britain; six times as high as France.

The Scandinavian commitment to culture can best be seen in adult education. People enrol on evening courses subsidised by the government to develop their knowledge and skills, or to gain extra qualifications. One in three takes up these opportunities for lifelong learning.

EXPENDITURE ON HEALTH ▶ AND EDUCATION
(as a percentage of GDP)

Health and equality

The consensus that exists in Scandinavian society, across the political spectrum, rests on two basic values: health and equality. By avoiding Utopian ideas, and using a great deal of common sense, the Nordic nations have managed to create harmonious societies where the equitable distribution of wealth allows everyone to share the benefits of a successful economy. Since the early 20th century, the poor, the sick and the disabled have been cared for with a generosity that has made the Scandinavian public health system the envy of the world. Only in recent years have many other European countries caught up with them. Yet the fact remains that prosperity creates its own health problems: lack of exercise, over-eating and stress make cardiovascular disease the greatest killer in Scandinavia, as in the rest of the developed world.

INFANT MORTALITY *(per 1000 births)*			
Denmark	4.2	Latvia	10.9
Estonia	8.1	Lithuania	7.9
Finland	4.2	Norway	3.9
Iceland	2.4	Sweden	3.2

NUMBER OF INHABITANTS PER DOCTOR			
Denmark	294	Latvia	357
Estonia	333	Lithuania	250
Finland	323	Norway	357
Iceland	307	Sweden	323

NUMBER OF STUDENTS IN HIGHER EDUCATION *(per 100 000 inhabitants)*			
Denmark	3301	Latvia	2341
Estonia	3105	Lithuania	2390
Finland	4355	Norway	4118
Iceland	2636	Sweden	3127

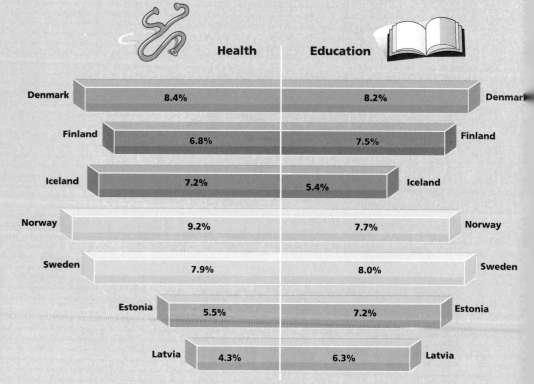

Health — Education

	Health	Education
Denmark	8.4%	8.2%
Finland	6.8%	7.5%
Iceland	7.2%	5.4%
Norway	9.2%	7.7%
Sweden	7.9%	8.0%
Estonia	5.5%	7.2%
Latvia	4.3%	6.3%

Work and the economy

Scandinavian prosperity is based on the successful exploitation of know-how, design, quality and innovation. Norway's economy has had a boost from the discovery of oil in the North Sea. Meanwhile, the Baltic States, a decade after liberation, are now competing in the global economy and preparing to join the European Union.

Towards a new unity?

For much of their history, the countries that lie around the Baltic Sea have maintained a close but competitive relationship. It was only when the Nazis invaded the region in 1939, opening up the way to Soviet domination, that a deep split was created. Denmark, Norway and Sweden saw the development of prosperous industrial economies coupled with all the services and infrastructures of an effective welfare state. Estonia, Latvia and Lithuania languished under the command economy of the Soviet Union, with poorly run industries, inefficient agricultural production and a corrupt bureaucracy. Neutral Finland, meanwhile, trod its own quiet path towards prosperity.

The collapse of the Soviet Union in 1991 meant the end of this division and the Baltic region became a free trade area once again, though the effects of the 50-year separation remain.

GROSS DOMESTIC PRODUCT (GDP) ▲
in order of size
(per inhabitant, in US dollars)

Norway 38,852
Denmark 30,433
Iceland 30,249
Sweden 25,733
Finland 23,419
Estonia 3,631
Lithuania 3,239
Latvia 3,052

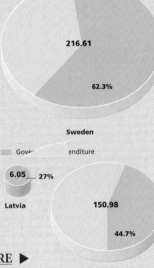

Sweden 216.61 — 62.3%
Government expenditure
Latvia 6.05 — 27%
Norway 150.98 — 44.7%

GOVERNMENT EXPENDITURE ▶
(as a percentage of GNP in billions of US dollars)

WOMEN IN PUBLIC LIFE AND THE ECONOMY

In Denmark, Sweden and Norway the right of succession to the throne belongs to the oldest child, male or female, of the reigning monarch. Equality of the sexes goes back a long way in Scandinavia. Divorce by mutual consent became legal in 1790 in the united kingdom of Norway and Denmark. The first women to take part in the Olympic Games, in Athens in 1896, were from Denmark – they were called 'Danish princesses' by the newspapers of the time. In 1906 women were granted the vote in Finland. In 1924 Nina Bang became minister of education in the Danish government, the first-ever female cabinet minister in a democratic state. Today, women are a powerful presence in the job market in Scandinavia at every level.

Percentage of women in work

Denmark	46.4%	Latvia	47.0%
Estonia	50.0%	Lithuania	48.4%
Finland	47.0%	Norway	44.2%
Iceland	46.6%	Sweden	48.0%

SOURCES OF INFORMATION
(per 1000 inhabitants)

	daily newspapers	radios	televisions
Denmark	311	1035	538
Estonia	174	673	361
Finland	455	996	504
Iceland	535	791	335
Latvia	247	651	460
Lithuania	93	385	383
Norway	590	798	427
Sweden	445	879	470

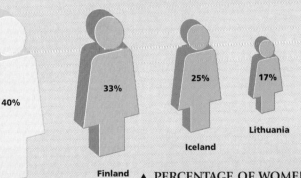

Sweden 40%
Finland 33%
Iceland 25%
Lithuania 17%

▲ PERCENTAGE OF WOMEN MEMBERS OF PARLIAMENT

Information highways and byways

The Scandinavians are great readers of newspapers: 80 per cent of homes take one daily. The first Scandinavian newspaper was printed in Denmark in 1666 – and it was written entirely in verse! Today, the national press faces tough competition both from regional newspapers and the new media. Radio and TV have been around for decades, of course, but hundreds of new stations and channels have sprung up in the past ten years, all clamouring for the public's money, time and attention. The Internet has made a huge impact, too: recent surveys of the use of information technology around the world have placed Norway, Sweden and Denmark as the top three, ahead of Germany, Japan, Britain and the USA.

NUMBER OF TOURISTS PER YEAR

Denmark	2 100 000	Latvia	490 000
Estonia	1 100 000	Lithuania	1 000 000
Finland	2 700 000	Norway	4 416 000
Iceland	303 000	Sweden	2 612 000

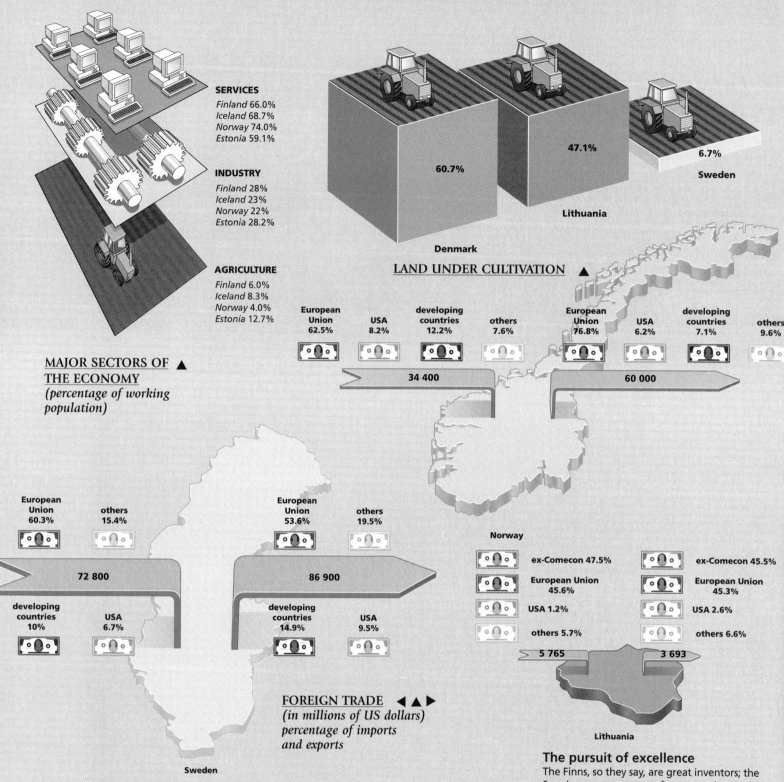

SERVICES
Finland 66.0%
Iceland 68.7%
Norway 74.0%
Estonia 59.1%

INDUSTRY
Finland 28%
Iceland 23%
Norway 22%
Estonia 28.2%

AGRICULTURE
Finland 6.0%
Iceland 8.3%
Norway 4.0%
Estonia 12.7%

**MAJOR SECTORS OF ▲
THE ECONOMY**
*(percentage of working
population)*

LAND UNDER CULTIVATION ▲

Denmark 60.7%
Lithuania 47.1%
Sweden 6.7%

Denmark

European Union 62.5%	USA 8.2%	developing countries 12.2%	others 7.6%

34 400

European Union 76.8%	USA 6.2%	developing countries 7.1%	others 9.6%

60 000

Sweden

European Union 60.3%	others 15.4%		

72 800

developing countries 10%	USA 6.7%		

European Union 53.6%	others 19.5%		

86 900

developing countries 14.9%	USA 9.5%		

Norway

	ex-Comecon 47.5%		ex-Comecon 45.5%
	European Union 45.6%		European Union 45.3%
	USA 1.2%		USA 2.6%
	others 5.7%		others 6.6%

5 765   3 693

Lithuania

FOREIGN TRADE ◀ ▲ ▶
*(in millions of US dollars)
percentage of imports
and exports*

TOTAL ROAD NETWORKS

Denmark 44 479 miles (71 579 km)
Estonia   10 209 miles (16 430 km)
Finland   48 407 miles (77 900 km)
Iceland   7880 miles   (12 682 km)
Latvia   14 194 miles (22 843 km)
Lithuania 45 766 miles (73 650 km)
Norway   56 473 miles (90 880 km)
Sweden   131 853 miles (212 188 km)

Scandinavia united

A glance at the map shows the difficulty of building roads in Scandinavia. For thousands of years, boats were the principal means of travel and transportation. More recently, bridges and tunnels have been built almost everywhere. In 1998, the eastern and western halves of Denmark, separated by the 10 mile (16 km) Store Baelt Strait, were joined by a bridge that was the longest in Europe and the second longest in the world. In the summer of 2000 another 10 mile (16 km) bridge was opened across the Øresund, linking Denmark with Sweden. Projects such as the Øresund bridge are the product of close economic and political ties between the Nordic countries. Another example is SAS (Scandinavian Airlines System), run jointly by Sweden, Norway and Denmark, with its headquarters at Kastrup Airport (Copenhagen), one of the fastest-growing air-transportation hubs in Europe.

The pursuit of excellence

The Finns, so they say, are great inventors; the Swedes are great manufacturers; the Danes great salesmen. Whatever the truth of this old saying, it points to the secret of Scandinavian economic success: imagination at the heart of enterprise, insistence on quality of manufacture, and a sound business sense.

NUMBER OF AIRPORTS

Denmark	28	Latvia	36
Estonia	5	Lithuania	25
Finland	69	Norway	67
Iceland	12	Sweden	147

Index

Page numbers in *italics* denote illustrations. Alphanumeric references in brackets are the co-ordinates for places in the map section, pages 140-9.

159

Acknowledgments

Abbreviations: t = top, m = middle, b = bottom, l = left, r = right.

Front cover: *Lofoten Islands, Norway:* DIAF/Y. Travert.
Back cover: *The old port of Nyhavn, Denmark:* HOA QUI/R. Manin.

Pages: 4/5: ALTITUDE/P. Bertrand; 6: COSMOS/SPL/Baum & Angus; 8t: HOA QUI/P. Bourseiller; 8b: HOA QUI/P. Bertrand; 9b: HOA QUI/P. Body; 10t: ALTITUDE/Y. Arthus-Bertrand; 10b: GAMMA; 11: ALTITUDE/Y. Arthus-Bertrand; 12t: ALTITUDE/ F. Jourdan; 12b: HOA QUI/C. Boivieux; 13b: ALTITUDE/Y. Arthus-Bertrand; 14t: HOA QUI/P. Bertrand; 14b: ALTITUDE/F. Jourdan; 15: HOA QUI/P. Bourseiller; 16t: HOA QUI/P. Body; 16m: GAMMA/R. Gaillarde; 16b: RAPHO/P. Kock; 17t: HOA QUI/C. Boivieux; 17m: RAPHO/G. Gerster; 17b: GAMMA/ E. Brissaud; 18: GAMMA/R. Gaillarde; 19t: BRIDGEMAN ART LIBRARY/*William of Normandy crosses the English channel*, Bayeux Tapestry/Tapestry Museum, Bayeux; 19m: GAMMA/R. Gaillarde; 19bl: EXPLORER/J.-L. Bohin/Museum of History, Stockholm; 19br: BRIDGEMAN ART LIBRARY/*Knut the Great,* in *Liber Kegum Antiquorum Regum,* 1321/British Library, London; 20tl: GAMMA/ R. Gaillarde; 20tr: HOA QUI/S. Grandadam; 20bl: EXPLORER/ A. Thomas/*Madonna of Vilkau,* 13th century/Museum of History, Stockholm; 20br: BRIDGEMAN ART LIBRARY/*Valdemar IV at Visby,* by Carl Gustav Hellqvist, 1882/Nationalmuseum, Stockholm; 21t: EXPLORER/C. Boivieux; 22t: BRIDGEMAN ART LIBRARY/*Gustave I Vasa receives the translation of the Bible,* by Julius Kronberg, 1870/Nationalmuseum, Stockholm; 22m: BRIDGEMAN ART LIBRARY/*Erik XIV,* by Domenicus Verwilt, 16th century/Nationalmuseum, Stockholm; 22b: BRIDGEMAN ART LIBRARY/*The Battle of Nordlingen II,* by Pieter Meulener, 17th century/Nationalmuseum, Stockholm; 23tl: RMN/ H. Lawandowski/*Queen Christina of Sweden and her court* (detail), by Louis Dumesnil, 17th century/Musée du Château, Versailles; 23tr: HARLINGUE-VIOLLET/*Charles XII leads his army into battle*/Bibliothèque nationale de France, Paris; 23b: HOA QUI/ C. Boivieux; 24t: BRIDGEMAN ART LIBRARY/*The arrival of Charles XIV,* by Axel Frederick Cederholm, 1818/Nationalmuseum, Stockholm; 24m: BRIDGEMAN ART LIBRARY/*Destruction of the Danish fleet at Copenhagen,* by Thomas Withcombe, 1816/The Stapelton Collection; 24b: RMN/*Jean-Baptiste Bernadotte in 1804,* by Joseph Nicolas Jouy, 1852/Musée du Château, Versailles; 25t: RMN/*Gateway to Dalby at Skåne,* by Hugo Frederick Salmson, 19th century/Musée d'Orsay, Paris; 25mt: RMN/*Coat of arms of the crown prince of Sweden and Norway*/Musée de la Voiture, Compiègne, France; 25mb: BRIDGEMAN ART LIBRARY/*Jean Sibelius,* by John Cooper, 20th century/Philips, The International Fine Arts Auctioneers; 25b: KIPA/Coll. CAT'S/Film *Pelle the Conqueror,* by Bille August, 1987; 26t, ml: HARLINGUE-VIOLLET; 26mr: KEYSTONE; 26b: COSMOS/B. & C. Alexander; 27t: GAMMA/Suomen; 27bl: CORBIS SYGMA/*L'Illustration;* 27br: CORBIS SYGMA/G. Pocius; 28-29: DIAF/R. Mazin; 30: COSMOS/G. Buthaud; 32: HOA QUI/C. Boivieux; 33t: HOA QUI/NF/Serena; 33m: COSMOS/VISUM/W. Steche; 34t: COSMOS/ B. & C. Alexander; 34b, 35tl: ALTITUDE/Y. Arthus-Bertrand; 35tr: COSMOS/ANZENBERGER/G. Hug-Fleck; 35b: GAMMA/ E.G. Hrafnsson; 36t: EXPLORER/A. Rainon; 36b: HOA QUI/ J.-B. Leroux; 37t: EXPLORER/P. Roy; 37m: HOA QUI/F. Latreille; 37b, 38, 39b: HOA QUI/P. Body; 39t: HOA QUI/P. Bertrand; 40t: HOA QUI/ZEFA/Ebeling; 40b: HOA QUI/P. Body; 41t: COSMOS/B. & C. Alexander; 41b: HOA QUI/F. Latreille; 42tl, tr: ALTITUDE /P. Bertrand; 42b: HOA QUI/P. Body; 43b: HOA QUI/C. Boivieux; 44t: BIOS/OKAPIA/Nevers; 44ml: DIAF/P. Cheuva; 44mr: BIOS/Hubert-Klein; 44b: BIOS/ F. Bruemmer; 45t, mr: BIOS/P. Henry; 45ml: BIOS/P. Weimann; 45b: BIOS/B. Lundberg; 46tl: ALTITUDE/Y. Arthus-Bertrand; 46tr: CORBIS SYGMA/J.-P. Amet; 46b: HOA QUI/Jouan-Rius; 47m: HOA QUI/C. Boivieux; 47b: HOA QUI/C. Sappa; 48l: COSMOS/B. & C. Alexander; 48r: COSMOS/SPL/P. Parviainen; 49tr: COSMOS/SPL/S. Fraser; 49br: ASK IMAGES/Aven; 50: HOA QUI/C. Boivieux; 52tl: COSMOS/G. Buthaud; 52tr: HOA QUI/ C. Boivieux; 52b: COSMOS/ANZENBERGER/G. Thoni; 53tr: HOA QUI/T. Perrin; 53b: HOA QUI/C. Sappa; 54t, m: HOA QUI/C. Boivieux; 54b: HOA QUI/P. Bertrand; 55t: HOA QUI/ C. Boivieux; 55b: HOA QUI/C. Sappa; 56t: ALTITUDE/Y. Arthus-Bertrand; 56m: DIAF/Pratt-Pries; 56b: GAMMA/LIAISON/B. Stern; 57t: CORBIS SYGMA/R. Reuter; 57m: CORBIS SYGMA/D. Van der Zwalm; 57b: ASK IMAGES/E. Doumic; 58l: DIAF/EURASIA PRESS; 58r: GAMMA/A. Ribeiro; 59t: ASK IMAGES/M. Cristofori; 59b: RAPHO/G. Sioen; 60t, b: with the authorisation of LEGO; 60m: CORBIS SYGMA/J.-P. Amet; 61t: CORBIS SYGMA/D. Van der Zwalm; 61m: GAMMA/LIAISON/B. Stern; 61b: GAMMA/ C. Hires; 62t: CORBIS SYGMA/R. Bossu; 62b: GAMMA/SCAN FOTO; 63t: HOA QUI/Jouan-Rius; 63m, b: GAMMA/E. Baitel;

64: HOA QUI/P. Bertrand; 66t: HOA QUI/C. Sappa; 66m: HOA QUI/B. Gérard; 66b: HOA QUI/ZEFA/Damm; 67: HOA QUI/NF/Serena; 68t: HOA QUI/R. Manin; 68m: DIAF/Pratt-Pries; 68b: DIAF/R. Mazin; 69b: HOA QUI/C. Boivieux; 70tl: ASK IMAGES/J. Viesti; 70tr: HOA QUI/LIAISON INTERNATIONAL/ P. Feibert; 70m: HOA QUI/T. Perrin; 70b: DIAF/J.-P. Garcin; 71: COSMOS/AURORA/J. Azel; 72tl: HOA QUI/P. Body; 72tr: HOA QUI/P. Bertrand; 72b: GAMMA/*Figaro Magazine;* 73b: HOA QUI/P. Bertrand; 74/79: HOA QUI/B. Wojtek; 74t, b: DIAF/Y. Travert; 74mt: DIAF/Pratt-Pries; 74mb: HOA QUI/ B. Wojtek; 75tl: HOA QUI/S. Grandadam; 75tr: HOA QUI/ B. Wojtek; 75bl: EXPLORER/P. Wysocki; 75br: DIAF/Y. Travert; 76tl: HOA QUI/P. Body; 76mtl, mtm: HOA QUI/S. Grandadam; 76mtr, mtl: HOA QUI/B. Wojtek; 76mbr: HOA QUI/C. Boivieux; 76br: DIAF/Y. Travert; 77rl: HOA QUI/B. Perousse; 77tr: EXPLORER/P. Wysocki; 77bl: HOA QUI/C. Boisvieux; 77bm: DIAF/Pratt-Pries; 77br: HOA QUI/C. Sappa; 78tl, tr: HOA QUI/B. Wojtek; 78mt: DIAF/Pratt-Pries; 78mb: EXPLORER/ P. Wysocki; 78bl: HOA QUI/P. Body; 78br: HOA QUI/ S. Grandadam; 79tl: HOA QUI/C. Boisvieux; 79tr: EXPLORER/ W. Rozbroj; 79m: HOA QUI/B. Wojtek/Statues by Carl Milles, outdoor museum on the island of Lidingo/© by ADAGP, Paris 2000; 79bl: HOA QUI/B. Wojtek/architect: Svante BERG; 79br: EXPLORER/W. Rozbroj; 80: HOA QUI/P. Bertrand; 81tl, tr: CORBIS SYGMA/B. Annebicque; 81b: DIAF/B. Regent; 82t: ORESUND/VISION/J. Kofod Winther; 82b: DIAF/Pratt-Pries; 83t: ASK IMAGES/Aven; 83bl, br: HOA QUI/C. Sappa; 84t: HOA QUI/C. Boivieux; 84mr: HOA QUI/C. Sappa; 84b: HOA QUI/ E. Bernager; 85t: HOA QUI/C. Boivieux; 85m: HOA QUI/ C. Sappa; 86l: HOA QUI/T. Perrin; 86m: HOA QUI/C. Boivieux; 86r: HOA QUI/P. Body; 87tl: COSMOS/VISUM/J. Noorow; 88: HOA QUI/P. Bertrand; 90tl: RAPHO/P. Neyrat; 90tr: COSMOS/ B. & C. Alexander; 90m: COSMOS/VISUM/T. Tomaszewski; 91r: ASK IMAGES/L. Sechi; 91b: CORBIS SYGMA/P. Le Segretain; 92t: ASK IMAGES/TRIP/T. Noorits; 92m: CORBIS SYGMA/Ephymov; 92b: HOA QUI/C. Boivieux; 93t: GAMMA/PRESSENS BILD AB; 93m: GAMMA/E. Baitel; 93b: ASK IMAGES/TRIP/B. Turner; 94t, m: COSMOS/VISUM/T. Tomaszewski; 94b: CORBIS SYGMA/P. Caron; 95t: CORBIS SYGMA/B. Annebicque; 95m: RAPHO/H. Donnezan; 96t: ASK IMAGES/Aven; 96m: COSMOS/P. Menzel; 96b: CORBIS SYGMA/J. Van Hasselt; 97t: COSMOS/WOODFIN CAMP/H. Sykes; 97m: COSMOS/ P. Menzel; 98t: HOA QUI/J. Durieux; 98m: COSMOS/VISUM/ J. Modrow; 98b, 99m: HOA QUI/P. Body; 99t: HOA QUI/ P. Bertrand; 100t: RAPHO/H. Donnezan; 100m: ASK IMAGES/ Aven; 100b: HOA QUI/P. Bertrand; 101tl: DIAF/G. Simeone; 101tr: HOA QUI/C. Boivieux; 101b: DIAF/R. Mazin; 102t: CORBIS SYGMA/Pasquini; 102m: RAPHO/K. Hart; 102b: CORBIS SYGMA/ B. Annebicque; 103l: COSMOS/ANZENBERGER/G. Ihoni; 103r: HAO QUI/C. Sappa; 104t: COSMOS/B. & C. Alexander; 104bl: CORBIS SYGMA/J.-P. Amet; 104br: CORBIS SYGMA/ F. Pagani; 105tr: HOA QUI/J. Durieux; 105b: HOA QUI/C. Sappa; 106t: COSMOS/ANZENBERGER/R. Riegler; 106bl: COSMOS/ B. & C. Alexander; 106br, 107ml: HOA QUI/C. Boivieux; 107mr: DIAF/G. Simeone; 108: HOA QUI/P. Bourseiller; 110t: CORBIS SYGMA/D. Fineman; 110b: VANDYSTADT/ ALL-SPORT/C. Brunskill; 111t: AFP/EPA-PRESSENBILD/ S. Almqvist; 111m: GAMMA/*Figaro Magazine;* 111b: COSMOS/ B. & C. Alexander; 112tm, m: HOA QUI/C. Boivieux; 112b: GAMMA/PRESSENS BILD AB; 113tl: COSMOS/IMPACT/ P. Cavendish; 113tr: DIAF/Pratt-Pries; 113b: HOA QUI/ALTITUDE/ P. Bertrand; 114tl, bl: HOA QUI/C. Boivieux; 114m: CORBIS SYGMA/Pasquini; 115t: HOA QUI/J.-D. Joubert; 115m: HOA QUI/P. Body; 115b: COSMOS/B. & C. Alexander; 116: ASK IMAGES/T. Nectoux; 118tl, b: HOA QUI/P. Body; 118tr: RAPHO/ G. Gerster; 119t: DIAF/Pratt-Pries; 119b: HOA QUI/S. Gourdin; 120t: DIAF/EURASIA PRESS; 120b, 121t, m: DIAF/G. Simeone; 121bl: DIAF/EURASIA PRESS; 121brr: DIAF/J.-P. Garcin; 122t: COSMOS/Snowdon-Hoyer; 122m: HOA QUI/C. Boivieux; 122b: COSMOS/ANZENBERGER/F. Giaccone; 123t: COSMOS/ F. Perri; 123m: HOA QUI/P. Bertrand; 123br: HOA QUI/ C. Boivieux; 124m: HOA QUI/S. Grandadam/*Mascot for movements in Art, 1960,* by Carl Fredrik Reuterswärd/Museum of Modern Art, Stockholm; 124b: HOA QUI/P. Body; 125t: DIAF/ Y. Travert/*Two Piece Reclinig Figure no. 5,* by Henry Moore, 1963-4/Museum of Louisiana, with permission from the Henry Moore Foundation; 125m: DIAF/R. Mazin/Museum of Dolungarvik; 125b: ASK IMAGES/M. Cristofori/Temporary exhibition of human rights, designed by the architect Lars Hostrup, National Museum of Copenhague; 126: EXPLORER/ E. Chrétien; 127t: HOA QUI/C. Boisvieux; 127m: HOA QUI/

C. Sappa; 127b: ASK IMAGES/TRIP/T. Noorits; 128: EXPLORER/ C. Boisvieux; 130t: COSMOS/VISUM/J. Modrow; 130m: CORBIS SYGMA/Davies & Davies; 130b: HOA QUI/P. Bertrand; 131tr: BRIDGEMAN ART LIBRARY/Gemeentemuseum, Haags; 131b: CORBIS SYGMA/T. Frank; 132t: BRIDGEMAN ART LIBRARY/*August Strindberg,* by Carl Larsson, 1899/ Nationalmuseum, Stockholm; 132mt: KIPA/S. Gaudenti/Play *Mademoiselle Julie,* by August Strindberg, with Niels Arestrup and Isabelle Adjani, directed by Niels Arestrup at the Théâtre Édouard-VII, Paris, in 1983; 132mb: HOA QUI/T. Perrin/ *Andersen,* by Henry Luckow Nielsen; 132b: HOA QUI/ C. Boisvieux; 133t: BRIDGEMAN ART LIBRARY/*Mother and daughter,* by Edvard Munch, 1897/Nasjonalgalleriet, Oslo/© Munch Museet/Munch Ellingsen Group/ADAGP, Paris 2000; 133m: BRIDGEMAN ART LIBRARY/*A woman sewing,* by Wilhelm Hammershoi/Christie's, London; 133b: BRIDGEMAN ART LIBRARY/*Erik Erikson, the blacksmith,* by Carl Larsson/Sundborn, Sweden; 134t: COLL. KIPA/Film *Festen,* by Thomas Vinterberg, 1998; 134b: COLL. KIPA/Film *Babette's Feast,* by Gabriel Axel, 1987, Panorama Productions; 135t: KIPA/SUNSET; 135m: KIPA/ Coll. CAT'S/Film *Pelle the Conqueror,* by Bille August, 1987; 135bl: KIPA; 135br: KIPA/SUNSET; 136t: PANTON DESIGN, Basel/Lampe 'Panthella', 1970, designer Verner Panton; 136b: HOA QUI/P. Bertrand; 137t: HOA QUI/P. Body; 137m: BRIDGEMAN ART LIBRARY/Armchair '41', 1931-2, designer Alvar Aalto/Bonhams, London; 138-139: ALTITUDE/ Y. Arthus-Bertrand.

Printed and bound in the EEC by Arvato Iberia
Colour separations: Station Graphique, Ivry-sur-Seine
Paper: Perigord-Condat, France

617-006-02